Mastering Clojure

From Basics to Expert Proficiency

Contents

Introduction

Clojure, a modern, dynamic, and functional programming language, offers a powerful toolset for developers aiming to leverage simplicity and robustness in their code. Originally developed by Rich Hickey, Clojure runs on the Java Virtual Machine (JVM) and is designed to interoperate seamlessly with Java. It inherits its syntactical roots from Lisp, providing both a familiar yet distinct approach towards functional programming.

This book, "Mastering Clojure: From Basics to Expert Proficiency", is crafted to guide developers through the essential concepts and advanced topics of Clojure. It is structured to cater to beginners while also presenting in-depth content for seasoned programmers seeking to refine their expertise. The foundational principles of Clojure are rooted in functional programming, emphasizing the use of immutable data structures, first-class functions, and a declarative style of coding that reduces side effects and enhances predictability.

Our journey begins with a comprehensive introduction to Clojure, establishing a solid groundwork by exploring its history and philosophical underpinnings. Understanding the context and rationale behind Clojure's design choices is crucial for appreciating its capabilities and benefits. We will then delve into the practical aspects of getting started with Clojure, including installation, basic syntax, and initial project setup. This early exposure will facilitate a smooth transition into more complex topics.

The subsequent chapters will systematically explore Clojure's syntax and basic data structures, ensuring a robust grasp of literals, keywords, symbols, and fundamental collections such as lists, vectors, maps, and sets. Mastery of these elements is imperative for effective Clojure programming. From there, we introduce functions and functional programming concepts, highlighting the elegance and power of higher-order functions, anonymous functions, and recursion.

Advanced data structures and collections receive their due attention, with discussions on persistent data structures, transients, zippers, and efficient sequence operations. The handling of state and concurrency in Clojure, particularly through atoms, refs, agents, and core.async, is addressed to provide tools for managing state changes in a multi-threaded environment.

Metaprogramming and macros open a realm of possibilities in Clojure, allowing for code that can generate and manipulate other code. This segment of the book emphasizes macro hygiene, code generation techniques, and real-world applications of macros. Given Clojure's seamless interoperability with Java, a dedicated chapter elucidates how to invoke Java methods, handle Java exceptions, and integrate Java libraries into Clojure projects.

Effective development in Clojure is bolstered by an understanding of available tools and a well-organized workflow. This book offers insights into setting up an optimal development environment, leveraging REPL-driven development, managing dependencies, and employing continuous integration and deployment strategies. Finally, building and deploying Clojure applications is addressed, encompassing structuring code, creating standalone JAR files, automating builds, and deploying to cloud platforms.

Each chapter and section within this book is meticulously curated to ensure that topics are covered comprehensively while maintaining accessibility for learners at different stages of their programming journey. By the conclusion of this book, readers will be well-equipped with the skills and knowledge required to utilize Clojure's full potential in developing robust and maintainable software applications.

Chapter 1

Introduction to Clojure and Functional Programming

This chapter provides an overview of Clojure, covering its origins, philosophy, and core principles of functional programming. It highlights the benefits of functional programming and Clojure's unique position in the programming ecosystem. The chapter also guides readers through the initial setup of their development environment, including the use of the REPL and basic Clojure syntax for creating a simple "Hello World" program. Additionally, it introduces foundational concepts such as immutable data structures and the essentials of Lisp and Clojure syntax.

1.1 What is Clojure?

Clojure is a dynamic, general-purpose programming language that operates on the Java Virtual Machine (JVM). It was created by Rich Hickey and released in 2007. Clojure is designed to be a functional language that integrates seamlessly with the vast ecosystem of Java libraries. As a dialect of Lisp, it inherits many of Lisp's beneficial features while introducing modern capabilities and robust integration with JVM.

One of the core attributes of Clojure is its emphasis on functional programming paradigms. Clojure encourages the use of functions as first-class citizens, supports immutability by default, and provides powerful tools for managing state in a safe and controlled manner. The syntax of Clojure is heavily influenced by Lisp, characterized by its use of parentheses to denote function application and its minimalist, consistent design.

```
(defn greet [name]
  (str "Hello, " name "!"))

(greet "World")
```

In this example, the greet function is defined with a single argument name. The function returns a concatenated string that includes a greeting. When the greet function is called with the argument "World", it evaluates to the string "Hello, World!".

To understand what makes Clojure unique, it's important to explore some of its defining characteristics:

- **Immutability:** By default, data structures in Clojure are immutable. This means that once a structure is created, it cannot be changed. This simplifies reasoning about code, avoids side effects, and enhances concurrency.
- **Homoiconicity:** In Clojure, code is represented as data structures (typically lists) which allows powerful metaprogramming capabilities. This allows developers to manipulate code with the same tools used to manipulate data.
- **Macros:** Leveraging its homoiconic nature, Clojure supports macros which enable syntactic extensions and code transformations at compile time, providing great flexibility and expressiveness.
- **Concurrency:** Clojure provides advanced constructs for concurrency, such as Atoms, Refs, and Agents. These tools help developers manage state changes in a thread-safe manner.
- **Interoperability:** Clojure is designed to interact seamlessly with Java. This allows Clojure to utilize the extensive set of libraries available in the Java ecosystem and to integrate easily with existing Java applications.

Example of an Immutable Data Structure Creating an immutable list and performing operations on it without altering the original list:

```
(def original-list [1 2 3])
(def new-list (conj original-list 4))

;; Output original-list and new-list
original-list ;; => [1 2 3]
new-list ;; => [1 2 3 4]
```

In this example, original-list remains unchanged after calling the conj function, which returns a new list new-list with the element 4 added. This demonstrates how Clojure's immutable data structures preserve original state and enable safe, functional transformations.

Concurrency with Atoms An example using Atoms for safe concurrent modifications:

```
(def counter (atom 0))

(defn increment-counter []
  (swap! counter inc))

(increment-counter)
(deref counter) ;; => 1
```

Here, counter is defined as an Atom with an initial value of 0. The increment-counter function uses swap! to safely increment the value of counter by applying the inc function. Using deref (or the shorthand @counter) we see that the counter value has been incremented to 1.

This focus on immutability and safe state management makes Clojure highly suitable for developing software in environments that require robust concurrent execution and predictable, maintainable codebases. With these foundational concepts, the language provides a powerful toolkit for developers seeking to leverage functional programming principles in their work on the JVM.

1.2 History and Philosophy of Clojure

Clojure is a functional, dynamic programming language that runs on the Java Virtual Machine (JVM) and is designed with an emphasis on simplicity and robustness. The language was created by Rich Hickey, a seasoned software developer, who officially released it in 2007. With a rich history encapsulated within its short existence, Clojure incorporates centuries of accumulated wisdom in computer science to address modern-day software development challenges.

Origins and Development

Rich Hickey conceived Clojure as a solution to complexities he was encountering in his professional work. Before developing Clojure, Hickey worked extensively with both Java and Common Lisp. He experienced firsthand the limitations of traditional imperative programming and recognized the power and expressiveness of Lisp dialects. However, he also identified a gap in the landscape: the lack of a Lisp-like language that could smoothly integrate with the JVM ecosystem while addressing the practical challenges of concurrency and state management in large-scale applications.

Hickey initiated the development of Clojure with the aim to synthesize the best features of Lisp with the practical benefits of the JVM. He closely examined the pitfalls of existing languages and environments and designed Clojure to eliminate or, at least, mitigate those issues. This pragmatic foundation philosophy is reflected in Clojure's efficient handling of immutable data structures and concurrency.

Philosophical Tenets

The philosophy of Clojure revolves around several core tenets:

- Simplicity and Power: Clojure is designed to be simple yet powerful. The simplicity comes from minimizing incidental complexity, which is extraneous complexity not directly related to solving the actual problem at hand. It embraces the expressive power of Lisp's macro system and its uniform syntax, enabling developers to extend the language naturally.

- Functional Programming Paradigm: Clojure's foundation is functional programming, emphasizing functions as first-class citizens, immutable data, and a declarative rather than imperative approach to computation. Functional programming ensures that functions do not cause side effects, making programs easier to reason about and maintain.

- Concurrency: Recognizing the growing importance of multicore processors, Clojure is built to handle concurrency gracefully. It provides abstractions such as Software Transactional Memory (STM) and agents, ensuring safe and efficient management of shared state.

- Interoperability: Clojure is designed to be highly interoperable with the vast ecosystem of Java libraries and frameworks. This allows Clojure programs to leverage existing Java code seamlessly, tapping into the mature and extensive resources available to the Java community.

- Lisp Philosophy: Clojure retains the traditional Lisp philosophy: code-as-data (homoiconicity) and macros for metaprogramming. Homoiconicity permits the seamless manipulation of code since the code itself is represented using the fundamental data structures of the language.

Clojure's Design Decisions

The language design reflects Hickey's philosophy and the practical needs of software development:

- Immutable Data Structures: By default, data structures in Clojure are immutable, meaning once created, they cannot be changed. This immutability helps prevent a class of errors related to unintended state changes and makes Clojure code inherently thread-safe.
- Functional Constructs: Clojure incorporates a rich set of higher-order functions and functional constructs. For instance, functions like map, reduce, and filter are staples in Clojure, allowing elegant transformations and reductions of data.
- Namespaces: Clojure uses namespaces to organize code and manage the scope of symbols. This helps in avoiding conflicts and promoting modular development.
- Macros: Leveraging macros allows the extension of language syntax. Unlike other languages, where metaprogramming could introduce complexity, in Clojure, macros enable powerful code transformations that adhere to the language philosophy of simplicity.
- Interop: Clojure's seamless interoperability with Java is a strategic decision that allows the reuse of Java libraries directly within Clojure programs. This interop support extends to JVM based languages, providing a conducive environment for mixed-language applications.

Community and Ecosystem

Since its release, Clojure has fostered a vibrant community and a growing ecosystem. This community-driven development has resulted in numerous libraries, frameworks, and tools that enhance the productivity of Clojure developers. The language's development is guided openly by Cognitect and community contributions are integral to its evolution.

Clojure embraces a minimalist approach where the language and its core libraries undergo minimal changes, ensuring stability and consistency for the users. This stable core is augmented by a robust set of libraries maintained by the community, catering to various needs ranging from web development to data analysis.

Clojure's history and philosophy are deeply intertwined with its design principles and community approach, which collectively contribute to its unique place in the programming ecosystem.

1.3 Introduction to Functional Programming

Functional programming is a programming paradigm where computation is treated as the evaluation of mathematical functions and avoids changing-state and mutable data. This paradigm emphasizes the application of functions, in contrast with imperative programming's emphasis on changes in state and explicit commands.

At the core of functional programming are several fundamental concepts:

- First-Class Functions: Functions are treated as first-class citizens. They can be assigned to variables, passed as arguments to other functions, or returned from other functions.
- Pure Functions: These functions have no side effects. A pure function's output value is determined only by its input values, without observable side effects on the program state.
- Immutability: Data structures are immutable, meaning once they are created, their state cannot change. Any modification to an immutable structure creates a new structure.
- Higher-Order Functions: These functions can take other functions as arguments or return them as results.
- Function Composition: Combining simple functions to build more complex ones.

- Recursion: Instead of using traditional looping constructs, recursion is often used for iteration.

First-Class Functions

In Clojure, as in other functional languages, functions are first-class citizens. This means you can manipulate functions just like any other data type. Here's an example:

```
(defn add [x y]
  (+ x y))

(defn apply-operation [f a b]
  (f a b))

(apply-operation add 5 10) ; Invokes (add 5 10)
```

In this example, the apply-operation function takes another function f as an argument and applies it to the arguments a and b. When apply-operation is called with add as the function and 5 and 10 as arguments, it returns 15.

Pure Functions

A function is considered pure if it meets the following criteria:

- It always produces the same output for the same input.
- It has no side effects (*e.g.*, it does not alter any external state).

Pure functions are easier to reason about and test. Consider the Clojure function below for calculating the area of a circle:

```
(defn area-of-circle [radius]
  (* Math/PI (* radius radius)))

(area-of-circle 5) ; produces 78.53981633974483
```

Given the same radius, area-of-circle will always return the same area.

Immutability

In functional programming, data structures are immutable. You cannot change them after they are created. Instead of modifying the existing data structure, you create a new one with the desired changes.

Clojure supports immutable data structures such as lists, vectors, sets, and maps. Here is how you might work with an immutable vector:

```
(def fruits ["apple" "banana" "cherry"])
(def new-fruits (conj fruits "date"))
```

```
(new-fruits) ; ["apple" "banana" "cherry" "date"]
(fruits) ; ["apple" "banana" "cherry"]
```

Here, conj is used to add "date" to the fruits vector, resulting in a new vector new-fruits, while the original fruits vector remains unchanged.

Higher-Order Functions

Functions that can take functions as arguments or return them are known as higher-order functions. An example of a higher-order function in Clojure is map, which applies a function to every item in a collection:

```
(defn square [x]
  (* x x))

(map square [1 2 3 4 5]) ; produces (1 4 9 16 25)
```

The map function applies the square function to each element of the vector [1 2 3 4 5].

Function Composition

Function composition entails combining two or more functions to produce a new function. Clojure's comp function is used for composing functions. Consider the following example:

```
(defn double [x]
  (* 2 x))

(defn add-ten [x]
  (+ 10 x))

(def compose-example (comp add-ten double))

(compose-example 5) ; produces 20
```

Here, compose-example is a composition of add-ten and double. The input 5 is first doubled to 10, and then 10 is added, resulting in 20.

Recursion

Functional programming relies heavily on recursion as opposed to traditional looping constructs like for or while. Consider the following example where we calculate the factorial of a number using recursion:

```
(defn factorial [n]
  (if (<= n 1)
    1
    (* n (factorial (- n 1)))))

(factorial 5) ; produces 120
```

In this example, the factorial function calls itself with n-1 until n is less than or equal to 1.

Functional programming emphasizes declarative over imperative programming, aiming for simplicity, conciseness, testability, and reliability. Mastery of these concepts is crucial for effective Clojure programming.

1.4 Benefits of Functional Programming

Functional programming (FP) offers numerous advantages over imperative paradigms, making it a compelling choice for modern software development. In this section, we delve into several key benefits of FP, particularly within the context of Clojure, to illustrate these points.

Immutability and State Management One of the core tenets of FP is immutability, which ensures that data structures cannot be altered once created. This paradigm fundamentally changes how state is managed within a program:

- **Simplicity:** Since data are immutable, functions do not produce side effects by altering existing states. This simplifies reasoning about the code since the output of a function depends solely on its input parameters.
- **Concurrency:** Immutability is particularly advantageous in concurrent and parallel programming, as it eliminates issues such as race conditions. Since data structures cannot be changed by multiple threads, thread safety is inherently achieved.
- **Predictability:** By ensuring that data structures are immutable, programs become more predictable. This is because the possibility of inadvertent changes to state is eliminated, leading to more reliable and maintainable code.

Pure Functions FP emphasizes the use of pure functions, which satisfy the criteria of being deterministic and free of side effects. The benefits derived from using pure functions include:

- **Referential Transparency:** Pure functions provide the property of referential transparency, meaning that an expression can be replaced with its value without changing the program's behavior. This contributes to the ease of understanding and reasoning about code.

- **Ease of Testing:** Since pure functions do not depend on or alter the state outside their scope, they are straightforward to test. Given the same inputs, a pure function will consistently produce the same output, enabling predictable and reproducible tests.

- **Cacheability:** The predictable nature of pure functions allows for memoization, where previous computations can be cached and reused, thereby optimizing performance.

Higher-Order Functions In FP, functions are first-class citizens, and higher-order functions (HOFs) are a powerful feature:

- **Abstraction and Reusability:** HOFs enable abstraction by allowing functions to be passed as arguments, returned from other functions, or stored in data structures. This enhances code reusability and modularity.

- **Composition:** Functions can be composed to build more complex operations from simple, reusable building blocks. Clojure, for instance, provides the comp function to achieve such compositions:

```
(defn square [x]
  (* x x))

(defn increment [x]
  (+ x 1))

(def square-and-increment (comp increment square))

(square-and-increment 2) ; => 5
```

In this example, the square-and-increment function is composed of square and increment. When applied to the value 2, it first calculates the square of 2 (which is 4) and then increments the result to 5.

Declarative Programming FP encourages a declarative style, where developers express *what* the program should accomplish rather than *how* to accomplish it:

- **Clarity:** By focusing on the *what*, code becomes more declarative and readable. This often results in clearer, more expressive code compared to imperative approaches.
- **Conciseness:** Declarative code tends to be more concise. Clojure, for example, allows expressing operations on collections succinctly using functions like map, filter, and reduce:

```
(def numbers [1 2 3 4 5])

(def even-numbers (filter even? numbers))
```

  In this snippet, filter is used in a declarative manner to select the even numbers from the list numbers.

Modularity and Maintainability The principles of immutability, pure functions, and higher-order functions contribute to a modular and maintainable codebase:

- **Separation of Concerns:** Functions in FP typically have a single responsibility, promoting the separation of concerns. Each function addresses a specific part of the problem, making the code easier to understand and maintain.
- **Modularity:** Clojure's standard library, which extensively uses functions and sequences, promotes modular design. Functions can be developed, tested, and reasoned about in isolation, then composed to form more complex operations.
- **Ease of Refactoring:** The predictability and modularity of FP make refactoring more straightforward. Changes are localized, reducing the risk of unintended side effects elsewhere in the code.

The intrinsic properties of functional programming align closely with modern software engineering practices, offering significant advantages in terms of code reliability, readability, and maintainability. Clojure, in leveraging these principles, provides a robust environment for building scalable and robust applications.

1.5 Clojure's Place in the Programming Ecosystem

Clojure, a modern dialect of the Lisp programming language, occupies a distinctive and influential position in the contemporary programming ecosystem. With its immutable data structures, functional programming capabilities, and seamless Java interoperability, Clojure has garnered a dedicated following among developers who value simplicity, robustness, and expressiveness in software design.

Clojure is designed to be a general-purpose language, but it particularly excels in domains where concurrency, fault tolerance, and ease of abstraction are critical. The language emphasizes immutability and immutable data structures, which result in safer, more maintainable code. This focus on immutability simplifies both reasoning about code and the development of concurrent applications.

Clojure's unique approach integrates smoothly with the Java Virtual Machine (JVM), leveraging the extensive ecosystem of Java libraries and tools. This interoperability allows developers to use existing Java frameworks and libraries within their Clojure applications, providing a seamless blend of the functional programming paradigm with the maturity and performance of the JVM.

To understand Clojure's place in the programming ecosystem, we must consider its characteristics compared to other functional languages and its application in various programming domains.

- **Interoperability:** Unlike many functional languages that operate in their silo, Clojure is designed from the ground up to interact seamlessly with the Java ecosystem. This interaction enables Clojure programmers to use Java libraries directly, call Java methods, and even implement Java interfaces. The ability to operate and integrate within the extensive Java ecosystem provides Clojure with a significant advantage in environments where Java is already entrenched.

```
;; Example of Java interoperability in Clojure
(import java.util.Date)

(def current-date (Date.))
(.toString current-date)
```

```
Output:
"Wed Oct 12 15:43:32 PDT 2022"
```

- **Expressiveness and Conciseness:** Clojure offers a high degree of expressiveness with minimal syntax, which is a hallmark of Lisp languages. This property enables developers to write more concise code without sacrificing readability or functionality. The emphasis on higher-order functions and pure functions allows for cleaner composition of operations and more modular code.

```
;; Example of Clojure's expressiveness using higher-order functions
(defn increase-by [amount]
  (fn [number] (+ number amount)))

(def add-five (increase-by 5))
(add-five 10)
```

```
Output:
15
```

- **Tooling and Ecosystem:** The Clojure ecosystem is supported by a variety of tools such as Leiningen (build automation), REPL environments, and integrative development environments (IDEs) with Clojure-specific extensions. Leiningen simplifies dependency management and builds processes, while the REPL encourages interactive development and rapid experimentation.

```
;; Example of a Leiningen project.clj file
(defproject my-clojure-app "0.1.0-SNAPSHOT"
  :dependencies [[org.clojure/clojure "1.10.3"]
                 [ring/ring-core "1.9.0"]])
```

  These tools, combined with robust library support from repositories like Clojars, create a well-rounded environment suited for both small scripts and large-scale applications.

- **Concurrency:** One of the core strengths of Clojure is its approach to concurrency. Clojure provides several powerful concurrency primitives and constructs such as atoms, refs, agents, and core.async. These constructs allow developers to write concurrent programs that are easier to reason about because they avoid the pitfalls of traditional shared-state concurrency.

```
;; Example of using atoms for state management
(def counter (atom 0))

(defn increment-counter []
  (swap! counter inc))

(increment-counter)
(increment-counter)
@counter
```

Output:
2

- **Domain Specific Languages (DSLs):** Clojure excels in the creation of internal Domain Specific Languages (DSLs) due to its homoiconic nature – the code and data share the same structure. This capability makes it an ideal choice for problems requiring custom language constructs or macros to simplify complex workflows.

```
;; Example of a simple DSL for describing a database schema
(defmacro defschema [name & fields]
  `(def ~name {:fields '~fields}))

(defschema user
  [id :integer
   name :string
   email :string])
```

These attributes make Clojure's place within the programming ecosystem particularly significant for a diverse array of applications, ranging from web development and data analysis to concurrent processing and systems programming. By offering a blend of functional programming with the practical benefits of the JVM ecosystem, Clojure continues to be a powerful and versatile tool for developers.

1.6 Setting Up Your Environment

To begin writing and running Clojure code, it is essential to set up a suitable development environment. This section outlines the necessary steps and tools required to create an efficient development ecosystem for Clojure. The components involved include installing Java, setting up Leiningen, and configuring an Integrated Development Environment (IDE) or text editor.

Step 1: Install Java

Clojure runs on the Java Virtual Machine (JVM), so the first step is to ensure that Java is installed. Clojure requires at least Java 8, but it is recommended to use the latest LTS (Long-Term Support) version, typically Java 11 or Java 17.

To check if Java is already installed, open a terminal and type the following command:

```
java -version
```

If Java is installed, the version number will be displayed. If not, download and install the appropriate version from the official Oracle website or the OpenJDK distribution. For example, to install OpenJDK 11 on a Unix-based system, you can use:

```
sudo apt-get install openjdk-11-jdk
```

After installation, verify the installation by running:

```
java -version
```

Step 2: Install Leiningen

Leiningen is the build automation and dependency management tool for Clojure. It simplifies project setup and management, including fetching dependencies, running tests, and building projects.

To install Leiningen, first download the lein script. On Unix-based systems, this can be achieved using curl or wget.

With curl:

```
curl https://raw.githubusercontent.com/technomancy/leiningen/stable/bin/lein -o lein
```

With wget:

```
wget https://raw.githubusercontent.com/technomancy/leiningen/stable/bin/lein
```

Make the script executable and move it to a directory included in your system's PATH:

```
chmod +x lein
sudo mv lein /usr/local/bin/
```

Run lein to complete the installation process:

```
lein
```

This command downloads the Leiningen self-installing package and sets up the necessary directories on your system.

Step 3: Configure an IDE or Text Editor

The choice of Integrated Development Environment (IDE) or text editor heavily influences productivity. Several editors support Clojure development, including IntelliJ IDEA with the Cursive plugin, VS Code with the Calva extension, and Emacs with CIDER.

- IntelliJ IDEA with Cursive: IntelliJ IDEA is a popular IDE that supports Clojure through the Cursive plugin. To install:

  - Download and install IntelliJ IDEA from the official JetBrains website.
  - Open IntelliJ IDEA and navigate to File > Settings > Plugins.
  - Search for Cursive and install the plugin.

- VS Code with Calva: Visual Studio Code (VS Code) is a lightweight text editor that supports Clojure development through the Calva extension. To set it up:
  - Download and install VS Code from the official website.
  - Open VS Code, and go to the Extensions view by clicking on the Extensions icon in the Activity Bar on the side of the window.
  - Search for Calva and click Install.

- Emacs with CIDER: Emacs is a powerful text editor with extensive Clojure development support through CIDER. To configure it:
  - Install Emacs from your system's package manager.
  - Add CIDER to your Emacs configuration file (.emacs or init.el):

```
(require 'package)
(add-to-list 'package-archives
             '("melpa" . "https://melpa.org/packages/") t)
(package-initialize)
(unless (package-installed-p 'cider)
  (package-refresh-contents)
  (package-install 'cider))
```

Step 4: Verify Clojure Installation

Once you have installed and configured the necessary tools, verify the entire setup by creating a new Clojure project and running it.

Create a new Leiningen project by navigating to the directory where you want the project to reside and running:

```
lein new app my-clojure-app
```

This command generates a new Clojure application template. Navigate into the project directory:

```
cd my-clojure-app
```

Compile and run the project with Leiningen:

```
lein run
```

The terminal should display the output:

```
Hello, World!
```

This confirms that your development environment is correctly set up to write and execute Clojure programs.

1.7 Hello World in Clojure

In this section, we will create the classical "Hello World" program using Clojure. This will offer a practical introduction to Clojure's syntax and its development environment. Successfully implementing this program will confirm that your development setup is functional and familiarize you with Clojure's basic structure.

To begin, ensure that your development environment is set up correctly as detailed in the preceding section. You should have Leiningen installed, which is a popular build automation and dependency management tool for Clojure.

Step 1: Create a New Leiningen Project

Open a terminal and execute the following command to create a new Leiningen project named hello-world:

```
lein new app hello-world
```

This command will generate a new Clojure project in a directory called hello-world. The directory structure will look like this:

```
hello-world/
  README.md
  doc/
    intro.md
  project.clj
  resources/
  src/
    hello_world/
      core.clj
  test/
    hello_world/
      core_test.clj
```

Step 2: Edit the core.clj File

Navigate to src/hello_world/ and open core.clj in your preferred text editor or IDE. The core.clj file should contain the following boilerplate code:

```
(ns hello-world.core
  (:gen-class))

(defn -main
  "I don't do a whole lot ... yet."
  [& args]
  (println "Hello, World!"))
```

The namespace declaration, (ns hello-world.core), defines the namespace for this file, which helps in organizing the code and preventing naming conflicts.

defn is a Clojure macro used to define a function. The -main function is the entry point of your program, analogous to main in Java. The println function prints the string "Hello, World!" to the console.

Step 3: Run the Program

To run your program, navigate to the root of your project directory (hello-world/) and execute:

```
lein run
```

You should see the following output:

```
Hello, World!
```

Step 4: Understanding the Project Configuration

The project.clj file contains configuration information for your Leiningen project. Open project.clj to inspect its contents:

```
(defproject hello-world "0.1.0-SNAPSHOT"
  :description "A simple Hello World project in Clojure"
  :url "http://example.com/FIXME"
  :license {:name "Eclipse Public License"
            :url "http://www.eclipse.org/legal/epl-v10.html"}
  :dependencies [[org.clojure/clojure "1.10.1"]]
  :main ^:skip-aot hello-world.core
  :target-path "target/%s"
  :profiles {:uberjar {:aot :all}})
```

Key lines in this file include: - :dependencies: Lists the libraries required by your project. The default dependency here is Clojure version 1.10.1. - :main: Specifies the namespace containing the -main function, hello-world.core, to be the entry point when running lein run. - :profiles: Contains the settings for building an uberjar (a standalone jar file that includes all dependencies).

Step 5: Build the Project

To create an uberjar, use the following Leiningen command:

```
lein uberjar
```

This command will compile your project and package it into a single JAR file, which can be found in the target/ directory. The JAR file can be executed using the command:

```
java -jar target/hello-world-0.1.0-SNAPSHOT-standalone.jar
```

This will produce the same output:

```
Hello, World!
```

Creating a "Hello World" program in Clojure involves setting up a new Leiningen project, defining a simple function, and running it. This exercise confirms that your development environment is properly configured and introduces you to fundamental elements of Clojure, such as namespaces, functions, and project configuration with Leiningen.

1.8 Basic REPL Usage

The Read-Eval-Print Loop (REPL) is an interactive programming environment that Clojure developers use extensively. It allows developers to enter expressions, evaluate them, and see the results immediately. This interactivity forms a key part of the Clojure development process, making it easier to experiment, test code snippets, and understand the behavior of functions and expressions in real time.

Starting the REPL

To start the REPL, ensure that you have Clojure installed and configured properly. Open a terminal or command prompt and execute the following command:

```
clojure
```

This command initiates the REPL environment, and typically, you will see a prompt similar to the following:

```
Clojure 1.10.3
user=>
```

user is the default namespace when you start the REPL. You can start typing Clojure expressions directly at this prompt.

Evaluating Expressions in REPL

Expressions entered into the REPL are evaluated immediately, and their results are displayed. For example:

```
user=> (+ 1 2 3)
6
user=> (* 5 4)
20
```

The REPL evaluates the arithmetic operations and returns the results directly. Note that Clojure uses prefix notation, meaning that the operator precedes its operands.

Defining Variables

You can define variables using the def special form. The definition associates a symbol with a value. For example:

```
user=> (def x 10)
#'user/x
user=> x
10
```

Here, x is defined with the value 10. Evaluating x thereafter returns 10.

Creating Functions

Functions can also be defined in the REPL using the defn macro. Functions in Clojure are first-class citizens, making their manipulation straightforward. For example:

```
user=> (defn add [a b]
         (+ a b))
#'user/add
user=> (add 4 5)
9
```

In this example, the function add takes two arguments, a and b, and returns their sum.

Working with Lists, Vectors, Maps, and Sets

The REPL allows the creation and manipulation of Clojure's core data structures easily. For example, you can create lists, vectors, maps, and sets as follows:

```
user=> (def my-list '(1 2 3 4))
#'user/my-list
user=> (def my-vector [1 2 3 4])
#'user/my-vector
user=> (def my-map {:a 1, :b 2})
#'user/my-map
user=> (def my-set #{1 2 3})
#'user/my-set
```

Evaluating these variables displays their contents:

```
user=> my-list
(1 2 3 4)
user=> my-vector
[1 2 3 4]
user=> my-map
{:a 1, :b 2}
user=> my-set
#{1 2 3}
```

Namespace Management

Namespaces in Clojure allow for the organization of code and help avoid symbol conflicts. The ns macro is used to manage namespaces. To switch to a different namespace or create a new one, you can use the following command:

```
user=> (ns my-namespace)
nil
my-namespace=>
```

Here, my-namespace becomes the current namespace, and any definitions made henceforth are local to this namespace.

Loading and Requiring Libraries

The Clojure REPL provides mechanisms to load and require libraries. The require function can be used to include libraries:

```
my-namespace=> (require '[clojure.string :as str])
nil
my-namespace=> (str/upper-case "hello")
"HELLO"
```

Here, the clojure.string library is required and given the alias str. The upper-case function from this library is then used to convert a string to uppercase.

Error Handling in REPL

When errors occur in the REPL, they are displayed immediately, and the REPL provides a stack trace to help diagnose the issue. For example:

```
user=> (/ 1 0)
Execution error (ArithmeticException) at user/eval1 (REPL:1).
Divide by zero
```

This error message indicates a division by zero and specifies the location of the error.

Exiting the REPL

To exit the REPL, you can use the exit or quit commands, or simply press Ctrl+D:

```
my-namespace=> (exit)
```

This command terminates the REPL session, returning you to the terminal or command prompt.

Understanding the efficient usage of the REPL is fundamental for Clojure development. It provides a dynamic and interactive programming environment essential for iterative development and quick feedback. "'

1.9 Understanding Immutable Data Structures

Immutable data structures form the foundation of functional programming languages like Clojure. Unlike traditional object-oriented or imperative programming languages where data can be modified after creation, immutable data structures ensure that once a value is created, it cannot be altered. This guarantees data consistency and can significantly simplify reasoning about program behavior.

In Clojure, common immutable data structures include lists, vectors, maps, and sets. Each of these data structures supports a range of functions that operate without altering the original data, instead creating new modified versions as needed.

Lists in Clojure are ordered collections that are particularly efficient for sequential access. They are denoted using parentheses and can store heterogeneous types of elements.

```
(def my-list '(1 2 3 4))
```

Adding an element to a list using the cons function creates a new list.

```
(def updated-list (cons 0 my-list))
```

The my-list remains unchanged, and updated-list becomes (0 1 2 3 4).

Vectors offer efficient indexed access and are denoted using square brackets.

```
(def my-vector [1 2 3 4])
```

Adding an element to a vector creates a new vector without altering the original.

```
(def updated-vector (conj my-vector 5))
```

Now, my-vector remains [1 2 3 4], and updated-vector becomes [1 2 3 4 5].

Maps associate keys with values and are denoted using curly braces.

```
(def my-map {:a 1 :b 2 :c 3})
```

To add an entry to a map or update the value of an existing key, you can use the assoc function.

```
(def updated-map (assoc my-map :d 4))
```

The original my-map remains :a 1 :b 2 :c 3 while updated-map becomes :a 1 :b 2 :c 3 :d 4.

Sets are collections of unique values and are also denoted using curly braces, but prefixed with a hash symbol.

```
(def my-set \#\{1 2 3 4\})
```

To add an element to a set or ensure an element is present, you use the conj function.

```
(def updated-set (conj my-set 5))
```

Here, my-set remains #{1 2 3 4}, and updated-set becomes #{1 2 3 4 5}.

Immutability in Clojure is facilitated by employing a technique called structural sharing. This aims to reuse parts of existing data structures, leading to significant memory and performance efficiency. For example, when a new vector is created by adding an element to an existing one, the majority of the vector can reference the original, unaltered vector, only substituting the specific parts that have changed.

```
(def my-large-vector (vec (range 1000)))
(def my-new-vector (conj my-large-vector 1001))
```

In this example, most of the data between my-large-vector and my-new-vector is shared, avoiding the need to duplicate the original 1000 elements.

Aligning with functional programming paradigms, immutability simplifies concurrent programming. Since immutable data cannot be changed after it is created, there are no concerns about race conditions or other side effects that can arise from concurrent modifications. Multiple threads can safely read the same data without needing locks or other synchronization primitives, significantly enhancing both performance and safety in multi-threaded applications.

For instance, consider a situation where multiple threads are accessing and updating a data structure. With immutable data structures, each thread can operate on its own version of the data, ensuring that one thread's operations do not interfere with another's.

```
(future
  (println (conj my-vector 6)))
(future
  (println (conj my-vector 7)))
```

Both futures execute concurrently, each producing a new vector without modifying my-vector. my-vector remains unchanged, and both threads can operate independently, avoiding the complexities of shared, mutable state.

The use of immutable data structures in Clojure encourages writing safer, more predictable code that is easier to understand and maintain. This aligns with Clojure's philosophy of simplicity and robustness, allowing developers to leverage the full benefits of functional programming principles.

1.10 Introduction to Lisp and Clojure Syntax

Clojure, as a dialect of Lisp, retains much of the Lisp syntax and philosophy. Understanding Clojure syntax begins with understanding Lisp's core principles and syntactic constructs. Lisp, which stands for "List Processing," is known for its simple and consistent syntax, where the primary syntax structure is the list. This section provides an in-depth examination of Clojure's syntax and its relationship to Lisp, offering clarity by exemplifying the central syntactic concepts essential for writing and comprehending Clojure code.

Lisp programs are composed of expressions, also known as forms, which are written as lists enclosed in parentheses. Each list begins with a function or operator followed by its arguments. For instance, the sum of two numbers in Lisp is written as:

```
(+ 1 2)
```

This is in contrast to most programming languages that use infix notation (e.g., 1 + 2).

Symbols and Data Types

Clojure, like Lisp, makes extensive use of symbols. Symbols are identifiers that name functions, variables, or any other entities. In Lisp expressions, symbols are used to refer to their values, functions, or operations. Clojure provides several basic data types:

- Numbers: Integers, floating-point numbers, and ratios. Example:

```
42
3.14159
22/7
```

- Strings: Enclosed in double quotes.

```
"Hello, World!"
```

- Keywords: Prefixed with a colon and are used as identifiers that evaluate to themselves.

```
:example
```

- Booleans: true and false

```
true
false
```

- Nil: Represents a null value.

```
nil
```

Lists, Vectors, Maps, and Sets

Clojure, staying true to its Lisp heritage, uses lists as a fundamental data structure. Lists are ordered collections of elements enclosed in parentheses.

```
(1 2 3 4)
```

Vectors in Clojure are also ordered collections but are indexed and enclosed in square brackets.

```
[1 2 3 4]
```

Maps in Clojure are key-value pairs and are enclosed in curly braces.

```
{:a 1 :b 2 :c 3}
```

Sets in Clojure are collections of unique values and are prefixed with a hash symbol before curly braces.

```
#{1 2 3 4}
```

Defining Functions

Functions are first-class citizens in Clojure, as in all Lisps. They are defined using the defn macro, which stands for "define function."

```
(defn add [x y]
  (+ x y))
```

This statement defines a function named add, which takes two arguments, x and y, and returns their sum.

Local Bindings

Local bindings in Clojure, akin to local variables in other languages, are typically created using let forms. The let form allows for the binding of values to symbols within an enclosed scope.

```
(let [a 10
      b 20]
  (+ a b))
```

This let expression binds the value 10 to the symbol a and the value 20 to the symbol b, and then adds a and b.

Conditionals

Conditional expressions in Clojure are constructed using if, cond, and other related forms. The if form is used to choose between two expressions based on a condition.

```
(if (> 2 1)
  "true"
  "false")
```

The cond form is a multi-branch conditional.

```
(cond
  (> 2 3) "greater"
  (< 2 3) "less"
  :else "equal")
```

Here, cond tests each condition sequentially and returns the value associated with the first true condition. The :else keyword is typically used as the default case.

Working with Sequences

Sequences (or seqs) are a core abstraction in Clojure for working with ordered collections. The seq function returns a sequence from a collection. Several higher-order functions are available for sequence manipulation, such as map, filter, and reduce.

```
(map inc [1 2 3 4])
; => (2 3 4 5)

(filter even? [1 2 3 4])
; => (2 4)

(reduce + [1 2 3 4])
; => 10
```

Understanding the sequence abstraction is vital for functional programming in Clojure since it allows the application of functional transformations across collections seamlessly.

Namespaces

Namespaces in Clojure provide a way to organize and manage symbols, mitigating naming conflicts. Namespaces are created using the ns macro.

```
(ns my-namespace
  (:require [clojure.string :as str]))

(defn greeting []
  (str/join ", " ["Hello" "world"]))
```

This example demonstrates a namespace called my-namespace, requiring the clojure.string library with an alias str. The function greeting then uses the str/join function to concatenate strings.

Carefully understanding these syntactic constructs is crucial to mastering Clojure. By exploring lists, vectors, maps, sets, function definitions, local bindings, conditionals, sequences, and namespaces, one builds a solid foundation for developing proficient, idiomatic Clojure programs.

Chapter 2

Getting Started with Clojure

This chapter details the initial steps for setting up and using Clojure, including the installation of Clojure and Leiningen, creating a basic project, and understanding project structure. It covers essential REPL commands, running Clojure scripts, and accessing documentation. Key concepts introduced include namespaces, basic data types, and working with core collections such as vectors, maps, and sets. Basic input and output operations, along with error handling and debugging techniques, are also discussed.

2.1 Installing Clojure and Leiningen

To begin working with Clojure effectively, it's critical to properly install both Clojure and Leiningen. These tools serve as the foundation for developing, building, and managing Clojure projects.

Clojure is a dynamic programming language that targets the Java Virtual Machine (JVM). It is designed to be a simple, yet robust tool for general-purpose programming, particularly excelling in functional programming paradigms.

Leiningen is a build automation tool for Clojure that simplifies project management, dependency handling, and other development tasks.

Both tools are necessary to streamline the Clojure development process.

Homebrew is a package manager for macOS and Linux which streamlines the installation process of Clojure and Leiningen. Assuming that Homebrew is installed, you can install Clojure using the following command:

```
brew install clojure/tools/clojure
```

This command installs the Clojure command-line tools, enabling you to run the clojure compiler and REPL. Verify the installation using:

```
clojure -e "(println 'Hello, World!)"
```

The expected output should be:

```
Hello, World!
```

If Homebrew is not installed, you can manually install Clojure by downloading and unzipping the distribution from the official Clojure website. Add the clojure binary to your system's PATH environment variable to make it accessible globally.

Next, install Leiningen. Using Homebrew, execute:

```
brew install leiningen
```

Verify the installation by executing:

```
lein
```

The expected output should be:

```
Leiningen is a tool for working with Clojure projects.
Several tasks are available:
<list of tasks>
```

For manual installation, download the lein script from the Leiningen website, place it in a directory within your system's PATH, and make it executable:

```
chmod +x /usr/local/bin/lein
```

Initialize Leiningen to download dependencies by running:

```
lein
```

This command sets up the local dependencies required by Leiningen for your user environment.

On Windows, both Clojure and Leiningen can be installed via the choco package manager. Ensure choco is already installed and run the following commands:

```
choco install clojure
choco install leiningen
```

After each installation, confirm the installation was successful by checking the version:

```
clojure --version
lein --version
```

The output should display the version numbers of the installed tools, confirming they are now available for use.

The installation of Clojure and Leiningen lays the groundwork for creating and managing Clojure projects. With these tools correctly set up, you are prepared to explore the core functionalities and capabilities of the language and its ecosystem seamlessly. The next steps will involve initiating your first Clojure project and familiarizing yourself with the project structure, setting the stage for advanced exploration and development.

2.2 Creating Your First Clojure Project

Creating a new Clojure project involves using Leiningen, a popular build automation tool for Clojure. Leiningen helps streamline project creation, dependency management, and deployment tasks. To create your first Clojure project, follow the steps outlined below.

First, ensure that Leiningen is installed on your system. If it is not yet installed, refer to the "Installing Clojure and Leiningen" section earlier in this chapter.

To start a new Clojure project, open your terminal or command prompt and navigate to the directory where you want your project to be located. Run the following command:

```
lein new app my-first-clojure-app
```

This command creates a new Clojure project named my-first-clojure-app using the app template. Leiningen generates a directory structure for your project, which will look like this:

```
my-first-clojure-app/
  CHANGELOG.md
  LICENSE
  README.md
  doc/
    intro.md
  resources/
  src/
    my_first_clojure_app/
      core.clj
  test/
    my_first_clojure_app/
      core_test.clj
  .gitignore
  project.clj
```

This structure contains several files and directories:

- CHANGELOG.md: A file for tracking the project's change log.
- LICENSE: The project license file.
- README.md: The readme file containing project information.
- doc/: A directory for documentation, including a sample intro.md file.
- resources/: A directory for static resources.
- src/: The source directory containing your Clojure code.
- src/my_first_clojure_app/core.clj: A sample Clojure file where the main application code resides.
- test/: The directory containing tests.
- test/my_first_clojure_app/core_test.clj: A placeholder for writing tests for your application.
- .gitignore: A file listing the content to be ignored by Git version control.
- project.clj: The Leiningen project configuration file.

Next, let's examine the project.clj file. This file is crucial as it defines your project's configuration, dependencies, and other settings. Open project.clj, and you will see content similar to:

```
(defproject my-first-clojure-app "0.1.0-SNAPSHOT"
  :description "FIXME: write description"
  :url "http://example.com/FIXME"
  :license {:name "Eclipse Public License"
            :url "http://www.eclipse.org/legal/epl-v10.html"}
```

```
:dependencies [[org.clojure/clojure "1.10.3"]]
:main ^:skip-aot my-first-clojure-app.core
:target-path "target/%s"
:profiles {:uberjar {:aot :all}})
```

Key elements in this file include:

- defproject: Defines the project name and version.
- :description: A brief description of the project; initially a placeholder.
- :url: The project's URL; also initially a placeholder.
- :license: The license under which the project is distributed.
- :dependencies: A vector of project dependencies. It includes Clojure itself, version 1.10.3 in this example.
- :main: Specifies the main namespace that contains the entry point for the application.
- :target-path: Defines the directory where compiled files will be placed.
- :profiles: Profiles are used to manage different build configurations. The :uberjar profile specifies settings for building a standalone jar.

To run the sample project, navigate to the project directory in your terminal:

```
cd my-first-clojure-app
```

Then, execute the following command to start a REPL connected to the project:

```
lein repl
```

You should see output similar to:

```
nREPL server started on port 57205 on host 127.0.0.1 - nrepl://127.0.0.1:57205
REPL-y 0.4.4, nREPL 0.6.0
Clojure 1.10.3
OpenJDK 64-Bit Server VM 11.0.3+7
...
my-first-clojure-app.core=>
```

This indicates that the REPL has started and you are now in the context of your new project.

To execute the main function defined in core.clj, modify the core.clj file located at src/my_first_clojure_app/core.clj. Initially, this file contains a simple hello-world function:

```
(ns my-first-clojure-app.core)

(defn -main
  "I don't do a whole lot ... yet."
  [& args]
  (println "Hello, World!"))
```

Update it to:

```
(ns my-first-clojure-app.core)

(defn -main
  "This is the main entry point for the application."
  [& args]
  (println "Welcome to your first Clojure project!"))
```

Save the file and return to your terminal. Exit the REPL by typing :quit.

Now, run the updated main function from the terminal with Leiningen:

```
lein run
```

You should see the following output:

```
Welcome to your first Clojure project!
```

This confirms that your first Clojure project is set up correctly and that the main function executes as expected.

2.3 Understanding Project Structure

A firm grasp of the typical project structure in Clojure is essential for efficient development and easy navigation. When creating a new Clojure project using Leiningen, for example with the command:

```
lein new app myproject
```

a standardized directory and file layout is generated. This layout adheres to conventions that aid in maintaining comprehensibility and organization in Clojure projects. We will dissect this structure to understand its components and their purposes comprehensively.

The general directory structure of a new Leiningen project looks like this:

```
myproject/
    README.md
    doc/
        intro.md
    project.clj
    resources/
    src/
        myproject/
            core.clj
    target/
    test/
        myproject/
            core_test.clj
```

Each directory and file serves a specific function in the development lifecycle:

- README.md: This file contains project documentation. It is commonly written in Markdown and provides an overview of the project's purpose, usage instructions, and any other information crucial to users and developers.
- doc/: The doc directory is intended for additional documentation. By default, it contains an intro.md file that can be used as a place to document specifics about the project or for extended instructions beyond the README.md.
- project.clj: This is the core configuration file for the project. It defines project metadata, dependencies, build configurations, and various hooks Leiningen uses during development and deployment. Here is an example structure of project.clj:

```
(defproject myproject "0.1.0-SNAPSHOT"
  :description "A simple Clojure project"
  :url "http://example.com/myproject"
  :license {:name "Eclipse Public License"
            :url "http://www.eclipse.org/legal/epl-v10.html"}
  :dependencies [[org.clojure/clojure "1.10.3"]]
  :main ^:skip-aot myproject.core
  :target-path "target/%s"
  :profiles {:uberjar {:aot :all}})
```

- resources/: This directory is used to store static files required by the application, such as configuration files, templates, or any other resources necessary for runtime. These files are included in the classpath and can be accessed by the application.
- src/: The src directory contains the source code of the project. Conforming to Java's package naming conventions, the code resides under a directory matching the project's namespace structure. For instance, in our example, myproject is the namespace, thus core.clj resides in src/myproject/.

Example content of src/myproject/core.clj:

```
(ns myproject.core
  (:gen-class))

(defn -main
  "A simple main function"
  [& args]
  (println "Hello, World!"))
```

- target/: The target directory is dynamically generated by Leiningen to store compiled assets, including .class files, JAR files, and any other artifacts produced during the build process. This directory is crucial for maintaining separation between source code and compiled code.
- test/: The test directory is structured similarly to the src directory but contains test files rather than application source files. The same namespace convention applies. For instance, test/myproject/core_test.clj contains the test cases for src/myproject/core.clj.

  Example content of test/myproject/core_test.clj:

```
(ns myproject.core-test
  (:require [clojure.test :refer :all]
            [myproject.core :refer :all]))

(deftest test-main
  (testing "main function"
    (is (= (with-out-str (-main)) "Hello, World!\n"))))
```

Understanding each component and its role within the project structure ensures smoother navigation, systematic coding practices, and improved collaboration among team members. Furthermore, adhering to these conventions facilitates integration with various development and deployment tools designed for Clojure projects.

2.4 Basic REPL Commands

The Read-Eval-Print Loop, or REPL, is an essential tool for working with Clojure. It allows for interactive programming, enabling rapid development and experimentation. REPL facilitates a dynamic workflow where expressions are read, evaluated, and their results printed back to you without requiring the formal structure of a complete program. This section covers the fundamental REPL commands that form the basis of effective Clojure development.

To start the REPL, navigate to your project directory and use Leiningen with the following command:

```
lein repl
```

Once the REPL is running, it waits for user input with the prompt user=>. You can now begin entering Clojure expressions. Below are some of the primary operations and commands you will use.

Evaluating Expressions:

In the REPL, you type a Clojure expression and press Enter. The REPL reads the expression, evaluates it, and prints the result. For instance:

```
user=> (+ 1 2 3)
6
```

Here, (+ 1 2 3) is an arithmetic expression that adds three numbers. The result is 6.

Defining Variables:

To define a variable, use the def keyword. This assigns a value to a symbol which can be used later.

```
user=> (def x 10)
#'user/x
user=> x
10
```

In this example, x is defined to hold the value 10. The REPL returns #'user/x, indicating that x is now bound in the user namespace. When x is evaluated, it returns 10.

Function Definitions:

Use defn to define a function. A function includes parameters and a body which is evaluated when the function is called.

```
user=> (defn add [a b]
         (+ a b))
#'user/add
user=> (add 3 4)
7
```

This code defines a function add that takes two parameters, a and b, and returns their sum. When (add 3 4) is invoked, it results in 7.

Namespaces:

Namespaces provide a way to group related functions and variables. The ns macro is used to create and switch to a new namespace.

```
user=> (ns mynamespace)
nil
mynamespace=> (def y 20)
#'mynamespace/y
mynamespace=> y
20
```

Here, a new namespace mynamespace is created and switched to. Within this namespace, the variable y is defined and evaluated.

Loading Files:

You can load and execute content from a Clojure file using the load-file function. Assume you have a file example.clj in your current directory.

```
user=> (load-file "example.clj")
nil
```

The contents of example.clj are executed in the REPL, and nil is returned if the file loads successfully.

Documentation and Source Code:

To access the documentation or the source code of a function, use the doc, source, or find-doc commands. For example:

```
user=> (doc +)
-------------------------
clojure.core/+
([x] [x y] [x y & more])
Returns the sum of nums.
user=> (source +)
(defn +
  "Returns the sum of nums. (+) returns 0. Does not auto-promote
  longs, will throw on overflow. See also: +'."
  {:added "1.2"
   :static true}
  ([x] x)
  ([x y] (. clojure.lang.Numbers (add x y)))
  ([x y & more]
   (reduce + (+ x y) more)))
nil
```

These commands are useful for understanding how functions work and ensuring you use them correctly. For example, (doc +) prints the documentation for the + function, while (source +) shows its actual source code.

Autocompletion and Command History:

The REPL supports command history and autocompletion for efficient coding. Use the Up and Down arrow keys to navigate through the history of commands you have previously entered. Press Tab to autocomplete partially-typed function names or variable names.

Exiting the REPL:

To gracefully exit the REPL, use the :quit command.

```
user=> :quit
```

The REPL session terminates, and you return to your terminal or command prompt.

Understanding and mastering these REPL commands will significantly enhance your Clojure development workflow, allowing you to test and iterate on your code quickly and efficiently.

2.5 Creating and Running Clojure Scripts

Creating and running Clojure scripts is an essential skill for any Clojure developer, as it allows for quick experimentation, prototyping, and automation of tasks. This section provides a detailed guide to writing Clojure scripts and executing them effectively.

To begin, ensure that you have a working Clojure environment. Verify the installation of Clojure and Leiningen on your system by executing the following commands in your terminal:

```
clojure -M --help
lein --version
```

These commands should display the help and version information, confirming that both tools are installed correctly. If not, refer back to the "Installing Clojure and Leiningen" section for detailed installation instructions.

Creating a Basic Clojure Script

Create a new file with a .clj extension. This extension is the standard for Clojure scripts. Open your preferred text editor or IDE and create a file named example-script.clj. Write the following simple script that prints "Hello, World!" to the console:

```
;; example-script.clj
(ns example-script.core)

(defn -main []
  (println "Hello, World!"))
```

In this script, we've defined a namespace example-script.core, which is a common practice in Clojure to prevent naming conflicts. The -main function is a convention for the entry point of the script, where execution begins.

Running the Script Using Clojure Command

To run this script using the Clojure CLI, use the following command in your terminal:

```
clojure example-script.clj
```

The output should be:

```
Hello, World!
```

The clojure command directly interprets and executes the script file specified.

Leiningen Approach

For more complex projects with dependencies, it is common to use Leiningen. Create a new Leiningen project by executing:

```
lein new app example-app
```

This command generates a new project named example-app with a standard directory structure. Navigate to the project directory and modify the core.clj file located in src/example_app/ by adding the following code:

```
(ns example-app.core
  (:gen-class))

(defn -main [& args]
  (println "Hello, World!"))
```

The :gen-class directive is added to generate a Java class from the namespace, which is necessary for creating an executable JAR file.

To run the script using Leiningen, execute:

```
lein run
```

The output should be:

```
Hello, World!
```

To create an executable JAR file, run:

```
lein uberjar
```

This command generates a JAR file in the target directory, which can be executed with:

```
java -jar target/example-app-0.1.0-SNAPSHOT-standalone.jar
```

The output should be:

```
Hello, World!
```

Script with Dependencies

For scripts that require external libraries, a deps.edn file can be created. Add the libraries to the dependencies map. For example, to use the Cheshire library for JSON parsing, create a deps.edn file with the following content:

```
{:deps {cheshire/cheshire {:mvn/version "5.10.0"}}}
```

Modify example-script.clj to use the Cheshire library:

```
;; example-script.clj
(ns example-script.core
  (:require [cheshire.core :as json]))

(defn -main []
  (println (json/encode {:greeting "Hello, World!"})))
```

Run the script using:

```
clojure -M:run
```

The output should be:

```
{"greeting":"Hello, World!"}
```

By incorporating these practices, you can effectively create and run Clojure scripts, catering to simple tasks or complex projects with dependencies.

2.6 Using Clojure Documentation

Effective use of documentation is critical when learning and working with Clojure. The Clojure environment offers a plethora of resources to help developers understand its core libraries and functions. Properly leveraging these resources can significantly enhance productivity and ensure correct usage of functions and methods. This section delves into the tools and methodologies for accessing and utilizing Clojure documentation effectively.

The primary resource for Clojure documentation is the official website, which houses detailed information about Clojure's core libraries, syntax, and functions. To access this documentation, you can visit https://clojure.org/. The website is structured into various sections, including "Getting Started," "API Reference," and "Community," each providing valuable information for novice and experienced developers alike.

Another critical tool for accessing documentation is the Clojure REPL (Read-Eval-Print Loop). The REPL not only serves as an interactive programming environment but also offers several built-in commands to fetch documentation for specific functions or macros. To illustrate, let's explore some essential REPL commands for documentation.

```
; To access documentation of a function, use the 'doc' command
(doc clojure.core/map)
```

Upon execution, the above command will return detailed documentation of the map function, including its signature, parameters, and a brief description of its behavior and usage.

```
-------------------------
clojure.core/map
([f] [f coll] [f c1 c2] [f c1 c2 c3] [f c1 c2 c3 & colls])
  Returns a lazy sequence consisting of the result of applying f to
  the set of first items of each coll, followed by applying f to the set
  of second items in each coll, until any one of the colls is
  exhausted. Any remaining items in other colls are ignored.
```

Additionally, the find-doc command is useful when the exact function name is unknown. This command searches for a specified term across all available documentation strings.

```
; To search for documentation containing a specific term
(find-doc "lazy sequence")
```

The find-doc command will return a list of functions and macros whose documentation includes the term "lazy sequence." This is particularly useful when users need to explore functions related to a specific concept without knowing the exact names.

```
-------------------------
clojure.core/lazy-seq
([& body])
Macro
  Returns a lazy sequence (works on any Iterable) of the values of a
  body of expressions repeated indefinitely.

-------------------------
clojure.core/map
([f] [f coll] [f c1 c2] [f c1 c2 c3] [f c1 c2 c3 & colls])
  Returns a lazy sequence consisting of the result of applying f to
  the set of first items of each coll, followed by applying f to the set
  of second items in each coll, until any one of the colls is
  exhausted. Any remaining items in other colls are ignored.
... more results ...
```

For cases where more granular information is required, the source command can be particularly insightful. It reveals the source code of a given function, providing a deeper understanding of its implementation.

```
; To view the source code of a function
(source clojure.core/filter)
```

The command will output the source code of the filter function, which can illuminate intricate details and the rationale behind its behavior.

```
(defn filter
  "Returns a lazy sequence of the items in coll for which (pred item)
  returns true. pred must be free of side-effects."
  [pred coll]
  (lazy-seq
    (when-first [s (seq coll)]
      (if (pred (first s))
        (cons (first s) (filter pred (rest s)))
        (filter pred (rest s))))))
```

Clojure also supports inline documentation through comments directly in the codebase. Properly documented code is crucial for maintenance and collaboration. Utilization of comments should follow the best practices, such as providing clear descriptions and ensuring the comments do not become outdated as the code evolves.

For instance, consider the following example of a documented function:

```
(defn add
  "Adds two numbers together and returns the result."
  [a b]
  (+ a b))
```

The string immediately following the function signature serves as an inline docstring, offering a succinct description of the function's purpose and parameters.

Interactive documentation tools like CIDER (Clojure Interactive Development Environment that Rocks) further enhance the developer experience. CIDER integrates seamlessly with Emacs and offers features such as interactive documentation lookup, allowing users to view function documentation directly within the editor.

```
; For example, within Emacs with CIDER running, use 'C-c C-d d' to view
    documentation.
```

This command invokes the documentation lookup for the symbol at the point, streamlining the process of acquiring necessary information without leaving the development environment.

Utilizing these documentation tools and techniques enables developers to seamlessly navigate and comprehend the Clojure ecosystem. Accessing reliable documentation supports efficient problem-solving and robust code creation, fostering a deeper grasp of Clojure's capabilities and best practices.

2.7 Understanding Namespaces

Namespaces in Clojure serve as a fundamental organizational unit, enabling developers to partition and manage code effectively. A namespace is a named context that holds a set of bindings between symbols and values, providing a way to group related functionalities and avoid name conflicts. This section will delve into the specifics of creating, using, and managing namespaces in Clojure.

To define a namespace in Clojure, the ns macro is used. It establishes a new namespace or switches to an existing one if the namespace already exists. The ns macro is typically placed at the top of a Clojure file to set the context for the subsequent code.

For example, the following code snippet creates a namespace named my-app.core:

```
(ns my-app.core)
```

When this line is executed, the namespace my-app.core is established, and any definitions that follow will reside within this namespace. This way, the my-app.core namespace can neatly encapsulate all functions, variables, and other entities associated with the core functionality of the application.

Namespaces also allow the inclusion and use of other namespaces, which is a common practice for code reuse and modularity. The require and use functions serve this purpose.

The require function imports symbols from another namespace. The following example demonstrates how to require the clojure.string namespace:

```
(ns my-app.core
  (:require [clojure.string :as str]))
```

In this example, the clojure.string namespace is required and aliased as str. The alias allows the functions within clojure.string to be accessed using the shorter str prefix. For instance, one can now use str/upper-case to call the upper-case function from the clojure.string namespace.

On the other hand, the use function also imports symbols from another namespace but differs in that it makes all the public symbols of the required namespace available directly, without needing a prefix. For example:

```
(ns my-app.core
  (:use clojure.string))
```

With the above usage of use, one can utilize the upper-case function directly without prefixing it with str/. However, overusing use can lead to potential name clashes, and as a result, require with aliases is preferred for clarity and to avoid conflicts.

Moreover, namespaces in Clojure can refer to functions, macros, and variables in other namespaces through the refer function. For example, to refer specific symbols from a namespace:

```
(ns my-app.core
  (:require [clojure.string :refer [blank? join]]))
```

Here, only the blank? and join functions from clojure.string are referred, making them available directly in the current namespace.

An important feature of namespaces is their ability to handle referential transparency and immutability, allowing symbols to be redefined within a namespace scope without affecting other namespaces. Clojure provides the alter-var-root and swap! functions to manage changes within namespaces efficiently.

Furthermore, temporary modifications to the namespace's environment can be made using the binding macro, ensuring that changes are local to the executed code block. For instance:

```
(binding [*out* *err*]
  (println "This will print to the error stream"))
```

This code temporarily binds the global output stream *out* to the error output stream *err* within the binding block, enhancing the ability to manage different output contexts gracefully.

Exploring advanced namespace functionalities, Clojure also supports dynamic environments through the ns-interns, ns-publics, and ns-resolve functions. These functions provide introspective capabilities to query and manipulate namespaces programmatically.

```
;; List all interned symbols within the 'my-app.core' namespace
(ns-interns 'my-app.core)

;; Retrieve public symbols from the current namespace
(ns-publics *ns*)

;; Resolve a symbol to its corresponding var within the current namespace
(ns-resolve *ns* 'my-app.core/some-function)
```

These introspection functions are pivotal in dynamic code analyses, facilitating the development of sophisticated algorithms that adapt based on the runtime environment while ensuring seamless namespace management.

Incorporating these namespace management strategies is imperative for building scalable, maintainable, and robust Clojure applications.

2.8 Basic Clojure Data Types

Clojure is a dynamically typed language that offers a variety of data types. Understanding these basic data types is fundamental for writing efficient and readable Clojure code. This section provides an in-depth look at the fundamental data types in Clojure: numbers, strings, keywords, symbols, and booleans. Each data type has specific characteristics and operations that you can perform on them.

Numbers

Clojure supports several types of numbers: integers, floating-point numbers, ratios, and arbitrary-precision numbers.

- Integer: Represents whole numbers. Examples of integers in Clojure are both positive and negative numbers like 42 and -3.
- Floating-point: Denoted by a decimal point, e.g., 3.14 or -0.001.
- Ratio: Represented using a fraction, such as 3/2.

- BigInteger and BigDecimal: Used for numbers that exceed the limits of standard integer or floating-point types.

Example operations on numbers:

```
(def a 10)
(def b 20.5)
(def c (/ 3 2)) ; Ratio, evaluates to 3/2 or 1.5 depending on usage
(def d (bigint "12345678901234567890"))
```

Strings

Strings in Clojure are sequences of characters enclosed in double quotes. They support various operations such as concatenation, splitting, and more, using functions from the clojure.string namespace.

```
(def my-string "Hello, Clojure!")
(defn concat-strings [str1 str2]
  (str str1 " " str2))

(concat-strings "Hello" "World") ; Outputs: "Hello World"
```

"Hello World"

For other common operations like splitting a string:

```
(require '[clojure.string :as str])

(str/split "apple,orange,banana" #",") ; ["apple" "orange" "banana"]
```

["apple" "orange" "banana"]

Keywords

Keywords are identifiers that begin with a colon. They are often used as keys in maps and are unique. Keywords are immutable and are compared by identity, making them efficient for key-based lookups.

```
(def my-map {:name "Alice" :age 30})

(:name my-map) ; Retrieves "Alice"
```

"Alice"

Symbols

Symbols are used to refer to variables or functions in Clojure. They are created implicitly when you define a variable or function and can be created explicitly using the quote function or the single-quote character.

```
(def myvar 100)
myvar ; Refers to the value of myvar, which is 100

'myvar ; Refers to the symbol itself
```

```
(quote myvar) ; Equivalent to 'myvar
```

```
100
'myvar
'myvar
```

Booleans

Booleans represent logical values and can be true or false. They are often used in control structures like if and cond.

```
(def my-bool true)

(if my-bool
  "This is true"
  "This is false")
```

```
"This is true"
```

Above code evaluates my-bool and based on its value, outputs the corresponding string.

Clojure's standard library provides many functions to manipulate these data types, enabling the development of complex programs through the composition of simple and well-understood operations. Understanding and utilizing Clojure's basic data types is a stepping stone towards mastering the language, facilitating effective programming with clear and concise expressions.

2.9 Introduction to Vectors, Maps, and Sets

Clojure provides a variety of core collection types that are essential for storing and manipulating data. Among the most commonly used are vectors, maps, and sets. Each of these collection types offers different characteristics and behaviors that make them suitable for certain tasks. Understanding these differences is crucial for writing efficient and effective Clojure code.

Vectors are ordered collections that maintain the insertion sequence of elements. They provide fast random access by index and are particularly useful for tasks where elements need to be accessed sequentially or in a specific order.

```
(def my-vector [1 2 3 4 5])
(println (get my-vector 2)) ; Output: 3
```

In the example above, my-vector is a vector containing five elements.

The get function retrieves the element at the specified index, in this case, index 2, which yields the value 3.

Maps are collections of key-value pairs, where each key is unique. They are analogous to dictionaries in other programming languages and are ideal for representing structured data where lookup by key is required.

```
(def my-map {:name "Alice" :age 30 :city "Wonderland"})
(println (get my-map :name)) ; Output: Alice
```

In this case, my-map is a map with keys :name, :age, and :city. The get function retrieves the value associated with the key :name, which is "Alice". Maps also support efficient addition, removal, and update of key-value pairs.

Sets are collections of unique elements, which means they do not allow duplicate items. Sets are unordered and are typically used when the membership of elements needs to be tested or when the uniqueness of elements is important.

```
(def my-set #{1 2 3 3 4 5})
(println my-set) ; Output: #{1 2 3 4 5}
(println (contains? my-set 3)) ; Output: true
```

Here, my-set is defined with duplicate elements, but the set itself stores each element uniquely, resulting in {1 2 3 4 5}. The contains? function checks for the presence of an element in the set, returning true if the element exists.

To further explore the nuances of these collections, consider their mutability and performance characteristics. Vectors, maps, and sets in Clojure are immutable by default. Any operation that modifies a collection actually returns a new collection with the modification applied, leaving the original collection unchanged.

For example, adding an element to a vector creates a new vector with the element appended:

```
(def my-vector [1 2 3])
(def new-vector (conj my-vector 4))
(println new-vector) ; Output: [1 2 3 4]
(println my-vector) ; Output: [1 2 3]
```

The conj function is used here to add the element 4 to my-vector, resulting in a new vector new-vector. The original vector remains unchanged, demonstrating immutability.

Similarly, adding a key-value pair to a map creates a new map with the pair added:

```
(def my-map {:name "Alice" :age 30})
(def new-map (assoc my-map :city "Wonderland"))
(println new-map) ; Output: {:name "Alice", :age 30, :city "Wonderland"}
(println my-map) ; Output: {:name "Alice", :age 30}
```

In this example, assoc is used to add the key :city with value "Wonderland" to my-map, producing a new map new-map while leaving my-map unchanged.

Sets also exhibit similar immutable behavior:

```
(def my-set #{1 2 3})
(def new-set (conj my-set 4))
(println new-set) ; Output: #{1 2 3 4}
(println my-set) ; Output: #{1 2 3}
```

Here, conj adds an element to my-set, resulting in new-set which includes the new element, while my-set remains as it was.

Understanding these fundamental collection types—vectors, maps, and sets—equips you with the tools to handle a wide variety of data manipulation tasks in Clojure. Their immutability ensures stability and predictability, which are highly valuable traits in functional programming.

2.10 Working with Sequences

Sequences are fundamental to Clojure and provide a uniform way to work with collections. Clojure's sequence library offers a rich set of functions to manipulate sequences efficiently. In Clojure, sequences can be created from various collection types such as lists, vectors, maps, and sets.

To start working with sequences, we need to understand the seq function. The seq function converts a collection into a sequence. If the collection is empty, seq returns nil. Here is an example.

```
(seq [1 2 3 4 5])
```

The above code will output:

```
(1 2 3 4 5)
```

Lists in Clojure are sequences by default, so calling seq on a list will return the list itself. Vectors, sets, and maps can also be turned into sequences. For example:

```
(seq '(1 2 3 4 5))
(seq #{1 2 3 4 5})
(seq {:a 1 :b 2 :c 3})
```

The output of these commands will be:

```
(1 2 3 4 5)
(1 2 3 4 5)
([:a 1] [:b 2] [:c 3])
```

Maps are converted into sequences of key-value pairs. Now, let's explore some common sequence operations.

One of the most frequently used sequence functions is first, which returns the first item in the sequence.

```
(first [1 2 3 4 5])
```

This will output:

```
1
```

Another essential function is rest, which returns a sequence of all elements except the first one.

```
(rest [1 2 3 4 5])
```

This will output:

```
(2 3 4 5)
```

The cons function is used to add an element at the beginning of the sequence.

```
(cons 0 [1 2 3 4 5])
```

This will result in:

```
(0 1 2 3 4 5)
```

We can perform transformations on sequences using functions like map. The map function applies a given function to each item in the sequence.

```
(map inc [1 2 3 4 5])
```

This will increment each element in the list:

```
(2 3 4 5 6)
```

The filter function creates a new sequence consisting of items that satisfy a predicate function.

```
(filter odd? [1 2 3 4 5 6 7])
```

This filters out even numbers:

```
(1 3 5 7)
```

We can also use reduce to combine all elements of the sequence using a binary function.

```
(reduce + [1 2 3 4 5])
```

This will return the sum of all elements:

```
15
```

Another useful function is into, which takes a target collection and a sequence, and returns the target collection with all elements from the sequence conjoined into it.

```
(into [] '(1 2 3 4 5))
```

This transforms a list into a vector:

```
[1 2 3 4 5]
```

In addition to sequence operations, we need to understand lazy sequences. Lazy sequences are not evaluated until they are used. The function lazy-seq can be used to create lazy sequences.

```
(defn lazy-range [n]
  (lazy-seq
    (when (> n 0)
      (cons n (lazy-range (dec n))))))
(lazy-range 5)
```

The lazy-range function creates a lazy sequence of numbers from n down to 1. To realize the sequence, we can use take function which takes a specified number of elements from the sequence:

```
(take 3 (lazy-range 10))
```

This will return:

```
(10 9 8)
```

Understanding and utilizing sequences is crucial for effective Clojure programming. Mastery of sequence operations provides powerful tools for data manipulation and transformation.

2.11 Basic Input and Output Operations

Basic input and output (I/O) operations are fundamental to any programming language, allowing interaction with users and external systems. In Clojure, I/O operations are designed to be simple and consistent with its functional programming paradigm. This section will cover methods for reading input from various sources and writing output to the console and files.

Reading from the console

To read input from the console, Clojure provides the read-line function, which reads a line of text input from the standard input stream (usually the keyboard). The function waits for the user to type a line and press Enter, then returns the input as a string.

The following example illustrates this:

```
(defn get-user-input []
  (println "Please enter your name:")
  (let [name (read-line)]
    (println "Hello," name)))

(get-user-input)
```

When executed, this program will display a prompt, wait for the user to input their name, and then greet them.

Reading from a file

Reading from a file in Clojure can be handled using the slurp function, which reads the entire contents of the specified file and returns it as a string. This function can be very useful when dealing with small to moderately sized files.

Example usage of slurp:

```
(defn read-file [filename]
  (slurp filename))

(def file-contents (read-file "example.txt"))
(println file-contents)
```

In this snippet, the read-file function takes the filename as an argument and uses slurp to read its contents. The contents are then printed to the console.

For more complex file reading operations, such as processing large files, it is more efficient to read the file line by line. This is achieved using the with-open macro in conjunction with clojure.java.io/reader.

Example of line-by-line file reading:

```
(require '[clojure.java.io :as io])

(defn read-file-line-by-line [filename]
  (with-open [reader (io/reader filename)]
    (doseq [line (line-seq reader)]
      (println line))))

(read-file-line-by-line "example.txt")
```

In this example, with-open ensures that the file is properly closed after its contents are read. The doseq macro iterates over each line of the file and prints it.

Writing to the console

Writing output to the console in Clojure is straightforward using the println and print functions. The println function outputs its arguments followed by a newline, while print outputs without adding a newline.

Examples of using println and print:

```
(println "Hello, World!")
(print "This is ")
(print "Clojure")
```

The first line will output "Hello, World!" followed by a newline, while the subsequent lines will output "This is Clojure" without any intervening newlines.

Writing to a file

For writing data to a file, Clojure provides the spit function, which writes a string to a specified file. By default, spit will overwrite the file, but it can be configured to append to an existing file by passing an additional :append true option.

Example usage of spit:

```
(defn write-to-file [filename content]
  (spit filename content))

(def my-content "This is a sample content.")
(write-to-file "output.txt" my-content)
```

This function writes the string "This is a sample content." to output.txt, creating the file if it does not exist.

Appending to an existing file:

```
(defn append-to-file [filename content]
  (spit filename content :append true))
```

```
(append-to-file "output.txt" "\nAdditional line of text.")
```

This snippet appends a new line of text to the existing contents of output.txt.

By understanding these basic I/O operations, you can effectively handle input and output in your Clojure programs, enabling interaction with users and integration with external data sources.

2.12 Error Handling and Debugging

Effective error handling and debugging are crucial aspects of software development in Clojure. This section will guide you through the fundamental techniques and best practices for catching and resolving runtime errors, as well as the methodologies for debugging your Clojure programs efficiently.

The try and catch constructs in Clojure are used for handling exceptions. The try block contains the code that may potentially fail, while the catch block specifies the type of exception to handle and the code to execute when that exception occurs.

```
(try
  (do-something-dangerous)
  (catch Exception e
    (println "An error occurred:" (.getMessage e))))
```

In this example, do-something-dangerous is a placeholder for any potentially risky operation. If an exception is thrown during the execution of this operation, the catch block catches the exception, and println outputs an error message. The variable e represents the caught exception object, allowing various exception methods to be accessed, such as .getMessage.

Error handling can be further refined using specific exception types. Consider a case where you handle multiple exception types differently:

```
(try
  (do-something-dangerous)
  (catch ArithmeticException e
    (println "Arithmetic error: " (.getMessage e)))
  (catch NullPointerException e
    (println "Null pointer error: " (.getMessage e)))
  (catch Exception e
    (println "General error: " (.getMessage e))))
```

Here, arithmetic errors and null pointer exceptions are each managed distinctly, providing specific error messages for each case. The final catch clause acts as a catch-all for any other exceptions not previously specified.

In addition to try and catch, the finally block can execute code irrespective of whether an exception is thrown, typically used for cleanup operations:

```
(try
  (do-something-dangerous)
  (catch Exception e
    (println "An error occurred:" (.getMessage e)))
  (finally
    (println "Cleanup operations")))
```

While handling exceptions is essential, being proactive in debugging is equally important for Clojure development. One primary tool for debugging is the Read-Eval-Print Loop (REPL). The REPL allows interactive code evaluation, making it easier to test individual functions and expressions in isolation.

Consider a function that exhibits unexpected behavior:

```
(defn divide [numerator denominator]
  (/ numerator denominator))
```

If an error occurs due to a divisor of zero, you can test and debug this function in the REPL:

```
user=> (divide 4 2)
2
user=> (divide 4 0)
; Execution error (ArithmeticException) at user/divide (REPL:1).
; Divide by zero
```

The REPL immediately informs you of the ArithmeticException caused by dividing by zero.

For more complex debugging, Clojure's clojure.tools.logging library can be integrated to log messages. First, add the dependency to your project.clj:

```
(defproject your-project "0.1.0-SNAPSHOT"
  :dependencies [[org.clojure/clojure "1.10.1"]
                 [org.clojure/tools.logging "0.5.0"]])
```

Then, include and configure the library in your code:

```
(ns your-namespace
  (:require [clojure.tools.logging :as log]))

(defn divide [numerator denominator]
  (try
```

```
  (/ numerator denominator)
  (catch ArithmeticException e
    (log/error e "Division by zero"))))
```

This implementation logs the error when a division by zero occurs, providing more context for troubleshooting.

Moreover, for developers seeking to debug without extensive reliance on Logs, the pstack utility can be used to print stack traces in a readable format. It's particularly useful for long stack traces:

```
(try
  (divide 4 0)
  (catch Exception e
    (clojure.pprint/pprint (.getStackTrace e))))
```

This code outputs a detailed stack trace, making it easier to pinpoint the exact source of an error.

Finally, the integration of external debugging tools and editors can significantly enhance the debugging process. Editors like Cursive for IntelliJ IDEA or Emacs with CIDER provide robust debugging features, including breakpoints, stepping through code, and inspecting variables.

Effective error handling and debugging are paramount for maintaining robust and reliable Clojure applications. Utilizing the described techniques, tools, and libraries will fortify your ability to diagnose and resolve issues efficiently, ensuring smoother development workflows.

Chapter 3

Clojure Syntax and Basic Data Structures

This chapter explores Clojure's syntax and basic data structures, providing detailed explanations of expressions, literals, and keywords. It covers the use of symbols and namespaces, and the definition of variables with 'def'. The chapter delves into fundamental collections such as lists, vectors, maps, and sets, and demonstrates their usage. Key topics include using keywords as functions, destructuring collections, equality and comparison operations, and control flow constructs.

3.1 Basic Syntax and Expressions

Clojure is a modern, dynamic, and functional dialect of the Lisp programming language on the Java platform. It emphasizes simple, elegant, and expressive code. Understanding the syntax and expressions is fundamental to mastering Clojure. Herein, we will explore the primary components of Clojure syntax and essential expressions.

Clojure code is composed of expressions. Every piece of Clojure code is an expression, which when evaluated, produces a value. This is a direct inheritance from Lisp, where the primary construct is the symbolic expression (s-expression).

Basic Syntax Structure

The core units of Clojure's syntax are forms. A form is any piece of code written using Clojure's data structures (lists, vectors, maps, sets). The most fundamental form in Clojure is the list. Lists are enclosed within parentheses, e.g., (1 2 3).

Forms can be either literal values or expressions that refer to data or functions. For example, the form (inc 1) is a function call where inc is the function and 1 is the argument. Clojure employs prefix notation, which is consistent across the language. This notation means that the operator or function always precedes its arguments.

```
(inc 1)
```

This expression translates to calling the function inc with an argument of 1. The result of evaluating this expression is:

```
2
```

Literals

Literals are the simplest forms in Clojure and include numbers, strings, characters, keywords, and symbols.

- Numbers can be integers, floating-point, ratios, or arbitrary precision.

```
42
3.14
7/22
9223372036854775807 ;; Arbitrary precision integer
```

- Strings are character sequences enclosed in double quotes.

```
"Hello, Clojure!"
```

- Characters are represented with a backslash followed by the character.

```
\A
\newLine
```

- Keywords are identifiers that typically serve as keys in maps and are prefixed with a colon.

```
:name
:age
```

- Symbols represent identifiers that refer to variables or functions.

```
foo
```

Expressions

Clojure expressions form the essence of the language's functionality. An expression can be any valid piece of Clojure code that the compiler can evaluate to yield a value. The simplest expressions are single literals, which evaluate to themselves.

Function calls are common expressions in Clojure. The general form of a function call expression is (function-name argument1 argument2 ... argumentN). Below are some examples:

```
(+ 2 3)
;; => 5

(* 4 5)
;; => 20

(/ 10 5)
;; => 2
```

Here, +, *, and / are functions that perform arithmetic operations, and the numbers following them are the arguments passed to these functions.

Special Forms

Clojure supports several special forms which are core constructs intrinsic to the language. These special forms cannot be redefined or overridden. Examples include def, if, fn, do, and let.

- def is used to define a variable.

```
(def x 10)
```

- if is used for conditional evaluation.

```
(if true
    "This is true"
    "This is false")
;; => "This is true"
```

- fn is used to create anonymous functions.

```
((fn [x] (* x x)) 5)
;; => 25
```

- do groups multiple expressions, evaluating them in sequence.

```
(do
    (println "Hello")
    (println "World"))
;; Outputs:
;; Hello
;; World
;; => nil
```

- let binds values to symbols in a local context.

```
(let [a 1
      b 2]
    (+ a b))
;; => 3
```

Evaluating Expressions

Clojure expressions are evaluated based on the context. When an expression is evaluated, it is processed according to the rules of the language. For instance, evaluating a simple number returns the number itself.

```
42 ;; => 42
```

Evaluating a list evaluates the first item as a function and applies it to the rest:

```
(+ 5 3) ;; => 8
```

Function calls can also be nested. For instance:

```
(+ (inc 2) (* 3 4))
;; => (+ 3 12)
;; => 15
```

Understanding and mastering the basic syntax and expressions in Clojure equips the reader with a solid foundation for exploring more advanced topics and utilizing the language's features effectively.

3.2 Literals and Keywords

In Clojure, literals are used to represent fixed values within the code. Literals include numbers, strings, characters, booleans, and collections. Understanding how to properly define and use these literals is fundamental in writing effective Clojure code. Alongside literals, Clojure provides keywords, which are a critical feature for both syntactic and idiomatic purposes.

Numbers: Clojure supports various numeric literals. These include integers, floating-point numbers, ratios, and arbitrary precision decimals.

```
;; Integer literals
42
-7

;; Floating-point literals
3.14
-0.001

;; Ratio literals
22/7
-4/3

;; Arbitrary precision decimals
3.14M
2.71828M
```

Strings: String literals in Clojure are sequences of characters enclosed in double quotes. Clojure strings are immutable and support escape sequences such as \n for newline, \t for tab, and \" for a quotation mark.

```
"Hello, world!"
"This is a Clojure string\nwith a newline character"
"This string contains a \"quote\"."
```

Characters: Character literals in Clojure are prefixed with a backslash.

```
\a
\newline
\space
\#
```

Booleans: Booleans are used to represent truth values and can take on one of two literals: true or false.

```
true
false
```

Collections: Clojure employs several collection types, including lists, vectors, maps, and sets. Each of these data structures can be defined using specific syntax.

```
;; List literals
'(1 2 3)
'(a b c)

;; Vector literals
[1 2 3]
[a b c]
```

```
;; Map literals
{:name "Alice" :age 30}
{1 "one" 2 "two"}

;; Set literals
#{1 2 3}
#{"apple" "banana"}
```

Keywords in Clojure are symbolic identifiers, beginning with a colon (:). They are used commonly as keys in maps and for various functional programming techniques. Keywords are unique in that they evaluate to themselves, making them efficient for tasks requiring constant-time checks.

Defining Keywords:

```
:some-key
:user/name
```

Unlike symbols, keywords are always namespaced by default to the current namespace, or they can include a namespace explicitly. Keywords provide an elegant solution for key-value pair access and for annotating data.

Using Keywords as Functions: One of the compelling features of keywords is their ability to function as functions themselves. This allows for direct retrieval of values from associative collections, particularly maps.

```
(def user-info {:name "John Doe" :email "john@example.com"})

;; Using the :name keyword as a function to retrieve the value associated with it
(:name user-info) ;; returns "John Doe"
(:email user-info) ;; returns "john@example.com"
```

In the above examples, the :name keyword acts as a function, taking the user-info map as its argument and returning the value associated with the :name key.

Keywords with Default Values: Keywords can also accept a default value to return if the key is not found in the collection.

```
(:phone user-info "N/A") ;; returns "N/A" since :phone key is not present
```

Understanding literals and keywords, and recognizing their appropriate usage, is essential for writing concise, readable, and maintainable Clojure programs. This foundational knowledge enables the effective manipulation and querying of data structures, providing the basis for more advanced Clojure techniques and functional programming paradigms.

3.3 Symbols and Namespaces

Symbols and namespaces are foundational constructs in Clojure, crucial for organizing and managing code. In this section, we will detail the creation and use of symbols, and how namespaces allow for the segregation and management of different parts of a program.

Symbols in Clojure are identifiers that typically refer to variables or functions. They represent named entities within a namespace and are created using simple text notations.

```
(def pi 3.14159)
(def radius 5)
(defn area-of-circle [r]
  (* pi r r))
```

In the example above, pi, radius, and area-of-circle are symbols. Symbols are case-sensitive and can include letters, numbers, a few special characters like _, * and ?, but cannot start with a number.

A namespace is a mapping from symbols to their corresponding values or functions. It allows for organizing code into logical, manageable units. Namespaces help avoid naming collisions by segregating symbols into different logical groups.

You create and switch between namespaces using the ns macro:

```
(ns myapp.core)
(def x 10)
(defn add [a b]
  (+ a b))
```

In this example, the myapp.core namespace is created. Every symbol defined thereafter belongs to this namespace. This way, the symbols x and add are stored in myapp.core.

Namespaces can be nested to allow for more organized code structuring. This involves creating namespaces within namespaces using a dot notation:

```
(ns myapp.math.operations)
(defn multiply [a b]
  (* a b))
```

This code snippet defines the multiply function within the myapp.math.operations namespace. The full path to the multiply function becomes myapp.math.operations/multiply.

When symbols from another namespace are required, they can be referred to using their full namespace-qualified name. Alternatively, namespaces can be imported partially or completely using aliasing:

```
(ns myapp.main
  (:require [myapp.math.operations :as ops]))

(defn use-multiply [a b]
  (ops/multiply a b))
```

Here, the myapp.math.operations namespace is required using the alias ops. Thus, the multiply function can be referred to as ops/multiply, simplifying the usage. This practice not only organizes code but also makes it more readable.

In addition to :require, the ns macro supports :use, which imports all symbols from a namespace directly, but it's generally discouraged due to potential naming conflicts. Aliasing with :require is preferred for clearer, more maintainable code.

Clojure offers several namespace-related functions for inspection and manipulation, e.g., ns-interns, ns-publics, and ns-aliases. These functions provide information about the symbols and mappings within a namespace, facilitating debugging and introspection.

Namespaces also allow for isolation and loading of libraries, modular development, and encapsulation. By logically grouping related symbols and ensuring they don't clash with similarly named symbols in other namespaces, the code remains clean, structured, and free from inadvertent conflicts.

```
(ns myapp.utils
  (:require [clojure.string :as str]))

(defn capitalize-words [s]
  (str/join " " (map str/capitalize (str/split s #" "))))
```

In this example, the clojure.string library is required as str, and its join, capitalize, and split functions are used to create a new function capitalize-words. The use of namespaces ensures these functions don't interfere with any similarly named functions in different contexts within the broader application.

By employing symbols and namespaces effectively, Clojure developers can create modular, reusable, and well-organized code. This structure enhances readability and maintainability, and facilitates collaborative and large-scale software development.

3.4 Defining Variables with def

In Clojure, variables are defined using the def special form. This form binds a symbol to a value or expression, creating a global binding that remains immutable unless explicitly changed. The syntax for def is straightforward:

```
(def symbol value)
```

Here, symbol is the name of the variable, and value is the data or expression assigned to it. Once a variable is defined, it can be referenced by its symbol name within the context of your program.

def can be used to bind simple data types such as numbers, strings, and booleans:

```
(def pi 3.14159)
(def greeting "Hello, World!")
(def is-valid true)
```

These definitions create global bindings for pi, greeting, and is-valid. It is important to understand that these variables, once bound, refer to the same value throughout their scope unless redefined.

Clojure allows for more complex expressions to be assigned to variables as well:

```
(def area (* pi 10 10)) ; Calculates the area of a circle with radius 10 using the earlier
    defined pi
(def message (str greeting " Clojure"))
```

In the above examples, area computes the area of a circle using the previously defined value of pi, and message concatenates the greeting with the string " Clojure".

Variable definition isn't restricted to primitive data types. You can also bind collections such as lists, vectors, maps, and sets:

```
(def a-list '(1 2 3 4 5))
(def a-vector [1 2 3 4 5])
(def a-map {:a 1 :b 2 :c 3})
(def a-set #{1 2 3 4 5})
```

With def, the collections are globally accessible with their associated symbols.

Rebinding Variables

Though bindings created with def are generally immutable, you can change them if needed by redefining them with another def:

```
(def pi 3.14) ; Updates the value of pi
(def greeting "Welcome to Clojure")
```

This rebinding updates the global value associated with each symbol. However, frequent rebinding is discouraged in functional programming in favor of immutable state.

Global variable definitions using def should be approached with care, particularly when working within larger systems or concurrent environments. Unintended changes to global state can lead to unpredictable behavior, hence Clojure emphasizes the use of local bindings via let for most use cases, which will be discussed in detail in another section.

Nil Value in Variable Binding

In Clojure, a variable can also be bound to nil, which represents the absence of a value:

```
(def no-value nil)
```

This can be useful in scenarios where variables are initialized without specific values, ensuring they can be utilized in expressions without generating errors related to undefined variables.

Interacting with Java Libraries

Clojure runs on the Java Virtual Machine (JVM), and variables in Clojure can be used to hold references to Java objects and invoke Java methods. Here's an example:

```
(def now (java.util.Date.)) ; Creates a Java Date object
(def formatted-date (.toString now)) ; Invokes the toString method on the Date object
```

The variable now holds a reference to a Java Date object, and formatted-date contains the result of calling the toString method on the Java object.

Understanding and effectively using def for variable definition is a foundational step for mastering Clojure's ability to manage state and construct complex programs. Mastery of def enhances code clarity and ensures that values are correctly bound, thus contributing to the creation of robust and maintainable code.

3.5 Working with Lists

In Clojure, a list is one of the primary data structures, and it is utilized to store a sequence of values. Lists are ordered collections and are essential for various computational paradigms, particularly functional programming. Lists in Clojure are denoted by parentheses. The elements of a list can be of any type, including other collections.

The basic structure of a Clojure list is as follows:

```
'(element1 element2 element3 ...)
```

The apostrophe (') before the parentheses indicates a literal list. If the apostrophe is omitted, Clojure will attempt to treat the first element of the list as a function or macro and evaluate it accordingly.

conj is a common operation used to add elements to a list. Unlike in many other languages where elements are appended to the end, conj adds elements to the front (beginning) of the list. This operation has a time complexity of O(1), making it very efficient.

```
(conj '(1 2 3) 4) ;=> '(4 1 2 3)
```

To create an empty list, you can use the list function:

```
(list) ;=> '()
```

Accessing elements in a list can be done using various functions. The first function retrieves the first element of the list:

```
(first '(1 2 3 4)) ;=> 1.
```

The rest function returns the list without its first element:

```
(rest '(1 2 3 4)) ;=> '(2 3 4)
```

If you need to access elements elsewhere in the list, the nth function can be employed:

```
(nth '(1 2 3 4) 2) ;=> 3
```

Note that lists in Clojure are singly linked lists. This linked-list nature means that accessing the nth element has a time complexity of O(n).

For random-access reads, consider using vectors, which will be discussed in the next sections.

Iterating through a list can be efficiently done using higher-order functions such as map, reduce, and filter. Let's look at how these functions operate on lists.

The map function applies a given function to each element of the list, returning a new list with the transformed values:

```
(map inc '(1 2 3 4)) ;=> '(2 3 4 5)
```

Here, inc is a function that increments a number by 1. The map function does not modify the original list but rather produces a new list with the result of applying inc to each element.

reduce is used to perform a cumulative operation on the elements of a list:

```
(reduce + '(1 2 3 4)) ;=> 10
```

This example uses the reduce function to sum all elements of the list. + is a binary function that adds its two arguments.

filter is used to create a list of elements that satisfy a predicate (a function returning a Boolean value):

```
(filter even? '(1 2 3 4 5 6)) ;=> '(2 4 6)
```

The even? predicate returns true for even numbers, so filter produces a list of even numbers from the original list.

The comprehension of list operations can be significantly enhanced by recognizing the immutability principle that Clojure enforces. Lists, like all other collections in Clojure, are immutable. Any operation on a list returns a new list without altering the original list.

Here is an example showing how list immutability works in Clojure. The original list remains unchanged after performing the conj operation:

```
(def my-list '(1 2 3))
(def new-list (conj my-list 4))

; Output the original list
my-list ;=> '(1 2 3)

; Output the new list
new-list ;=> '(4 1 2 3)
```

Working with lists also involves the concept of list destructuring, which allows a more elegant extraction of elements. In the context of a let binding or a function parameter list, destructuring syntax can be used to assign values from a list to named variables:

```
(let [[a b & rest] '(1 2 3 4 5)]
  (println a) ; 1
  (println b) ; 2
  (println rest)) ; '(3 4 5)
```

In this example, a is bound to the first element (1), b is bound to the second element (2), and rest is bound to a list of the remaining elements $(3, 4, 5)$.

Understanding how to manipulate and traverse lists effectively forms a core competency in Clojure programming. Whether used within pure functions or as part of larger data structures, lists provide a versatile and powerful means of aggregating elements in a specified order.

3.6 Working with Vectors

Vectors in Clojure are sequential collections that provide efficient access and modification operations. They are similar to arrays in other programming languages but offer richer functionality. Vectors maintain the order of their elements and are indexed by contiguous integers starting from zero.

Vectors can be created using the vector function or the literal syntax, which uses square brackets. Here is an example of creating vectors with both methods:

```
(def vec1 (vector 1 2 3 4 5))
(def vec2 [1 2 3 4 5])
```

To access elements in a vector, the nth function is commonly used. The index passed to nth is zero-based:

```
(nth vec1 2)
; Returns: 3
```

Additionally, vectors can be indexed with a different syntax using the vector itself as a function, passing the index as an argument:

```
(vec2 2)
; Returns: 3
```

Modifying a vector can be done with the assoc function, which returns a new vector with the specified index updated to a new value:

```
(def vec3 (assoc vec1 2 42))
```

Note that Clojure's data structures are immutable, so assoc does not alter the original vector but rather creates a new one. vec1 remains unchanged:

vec1: [1 2 3 4 5]
vec3: [1 2 42 4 5]

Vectors support common collection operations such as conj, pop, and peek. conj appends an element to the end of the vector:

```
(def vec4 (conj vec1 6))
```

vec4: [1 2 3 4 5 6]

The pop function removes the last element from the vector, while peek returns the last element without removing it:

```
(def vec5 (pop vec4))
(peek vec4)
; Returns: 6
```

vec5: [1 2 3 4 5]

Vectors can be nested within other vectors or any other Clojure collections, providing multi-dimensional data structures:

```
(def nested-vec [[1 2 3] [4 5 6] [7 8 9]])
```

To access elements within nested vectors, apply multiple nth functions or use the get-in function for more structured access:

```
(nth (nth nested-vec 1) 2)
; Returns: 6

(get-in nested-vec [1 2])
; Returns: 6
```

Iteration over vectors can be efficiently handled using Clojure's looping constructs or sequence library functions. The map function applies a given function to each element in the vector:

```
(map inc vec1)
; Returns: (2 3 4 5 6)
```

The reduce function collapses the vector elements into a single value based on a provided reducing function:

```
(reduce + vec1)
; Returns: 15
```

Partitioning a vector into smaller chunks can be achieved with the partition function, which divides the vector into sub-vectors of a specified size:

```
(partition 2 vec1)
; Returns: ((1 2) (3 4))
```

When working with vectors of known sizes, using into-array allows converting a Clojure vector into a Java array to leverage Java interop:

```
(def java-array (into-array Integer/TYPE vec1))
```

This brief overview touches on the primary operations and characteristics of vectors in Clojure, highlighting the efficiency and versatility they offer for many programming tasks.

3.7 Working with Maps

Clojure maps represent collections of key-value pairs. This data structure provides fast lookups, additions, and deletions, making it ideal for representing associative arrays or dictionaries. Maps in Clojure are immutable, which means each operation on a map results in a new map rather than modifying the original. Maps can be created using several literals or functions.

A map is represented with curly braces {}, and key-value pairs are separated by spaces. Here is an example of a simple map:

```
(def my-map {:name "Alice" :age 30 :city "Wonderland"})
```

In this example, my-map is a map with three key-value pairs. Keys are typically keywords, which are preceded by a colon. However, keys can also be other data types such as strings, symbols, or numbers. The values can be of any type.

To access a value associated with a key, use the key as a function applied to the map:

```
(def name (:name my-map))
(println name) ; Output: Alice
```

Alternatively, the get function retrieves the value for a specified key, with an optional default value if the key does not exist:

```
(def age (get my-map :age))
(def country (get my-map :country "Unknown"))
```

```
(println age) ; Output: 30
(println country) ; Output: Unknown
```

Maps support a variety of operations, including adding, updating, and removing key-value pairs. Use the assoc function to add a new key-value pair or update an existing key:

```
(def updated-map (assoc my-map :country "Wonderland"))
(println updated-map) ; Output: {:name "Alice", :age 30, :city "Wonderland", :country
    "Wonderland"}
```

To remove a key from a map, use the dissoc function:

```
(def reduced-map (dissoc my-map :age))
(println reduced-map) ; Output: {:name "Alice", :city "Wonderland"}
```

For accessing nested maps, the get-in function retrieves a value based on a sequence of keys:

```
(def nested-map {:user {:name "Alice" :details {:age 30 :city "Wonderland"}}})
(def city (get-in nested-map [:user :details :city]))
(println city) ; Output: Wonderland
```

To update values within nested maps, the update-in function is used along with a sequence of keys and an update function:

```
(def updated-nested-map (update-in nested-map [:user :details :age] inc))
(println updated-nested-map)
; Output: {:user {:name "Alice", :details {:age 31, :city "Wonderland"}}}
```

Merging maps can be achieved using the merge function or merge-with for combining values of the same key with a custom function:

```
(def map1 {:a 1 :b 2})
(def map2 {:b 3 :c 4})
(def merged-map (merge map1 map2))
(println merged-map) ; Output: {:a 1, :b 3, :c 4}
```

merge-with allows more control for handling the merging of values for shared keys:

```
(def merged-map-with (merge-with + map1 map2))
(println merged-map-with) ; Output: {:a 1, :b 5, :c 4}
```

Using maps as functions by supplying a key to obtain its value streamlines the interaction with this data structure while leveraging Clojure's focus on functional programming principles. Understanding these various operations equips programmers to efficiently manage associative data with immutability at its core.

3.8 Working with Sets

Clojure sets are collections that maintain unique elements and support efficient membership tests. Sets are highly useful for situations where you need to ensure the uniqueness of items and perform operations like union, intersection, and difference. In this section, we shall explore how to create sets, perform set operations, and utilize common set functions.

Clojure supports both hashed sets and sorted sets. In most cases, hashed sets will be more commonly used due to their typical O(1) complexity for membership checks. Sorted sets, on the other hand, maintain elements in a sorted order and use a different underlying implementation.

Creating Sets

A set can be created using the hash-set function or by using the set literal syntax, which encloses elements within curly braces.

```
(hash-set 1 2 3 4)
#{1 2 3 4}
```

Both of the above expressions create a set with the elements 1, 2, 3, and 4. The hash-set function can be used programmatically to create sets from other collections.

```
(def my-set (hash-set 1 2 3 3 4))
(println my-set)
```

#{1 2 3 4}

Note that the duplicate 3 is automatically omitted, thus preserving the uniqueness property of sets.

Similarly, you can create sorted sets using the sorted-set function:

```
(def my-sorted-set (sorted-set 4 3 2 1 1))
(println my-sorted-set)
```

#{1 2 3 4}

Here, the elements are stored in a sorted order, again with duplicates removed.

Common Set Functions

Clojure provides several core functions for working with sets:

- conj - Adds an element to a set.
- disj - Removes an element from a set.
- union - Computes the union of two sets.
- intersection - Computes the intersection of two sets.
- difference - Computes the difference between two sets.

Let us review how these functions operate on sets through concrete examples.

```
(def a #{1 2 3})
(def b #{3 4 5})

(conj a 4)
(disj a 2)
(clojure.set/union a b)
(clojure.set/intersection a b)
(clojure.set/difference a b)
```

```
; Adding 4 to the set a
#{1 2 3 4}

; Removing 2 from the set a
#{1 3}

; Union of sets a and b
#{1 2 3 4 5}

; Intersection of sets a and b
#{3}

; Difference between sets a and b
#{1 2}
```

The conj function is used to add elements, whereas disj is used to remove elements. The set-specific functions union, intersection, and difference are part of the clojure.set namespace, and they perform union, intersection, and difference operations, respectively.

Membership Testing

Testing for the presence of an element in a set can be efficiently done using the contains? function:

```
(def my-set #{1 2 3})
(contains? my-set 2) ; true
(contains? my-set 4) ; false
```

```
true
false
```

The contains? function returns a boolean value indicating whether the specified element is in the set.

Using Sets for Membership Checking

One useful pattern is using sets to filter collections based on membership.

```
(def valid-ids #{1001 1002 1003 1004})
(def input-ids [999 1002 1004 1005])

(filter valid-ids input-ids)
```

```
(1002 1004)
```

In this example, valid-ids is a set of acceptable IDs, and input-ids is a list of IDs to check. Using the set directly in the filter function efficiently keeps only the valid IDs.

These fundamental operations and usage patterns with sets are vital when dealing with unique collections and performing typical set-related tasks in Clojure programs.

3.9 Using Keywords as Functions

In Clojure, keywords can be used not only as identifiers or constant values but also as functions. This capability stems from Clojure's design where keywords, being instances of the clojure.lang.Keyword class, implement the IFn interface. This allows a keyword to be called as a function that takes a data structure and returns the value associated with the keyword within that structure.

Keywords in Clojure are prefixed with a colon (:), and they are commonly used as keys in maps. When used as functions, they provide a concise way to retrieve values from maps, which can be particularly useful in reducing boilerplate code and improving readability.

To understand the functional aspect of keywords better, consider the following example where a map is defined, and the keyword :name is used to retrieve the value associated with it.

```
(def person {:name "Alice" :age 30 :city "Wonderland"})
(:name person)
```

The execution of the above code will output:

```
"Alice"
```

In this example, the :name keyword is used as a function to access the corresponding value in the person map. This operation is equivalent to the map lookup operation performed using the get function.

```
(get person :name)
```

Both approaches yield the same result. Using keywords as functions is a more idiomatic way that Clojure programmers often prefer due to its succinctness.

In addition to simple value retrieval, keywords as functions offer flexibility with an optional second argument. This second argument serves as a default value if the keyword is not present in the map. This feature is especially useful for ensuring that a retrieval operation does not result in nil if a key is absent.

```
(:nickname person "No nickname found")
```

Given that the person map does not contain the :nickname keyword, the execution of this code will output:

```
"No nickname found"
```

Not only do keywords work with maps, but they also function with any associative data structures such as vectors and sets. When used with vectors, the keyword's numeric value is treated as the index.

```
(def colors [:red :green :blue])
(:1 colors)
```

Here, the keyword :1 attempts to access the first index in the colors vector, resulting in the output:

```
:green
```

With sets, the keyword functions as an existence test, returning the keyword itself if it is present in the set.

```
(def fruits #{:apple :banana :cherry})
(:banana fruits)
```

The execution of this snippet will yield:

```
:banana
```

Alternatively, attempting to retrieve a keyword not in the set yields nil unless a default value is provided:

```
(:pineapple fruits "Not found")
```

This results in the output:

```
"Not found"
```

The capacity of keywords to act as functions extends beyond trivial lookups and default values. Keywords as functions seamlessly integrate with Clojure's higher-order functions. Consider the common use case of applying a function to each element within a sequence using map:

```
(def persons [{:name "Alice" :age 30}
              {:name "Bob" :age 25}
              {:name "Charlie" :age 35}])

(map :name persons)
```

The execution of the above code yields:

```
("Alice" "Bob" "Charlie")
```

This example demonstrates the utility of keywords as efficient tools for transforming sequences of maps. Each map in the persons vector is processed, and the :name keyword function extracts the corresponding names, producing a sequence of names.

The above approach can enhance clarity and reduce verbosity compared to manually defining functions for these operations. By leveraging keywords as functions, Clojure practitioners can often achieve more concise, readable, and expressive code.

3.10 Destructuring Collections

Destructuring is a powerful feature in Clojure that allows for the binding of names to parts of data structures. It simplifies the process of extracting values from collections, leading to more readable and concise code. Destructuring can be used in various constructs, such as function parameters, let bindings, and for loops. Here, we examine how to destructure lists, vectors, maps, and nested structures.

Lists and Vectors

Clojure provides a straightforward way to destructure lists and vectors. Given a collection, you can extract the elements by specifying a vector of symbols corresponding to the positions of the elements you wish to bind. Consider the following example:

```
(let [[a b c] [1 2 3]]
  (+ a b c))
```

In this let binding, the vector [a b c] on the left-hand side is matched with the vector [1 2 3] on the right-hand side. Consequently, a is bound to 1, b to 2, and c to 3. The sum of a, b, and c is 6, which is the result of the expression.

Destructuring supports various forms to handle different scenarios, such as when dealing with the remainder of a collection or binding only specific elements:

```
(let [[a b & rest] [1 2 3 4 5]]
  [a b rest])
```

Here, a is bound to 1, b to 2, and the rest of the elements, [3 4 5], are collected in the rest binding. The resulting vector is [1 2 [3 4 5]].

Maps

Destructuring maps involves specifying keys whose associated values you wish to bind. This can be done using a map within a let binding or function parameter list. The following example demonstrates basic map destructuring:

```
(let [{:keys [x y]} {:x 10 :y 20}]
  (* x y))
```

In this example, :keys [x y] indicates that x should be bound to the value associated with the :x key (10) and y to the value associated with the :y key (20). The product of x and y (200) is the result of the expression.

When dealing with default values, map destructuring can include a fall-back for missing keys:

```
(let [{:keys [a b] :or {a 1 b 2}} {:a 10}]
  [a b])
```

Here, a is present in the map with the value 10, but b is not. Therefore, a is bound to 10, and b falls back to its default value 2, resulting in the vector [10 2].

Nested Structures

Destructuring can be applied to nested data structures, allowing for deep extraction of values. Consider a nested map as follows:

```
(let [{:keys [name address]
       :or {name "Unknown"}
       :as person}
      {:name "Alice"
       :address {:city "Wonderland"
                 :street "Rabbit Hole"}}]
  [name (:city address) person])
```

This binding destructures the keys :name and :address from the top-level map. Additionally, the entire map is captured in the person binding using :as. The nested map under :address is further destructured to extract the :city key. Therefore, name is "Alice", :city under address is "Wonderland", and person retains the entire original map. The result is the vector ["Alice" "Wonderland" :name "Alice" :address :city "Wonderland" :street "Rabbit Hole"].

Function Parameters

Destructuring also streamlines function definitions by directly binding parts of argument collections to parameter names. For example:

```
(defn greet [{:keys [name title]}]
  (str "Hello, " title " " name "!"))

(greet {:name "Alice" :title "Dr."})
```

The greet function expects a map with :name and :title. When called with {:name "Alice" :title "Dr."}, it returns the string "Hello, Dr. Alice!" by using the destructured values.

In scenarios where functions accept vectors, destructuring also applies efficiently:

```
(defn calculate [[a b c]]
  (+ a (* b c)))

(calculate [1 2 3])
```

Here, the calculate function expects a vector and destructures it directly into bindings a, b, and c. Thus, calling calculate with the vector [1 2 3] results in $1 + (2 * 3)$ which evaluates to 7.

By leveraging destructuring, Clojure developers simplify data handling and enhance code readability while maintaining robust functionality.

3.11 Equality and Comparison

Clojure provides a robust set of functions for equality and comparison that we use to write expressive and accurate code. Understanding how to compare values efficiently and correctly is pivotal for developing reliable and maintainable Clojure applications. We shall discuss the primary methods for evaluating equality and performing comparisons: =, ==, identical?, compare, and the relational operators.

The = function is the primary tool for testing equality in Clojure. It assesses structural equality, meaning it checks whether two collections of data have the same shape and content. Here is an example demonstrating its use:

```
(= [1 2 3] [1 2 3]) ; => true
(= {:a 1 :b 2} {:b 2 :a 1}) ; => true
(= '(4 5 6) [4 5 6]) ; => false
(= 42 42.0) ; => true
```

Notice that = can evaluate the equality of different types of collections, such as lists and vectors. However, in some cases, it performs type conversion for comparison, such as treating integers and floating-point numbers as equal if their values are the same numerically.

The == function is used for numerical equality, ensuring that the values are equal without considering their types. It exclusively works for numbers and is beneficial when we need to disregard type differences:

```
(== 42 42.0) ; => true
(== 42 43) ; => false
```

When identity comparison is required, the identical? function is appropriate. This function evaluates whether two references point to the exact same object in memory. It does not consider the values or structure but the actual objects' identity:

```
(def a [1 2 3])
(def b a)
(def c [1 2 3])
(identical? a b) ; => true
(identical? a c) ; => false
```

In the case above, a and b refer to the same vector, so identical? returns true, whereas a and c are different vectors with the same content, so it returns false.

The compare function provides a more nuanced comparison and returns a value indicating the order of the arguments. It returns -1 if the first argument is less than the second, 0 if they are equal, and 1 if the first is greater. This is particularly useful in sorting operations or comparisons where ordering is necessary:

```
(compare 10 20) ; => -1
(compare 20 20) ; => 0
(compare 30 20) ; => 1
```

compare can be extended to other types such as strings and collections that can be consistently ordered:

```
(compare "apple" "banana") ; => -1
```

```
(compare [1 2] [1 2 3]) ; => -1
(compare {:a 1} {:a 1 :b 2}) ; => -1
```

Clojure includes a set of relational operators that we use for numerical comparisons, extending to other comparable entities, such as dates or strings. These include <, <=, >, and >=:

```
(< 10 20) ; => true
(<= 20 20) ; => true
(> 30 20) ; => true
(>= 30 30) ; => true
```

Moreover, comparisons in Clojure retain their chaining property, allowing multiple comparisons within a single expression:

```
(< 1 2 3 4) ; => true
(<= 1 2 2 3) ; => true
(> 4 3 2) ; => true
(>= 4 4 3) ; => true
```

These tools provide a comprehensive suite of comparison functions to work efficiently with various data types, ensuring both simplicity and precision in Clojure's operations for equality and comparison. These operations lay the groundwork for complex decision-making processes, conditional execution, and data structure manipulations that hinge on accurate assessments of equality and order.

3.12 Control Flow Constructs

In any programming language, the ability to control the flow of execution is crucial for developing logical and efficient code. Clojure provides several constructs to manage control flow, including conditional expressions, looping, and exception handling. This section will cover the use of if, if-not, when, when-not, cond, case, loop/recur, for, and try/catch/finally constructs.

Conditional Expressions

if is the most basic control flow construct that evaluates a condition and returns one value if the condition is true and another value if the condition is false. The syntax of the if expression is as follows:

```
(if condition
  then-expression
  else-expression)
```

The else-expression is optional. If it is not provided, nil is returned when the condition is false. Here's a simple example:

```
(if (< 3 5)
  "3 is less than 5"
  "3 is not less than 5")
```

```
"3 is less than 5"
```

The if-not expression is similar to if but negates the condition:

```
(if-not condition
  then-expression
  else-expression)
```

The when expression simplifies the if expression when there is no else-expression. It is used to execute a series of expressions if the condition is true. The syntax is as follows:

```
(when condition
  expression1
  expression2
  ...)
```

This can be useful for side-effects. For instance:

```
(when (> 5 3)
  (println "5 is greater than 3")
  (println "Another statement"))
```

```
5 is greater than 3
Another statement
```

The when-not expression is used in a similar way to when, but it negates the condition:

```
(when-not condition
  expression1
  expression2
  ...)
```

Complex Conditionals

For complex conditionals involving multiple branches, Clojure provides the cond expression. The cond expression evaluates each test in turn and returns the value corresponding to the first true test:

```
(cond
  test1 result1
  test2 result2
  ...
  :else fallback-result)
```

For example:

```
(cond
```

```
  (> 3 5) "3 is greater than 5"
  (< 3 5) "3 is less than 5"
  :else "3 is equal to 5")
```

"3 is less than 5"

The case expression is another conditional construct that is used when the condition is a discrete value. It provides a way to compare an expression against a set of constants:

```
(case expression
  value1 result1
  value2 result2
  ...
  :else fallback-result)
```

For instance:

```
(case 2
  1 "one"
  2 "two"
  3 "three"
  :else "other")
```

"two"

Looping Constructs

Clojure features iterative constructs such as loop/recur that support efficient looping through tail-call optimization. The loop expression establishes a recursion point, and recur is used to jump back to that point.

Here is a simple example where we calculate the factorial of a number using loop/recur:

```
(defn factorial [n]
  (loop [i n acc 1]
    (if (zero? i)
      acc
      (recur (dec i) (* acc i)))))
```

(factorial 5)

120

The for expression is used for list comprehensions, enabling a concise way to generate and transform sequences. The general syntax is:

```
(for [binding-form sequence-expression]
  body-expression)
```

For example:

```
(for [x (range 5) y (range 3)]
```

```
[x y])
```

([0 0] [0 1] [0 2] [1 0] [1 1] [1 2] [2 0] [2 1] [2 2] [3 0] [3 1] [3 2] [4 0] [4 1] [4 2])

Exception Handling

Clojure handles exceptions similarly to Java, providing the try, catch, and finally constructs. The try block contains code that may throw exceptions, while the catch block handles specific exceptions. The optional finally block executes code irrespective of whether an exception was thrown.

The syntax is as follows:

```
(try
  tr-expr
  (catch ExceptionType e catch-expr)
  (finally fin-expr))
```

For instance:

```
(try
  (/ 10 0)
  (catch ArithmeticException e
    (str "Caught exception: " (.getMessage e)))
  (finally (println "In finally block")))
```

In finally block
"Caught exception: Divide by zero"

Understanding and implementing these control flow constructs are fundamental to writing robust and efficient Clojure code. Each construct serves a specific purpose and, when used appropriately, can greatly enhance code readability and performance.

Chapter 4

Functions and Functional Programming Concepts

This chapter introduces the fundamentals of defining and using functions in Clojure, including the ‘defn‘ syntax, function parameters, and arity. It explores higher-order functions, anonymous functions with ‘fn‘, and common functional programming operations such as ‘map‘, ‘reduce‘, and ‘filter‘. Key concepts such as function composition, recursion, pure functions, side effects, closures, lexical scope, and lazy sequences are discussed. The chapter also highlights functional programming strategies and the use of ‘core.async‘ for concurrency.

4.1 Defining Functions with defn

In Clojure, functions are first-class citizens, meaning they can be passed as arguments, returned from other functions, and assigned to variables. The primary method to define functions in Clojure is by using the defn macro. The defn macro not only simplifies function definition but also integrates seamlessly with Clojure's emphasis on immutability and functional programming.

To define a basic function using defn, you specify the function's name, an optional docstring, the parameter list, and the function body. The basic syntax is as follows:

```
(defn function-name
  "Optional docstring describing the function"
  [parameters]
  body)
```

The following example demonstrates a simple function that adds two numbers:

```
(defn add-two-numbers
  "Adds two numbers together."
  [a b]
  (+ a b))
```

To call this function, simply use its name followed by the arguments:

```
(add-two-numbers 3 5)
```

This would yield the output:

```
8
```

It is important to note that the function body can consist of multiple expressions, and the value of the last expression in the body is returned as the result. Here is an example with multiple expressions in the function body:

```
(defn complex-operation
  "Performs a complex operation involving multiple steps."
  [x y]
  (let [sum (+ x y)
        product (* x y)]
    (/ sum product)))
```

In this function, the let binding creates local variables sum and product, and the last expression (/ sum product) is evaluated and returned.

Clojure allows the definition of functions that can accept a variable number of arguments by using the variadic syntax. This is accomplished by including a & symbol followed by a parameter name in the parameter list. All extra arguments passed to the function are collected into a list assigned to this parameter. For instance:

```
(defn sum
  "Sums a variable number of arguments."
  [& numbers]
  (reduce + numbers))
```

Here, the sum function takes any number of arguments and uses reduce to compute their sum. When calling this function:

```
(sum 1 2 3 4 5)
```

The output would be:

```
15
```

Functions in Clojure can also have multiple arities. This means that a single function name can be defined to accept different numbers of arguments, and each arity can have a distinct implementation. The definition of a multiple-arity function is achieved by providing separate parameter lists and bodies for each arity:

```
(defn greet
  "Greets a person. Accepts either one or two arguments."
  ([name]
   (str "Hello, " name "!"))
  ([greeting name]
   (str greeting, " " name "!")))
```

In the above greet function, there are two arities: one that takes a single argument and another that takes two arguments. Calling these functions would produce:

```
(greet "Alice")
(greet "Good morning" "Alice")
```

The corresponding outputs would be:

```
"Hello, Alice!"
"Good morning, Alice!"
```

Clojure's defn macro also supports metadata, which can be attached to functions to provide additional information such as the function's purpose, author, and more. To attach metadata to a function, use the^ symbol followed by a data map. Here is an example:

```
(defn ^{:author "John Doe" :date "2023-10-01"} documented-function
  "A function with metadata."
  [x]
  (* x x))
```

The attached metadata does not affect the function's behavior but can be accessed using the meta function:

```
(meta #'documented-function)
```

This yields:

```
{:author "John Doe", :date "2023-10-01"}
```

Clojure's approach to function definitions with defn emphasizes clarity and brevity while providing powerful tools for creating versatile and reusable code. Using defn, functions can be defined with documented purpose, varying arities, and rich metadata, adhering to the principles of functional programming.

4.2 Function Parameters and Arity

In Clojure, defining function parameters is a critical aspect of creating versatile and reusable functions. The number of parameters that a function can accept is referred to as its "arity." Understanding how to manage and utilize function parameters and varying arities allows you to write more general, flexible, and concise functions.

To define a function with specific parameters, you use the defn macro. Here is a basic example of a function that takes two parameters:

```
(defn add [x y]
  (+ x y))
```

In this example, the add function accepts two parameters, x and y, and returns their sum. The parameters are specified within square brackets immediately after the function name.

Clojure functions can also be defined to handle different numbers of parameters. This is known as defining functions with multiple arities. To define a function with multiple arities, you provide separate parameter lists and corresponding function bodies for each arity. Consider the following example:

```
(defn add
  ([] 0)
  ([x] x)
  ([x y] (+ x y)))
```

Here, the add function is defined with three arities:

- No parameters: returns 0.
- One parameter: returns the value of that parameter.
- Two parameters: returns the sum of the two parameters.

When calling the function, Clojure will automatically dispatch to the correct arity based on the number of arguments provided. Here is an example of calling the add function with different numbers of arguments:

```
(add) ; returns 0
```

```
(add 5) ; returns 5
(add 2 3) ; returns 5
```

The function calls demonstrate how Clojure selects the appropriate function body to execute based on the arguments' count.

Clojure also supports functions with variable numbers of arguments, often referred to as variadic functions. You can define a variadic function using the & symbol followed by a parameter name. This parameter is bound to a sequence of all additional arguments passed to the function. Here is an example:

```
(defn sum [x & more]
  (reduce + x more))
```

In this sum function:

- The first parameter, x, is required.
- The & more parameter collects any additional arguments into a sequence.
- The reduce function is used to sum x and all elements in more.

Examples of calling the sum function with varying numbers of arguments:

```
(sum 1) ; returns 1
(sum 1 2) ; returns 3
(sum 1 2 3 4); returns 10
```

Another important concept regarding function parameters is the destructuring of compound data structures. Destructuring allows you to bind names to elements of a collection directly within the parameter list. Here is an example with a vector:

```
(defn greet [[first-name last-name]]
  (str "Hello, " first-name " " last-name))
```

When calling greet, you pass in a vector, and the elements of the vector are destructured into first-name and last-name:

```
(greet ["John" "Doe"]) ; returns "Hello, John Doe"
```

Destructuring can also be applied to maps. Here is an example:

```
(defn greet-map [{:keys [first-name last-name]}]
  (str "Hello, " first-name " " last-name))
```

In the greet-map function, the map's keys :first-name and :last-name are destructured into the corresponding variables:

```
(greet-map {:first-name "John" :last-name "Doe"}) ; returns "Hello, John Doe"
```

Managing function parameters and arity effectively is essential in functional programming with Clojure. By understanding and applying these concepts, you can create more expressive and adaptable code.

4.3 Higher-Order Functions

Higher-order functions are fundamental to functional programming and are a key feature of Clojure. A higher-order function is defined as one that either takes one or more functions as arguments or returns a function as its result. This capability promotes code modularity, reusability, and expressive power.

In Clojure, functions are first-class citizens, which means they can be used as values in various places where other data types can be used. This section elaborates on how higher-order functions work and how they can be utilized effectively.

```
;; Example of a higher-order function
(defn apply-twice [f x]
  (f (f x)))

;; Using the higher-order function 'apply-twice'
(apply-twice inc 5) ;; => 7
```

In the example above, apply-twice is a higher-order function because it takes another function f as an argument. The inc function is passed to apply-twice, resulting in the value being incremented twice.

```
(apply-twice inc 5)
=> 7
```

Clojure's standard library provides numerous higher-order functions, such as map, reduce, and filter, which are essential tools for functional programming.

map applies a given function to each item in a collection and returns a new collection comprising the results.

```
;; Example of using 'map'
(defn square [x]
  (* x x))

(map square [1 2 3 4 5]) ;; => (1 4 9 16 25)
```

```
(map square [1 2 3 4 5])
=> (1 4 9 16 25)
```

reduce is another higher-order function that successively applies a function to the elements of a collection, reducing it to a single value.

```
;; Example of using 'reduce'
(reduce + [1 2 3 4 5]) ;; => 15
```

```
(reduce + [1 2 3 4 5])
=> 15
```

filter takes a predicate function and a collection, returning a new collection of items that satisfy the predicate.

```
;; Example of using 'filter'
(defn even? [x]
  (zero? (mod x 2)))

(filter even? [1 2 3 4 5 6]) ;; => (2 4 6)
```

```
(filter even? [1 2 3 4 5 6])
=> (2 4 6)
```

Higher-order functions enable you to create more abstract forms of reusable code. Consider the following example where a higher-order function make-adder returns a new function:

```
;; Example of higher-order function returning a function
(defn make-adder [n]
  (fn [x] (+ x n)))

;; Creating a new function by calling make-adder
(def add-five (make-adder 5))

(add-five 10) ;; => 15
```

```
(add-five 10)
=> 15
```

In this case, make-adder accepts a number n and returns a new function that adds n to its argument. Calling (make-adder 5) gives us a new function add-five which, when applied to 10, returns 15.

Higher-order functions provide significant advantages in enabling code reuse, improving modularity, and allowing generic programming. They allow operations to be abstracted in a way that their implementation can be easily reused in different contexts.

4.4 Anonymous Functions with fn

Anonymous functions, often referred to as lambda functions in the context of various programming languages, are functions defined without a name. In Clojure, anonymous functions are created using the fn special form. These functions can be passed as arguments, returned from other functions, and assigned to variables, allowing for a highly flexible and functional programming approach.

The outermost form for an anonymous function is (fn [params] (body)), where params represents one or more parameters, and body consists of the expressions that define the function's behavior. Unlike named functions created using defn, anonymous functions are not bound to a symbol within the namespace; instead, they exist independently and are typically used in place.

To illustrate the creation and utilization of anonymous functions, consider the following example, where an anonymous function is defined and immediately invoked:

```
(fn [x] (+ x 1)) ; This defines a function that adds 1 to its argument
```

The above example defines a function that takes one parameter x and returns the result of adding 1 to x. Since the function is anonymous, it can be passed directly as an argument to another function or be immediately invoked:

```
((fn [x] (+ x 1)) 5) ; => 6
```

Anonymous functions are particularly useful in higher-order functions, such as map, reduce, and filter. Here, they provide inline functionality without the need to define a separate named function. Consider the following application of map to increment each element in a list:

```
(map (fn [x] (+ x 1)) [1 2 3 4 5]) ; => (2 3 4 5 6)
```

For even more succinct syntax, Clojure offers a shorthand notation for anonymous functions using the #() form, where parameters are represented by %, %1, etc. This shorthand makes the use of anonymous functions even more concise and readable:

```
(map #(+ % 1) [1 2 3 4 5]) ; => (2 3 4 5 6)
```

Here, % represents the argument to the anonymous function, allowing for a compact expression of the increment operation within the map function.

When an anonymous function requires multiple parameters, you can specify these parameters using %1, %2, and so forth. The following code snippet demonstrates a reduction operation with a custom addition function:

```
(reduce #(+ %1 %2) [1 2 3 4 5]) ; => 15
```

In this example, %1 and %2 are the parameters to the anonymous function, representing two elements from the list being reduced.

Beyond simple operations, anonymous functions can also contain more complex logic and multiple expressions. For instance, an anonymous function that checks if a number is even and returns a corresponding message can be written as follows:

```
(fn [x]
  (if (even? x)
    (str x " is even")
    (str x " is odd")))
```

When used within a higher-order function, this anonymous function provides a contextual operation without the overhead of a named definition:

```
(map (fn [x]
       (if (even? x)
         (str x " is even")
         (str x " is odd")))
     [1 2 3 4 5])
; => ("1 is odd" "2 is even" "3 is odd" "4 is even" "5 is odd")
```

Anonymous functions encapsulate transient behavior suited for inline and one-off use cases. They are instrumental in enabling functional programming paradigms, offering significant flexibility and succinctness, particularly when combined with higher-order functions and other functional constructs in Clojure.

4.5 Using map, reduce, and filter

The map, reduce, and filter functions are fundamental tools in functional programming and are central to many operations in Clojure. These functions operate on collections and allow for expressive data transformations and aggregations.

map applies a given function to each element of a collection, producing a new collection of the results. The syntax is straightforward:

```
(map f coll)
```

Where f is the function to apply, and coll is the collection to process. For example, to double each number in a list:

```
(map (fn [x] (* 2 x)) [1 2 3 4 5])
```

This code returns:

```
(2 4 6 8 10)
```

One advantage of map is that it preserves the structure of the collection. If the input is a list, the output will be a list; if the input is a vector, the output will also be a vector.

reduce performs a reduction on a collection, applying a binary function consecutively to the collection's elements, producing a single accumulated value. The syntax is:

```
(reduce f init coll)
```

Where f is the binary function, init is the initial value for the accumulator, and coll is the collection. For example, to sum all numbers in a list:

```
(reduce + 0 [1 2 3 4 5])
```

This code returns:

```
15
```

Choosing appropriate initial values for the accumulator is crucial to prevent errors, especially for non-commutative or non-associative functions.

filter creates a new collection containing only those elements of the input collection that satisfy a given predicate function. The syntax is:

```
(filter pred coll)
```

Where pred is the predicate function and coll is the collection to process. For example, to filter out all even numbers from a list:

```
(filter odd? [1 2 3 4 5 6 7 8])
```

This code returns:

```
(1 3 5 7)
```

The filter function also preserves the type of the input collection.

Combining these functions enables more complex operations, promoting readability and reducing the need for imperatively looping through collections. For instance, to find the sum of the squares of odd numbers from 1 to 10:

```
(reduce + 0 (map (fn [x] (* x x)) (filter odd? (range 1 11))))
```

This code performs three steps: filtering, mapping, and reducing. It returns:

```
165
```

Understanding how map, reduce, and filter operate is pivotal for leveraging the full power of Clojure's functional programming paradigm. They allow for concise, readable, and maintainable code, making them indispensable tools for any Clojure programmer.

4.6 Composing Functions

Function composition is a fundamental concept in functional programming and a powerful tool for building complex operations from simpler ones. In Clojure, you can achieve function composition using the comp function, which takes a variable number of functions as arguments and returns a new function. The resulting composed function represents the application of the provided functions in the reverse order.

Consider the following example, where we define three simple functions: inc, double, and square.

```
(defn inc [x]
  (+ x 1))

(defn double [x]
  (* x 2))

(defn square [x]
  (* x x))
```

We can compose these functions to create a new function that increments a number, doubles it, and then squares the result. Using comp, the composed function can be created as follows:

```
(def inc-double-square (comp square double inc))
```

When inc-double-square is called with an argument, it will execute inc, then double, and finally square:

```
(inc-double-square 2)
```

Output:

```
36
```

The composition process is equivalent to executing the following expression:

```
(square (double (inc 2)))
```

This reverse application order is crucial to understand in function composition. It allows for the creation of pipeline-like transformations where each composed function processes the results of the previous one.

Function composition isn't limited to unary functions. Consider if each function can accept multiple arguments; you can still compose them as long as the output of one function can be matched with input parameters of the next one. For more complex pipelines, we use the partial function to bind values to specific parameters or use anonymous functions to adapt outputs to required inputs.

Here is an example using partial for function composition:

```
(defn subtract [x y]
  (- x y))

(defn divide [x y]
  (/ x y))

(def sub5 (partial subtract 5))

(def sub5-and-divide-by-2 (comp (partial divide 2) sub5))
```

The composed function sub5-and-divide-by-2 will first subtract 5 from the input value and then divide the result by 2:

```
(sub5-and-divide-by 10)
```

Output:

```
2.5
```

Moreover, to better express pipelines, Clojure offers the -> and -» threading macros, simplifying nested calls by restructuring them into a linear sequence.

Consider transforming the above using the -» threading macro, which threads the last argument of each function call:

```
(->> 2 inc double square)
```

This expression achieves the same result as the inc-double-square composition but is generally more readable, especially when dealing with longer pipelines.

Function composition, threading macros, and partial application together enable highly modular, readable, and maintainable functional programs. Understanding and leveraging these capabilities is essential for mastering functional programming in Clojure and effectively solving complex problems with elegant solutions.

4.7 Recursion in Clojure

Recursion is a fundamental concept in functional programming and plays a significant role in Clojure due to its immutable data structures. Unlike traditional iterative constructs found in imperative languages, recursion provides a way to solve problems by having a function call itself, breaking the problem into smaller, more manageable parts. This section delves into the mechanics of recursion in Clojure, illustrating how it can be effectively employed to solve various problems.

In Clojure, recursion can be implemented using standard function calls. Recursive functions must include a termination condition to prevent infinite loops. These functions repeatedly call themselves with modified arguments, converging towards this termination condition. As an example, consider the classic problem of calculating factorials.

```
(defn factorial [n]
  (if (<= n 1)
    1
    (* n (factorial (dec n)))))
```

In this example, factorial is a recursive function that computes the factorial of a given number n. The base case is defined when n is less than or equal to 1, returning 1. Otherwise, the function multiplies n by the factorial of (dec n), effectively reducing the problem size by one on each recursive call.

Tail Recursion

Tail recursion is an optimization technique where the recursive call is the last operation the function performs. Clojure optimizes tail-recursive functions using the recur special form, which eliminates the risk of stack overflow errors by reusing stack frames.

Let us rewrite the earlier factorial function using recur to ensure tail recursion.

```
(defn factorial [n]
  (loop [acc 1
         n n]
    (if (<= n 1)
      acc
      (recur (* acc n) (dec n)))))
```

Here, we use the loop construct to create an initial context with acc set to 1 (the accumulator for the result) and n unchanged. The termination condition checks if n is less than or equal to 1, at which point it returns the accumulator. Otherwise, recur is called with the new accumulator and the decremented n. The recur form guarantees a tail call by reinitializing the loop variables instead of making an actual recursive call.

Mutual Recursion

Mutual recursion involves multiple functions calling each other in a cyclic manner. These functions must also include proper termination conditions to avoid infinite recursions. Consider an example involving two mutually recursive functions to determine whether a number is even or odd.

```
(defn is-even? [n]
  (if (zero? n)
    true
    (is-odd? (dec n))))

(defn is-odd? [n]
  (if (zero? n)
    false
    (is-even? (dec n))))
```

In this example, is-even? calls is-odd? and vice versa. The base case for is-even? checks if the number is zero, returning true. Otherwise, it decrements the number by one and calls is-odd?. Similarly, is-odd? has a base case returning false if the number is zero and calls is-even? with the decremented number otherwise. This structure ensures that eventually, one of the functions will reach a base case as they approach zero.

Recursive Data Structures

Clojure functions can also handle recursive data structures like lists and trees. When working with lists, recursion can traverse and manipulate elements effectively. Consider a function to reverse a list using recursion.

```
(defn reverse-list [lst]
  (loop [acc []
```

```
      lst lst]
  (if (empty? lst)
    acc
    (recur (cons (first lst) acc) (rest lst)))))
```

In this scenario, reverse-list uses a loop to manage the accumulator acc and the list lst. The base case checks if lst is empty, at which point the reversed list (accumulator) is returned. Otherwise, recur prepends the first element of lst to acc and processes the remainder of the list.

Recursive Functions and Lazy Evaluation

Clojure's support for lazy evaluation can also intersect with recursion. When defining potentially infinite sequences, recursion pairs well with Clojure's lazy sequence capabilities. Consider generating an infinite sequence of Fibonacci numbers.

```
(defn fib-seq []
  ((fn rfib [a b]
     (lazy-seq
       (cons a (rfib b (+ a b)))))
   0 1))
```

In this case, the inner function rfib recursively generates the next Fibonacci number, using lazy-seq to defer computation until needed. The sequence begins with 0 and 1, and each subsequent pair of numbers is generated by adding the last two numbers. This approach leverages both recursion and lazy evaluation to create an efficient, potentially infinite sequence of Fibonacci numbers.

Utilizing recursion in Clojure enables solutions that are elegant and inherently functional. By properly managing base cases and employing tail recursion or mutual recursion when appropriate, recursive functions can solve complex problems while maintaining clarity and efficiency.

4.8 Pure Functions and Side Effects

Pure functions are a fundamental concept in functional programming, including Clojure. A *pure function* is a function that meets two primary criteria: it always produces the same output given the same input, and it produces no observable side effects. These characteristics make pure functions predictable, testable, and composable.

Pure functions have the following properties:

- Determinism: Given the same inputs, a pure function will always return the same output. This property simplifies reasoning about the function's behavior.

- No Side Effects: A pure function does not alter any state outside its scope or interact with the outside world (no modifying global variables, no I/O operations, etc.). This ensures that its execution does not depend on or change the state of the system.

```
(defn add
  "A pure function that adds two numbers."
  [x y]
  (+ x y))
```

In the above add function, given the same input values x and y, the function will always return $x + y$. Moreover, it does not modify any global state or perform any I/O operations.

Contrast this with impure functions, which do not hold the same guarantees. Impure functions may produce different outputs given the same inputs due to reliance on external state or may cause side effects that impact the system.

```
(def counter (atom 0))

(defn increment-counter
  "An impure function that increments a global counter."
  []
  (swap! counter inc))
```

In this example, the function increment-counter is considered impure. It modifies the state of the counter atom every time it is called, which constitutes a side effect. Additionally, its output (the new value of counter) is not solely dependent on its inputs but also on the current state of counter.

```
Examples of pure and impure function calls:
(let [result1 (add 1 2)
      result2 (add 1 2)]
  [result1 result2])
; => [3 3]

(let [counter1 @counter
      _ (increment-counter)
      counter2 @counter]
  [counter1 counter2])
; If the initial value of counter was 0:
; => [0 1]
```

Functional programming emphasizes the use of pure functions due to several advantages:

- Ease of Testing: Since pure functions do not depend on or modify external state, testing them in isolation is straightforward.

- Reasoning and Debugging: Pure functions' deterministic nature simplifies understanding and debugging—knowing that the same input always produces the same output reduces complexity.
- Concurrency: Inherent thread-safety of pure functions makes them well-suited for concurrent and parallel execution, as they do not introduce race conditions or require synchronization.

However, side effects are sometimes necessary for practical programming tasks, such as updating a database, writing to a file, or interacting with the user. In Clojure, these are managed carefully using constructs like atoms, refs, agents, and core.async channels, which are explored in other sections of this chapter.

By encapsulating side effects and limiting their spread, functional programming in Clojure strikes a balance, maintaining as much of the code base as pure as possible while managing necessary impure operations in a controlled manner. This approach leverages the advantages of pure functions while allowing essential interactions with the system's outside world.

4.9 Closures and Lexical Scope

Closures and lexical scope are essential concepts in Clojure, enabling powerful and flexible programming patterns. These concepts facilitate encapsulation, maintaining state across function calls, and leveraging the lexical environment where functions are created. Understanding closures helps grasp the deeper mechanics of function behavior and scope in Clojure.

Lexical scope, also known as static scope, refers to the region in the source code where a binding (variable and its value) is valid. In Clojure, variables are bound within the smallest enclosing set of braces or parentheses, whether it be in a let form, a function definition using fn or defn, or any other block structure. This binding is resolved at compile-time.

To illustrate, consider the following example of lexical scope using let:

```
(let [x 10
      y 20]
  (+ x y)) ; Returns 30
```

In this example, x and y are bound within the let form. These bindings are not accessible outside of the let block, demonstrating the concept of lexical scope clearly.

A closure in Clojure is a function that captures the bindings from its surrounding lexical context. The captured bindings are accessible and can be used even after the block, where they were defined, has exited. This ability allows closures to "remember" the environment in which they were created. The simplest example of a closure involves a function capturing a local binding:

```
(defn make-adder [x]
  (fn [y] (+ x y)))

(def add-five (make-adder 5))
(add-five 10) ; Returns 15
```

Here, make-adder returns an anonymous function that adds x to its argument y. When make-adder is called with 5, it returns a new function that adds 5 to its input. This returned function is a closure that retains the binding of $x = 5$.

add-five is effectively a new function (fn [y] (+ 5 y)), showcasing how the closure retains access to the binding x even after make-adder has finished executing. The binding of x is "closed over," forming a closure.

This capture of the lexical environment is powerful for creating functions with state:

```
(defn make-counter []
  (let [count (atom 0)]
    (fn []
      (swap! count inc)
      @count)))

(def counter (make-counter))
(counter) ; Returns 1
(counter) ; Returns 2
(counter) ; Returns 3
```

In this example, make-counter creates a closure over the count variable, an atom initialized to 0. Each call to the inner function increments count and returns its value. The closure captures and maintains the count state across multiple function calls.

Closures are essential in scenarios where function state persistence is required, such as managing counters, memoization, and functional data structures. They are also a cornerstone in many advanced functional programming techniques.

When discussing lexical scope and closures, it's important to understand that Clojure follows the principle of immutability extensively, though it provides constructs like atom, ref, agent, and var for managing mutable state safely in a controlled manner.

Lexical scoping and closures also interplay tightly with other functional programming concepts such as:

* Higher-order functions: Functions that return closures often produce higher-order functions. * Lazy sequences: Closures can capture their lexical environment to generate elements of a sequence lazily. * Recursion: Closures can encapsulate and recursively call themselves while maintaining state.

Incorporating these concepts correctly can lead to efficient, clean, and maintainable code, enhancing your proficiency as a Clojure developer.

4.10 Lazy Sequences

Lazy sequences are a powerful feature in Clojure, enabling the handling of potentially infinite data sets and optimizing performance by deferring computation. In contrast to eager evaluation, where expressions are evaluated immediately, lazy evaluation delays the computation until the value is actually needed. This approach is particularly beneficial when dealing with large or infinite sequences, ensuring that only the necessary elements are computed.

In Clojure, many sequence-generating functions produce lazy sequences. For example, the range function can generate a series of numbers either finite or infinite:

```
(def infinite-range (range))
(def finite-range (range 10))
```

The infinite-range is an example of an infinite lazy sequence, while finite-range is a lazy sequence containing the first ten non-negative integers. When working with lazy sequences, Clojure doesn't immediately compute the sequence. Instead, it creates a recipe to generate the sequence elements as needed.

To observe this lazy behavior, consider the following transformation using the map function:

```
(def transformed-range (map #(* % %) (range 10)))
```

Here, map applies the squaring function to each element of the range.

However, the computation is deferred until the sequence elements are accessed. To illustrate this laziness, we use the take function to retrieve elements from the lazy sequence:

```
(take 5 transformed-range)
```

The take function only computes the first five elements of transformed-range, demonstrating that the remaining elements are not evaluated. This deferral allows us to handle large or infinite sequences efficiently, as only the required portion is computed on demand.

Another common function that demonstrates lazy sequence behavior is iterate. This function repeatedly applies a given function to an initial value, generating an infinite sequence. For instance:

```
(def powers-of-2 (iterate #(* 2 %) 1))
```

The powers-of-2 sequence generates powers of 2 starting from 1. Similar to the previous example, the sequence is computed lazily. Accessing the first ten elements can be done as follows:

```
(take 10 powers-of-2)
```

Lazy sequences are seamless when combined with other sequence operations. The filter function, which lazily filters elements based on a predicate, is a perfect example. Suppose we need all even numbers from an infinite sequence:

```
(def even-numbers (filter even? (range)))
```

To retrieve the first ten even numbers:

```
(take 10 even-numbers)
```

This example verifies that only the necessary elements to satisfy take 10 are evaluated, maintaining efficiency.

When defining custom lazy sequences, Clojure provides the lazy-seq macro. This macro ensures that the sequence is lazily constructed and evaluated. Consider a function to generate a lazy sequence of Fibonacci numbers:

```
(defn fib
  ([] (fib 0 1))
  ([a b]
   (lazy-seq
     (cons a (fib b (+ a b))))))
```

The fib function initializes the sequence starting with 0 and 1. Using lazy-seq, it constructs the sequence lazily, with each subsequent pair computed as required:

```
(take 10 (fib))
```

This retrieves the first ten Fibonacci numbers efficiently.

Lazy sequences provide distinct advantages, such as handling large data, constructing infinite sequences, and optimizing performance by deferring computation. By leveraging Clojure's rich suite of lazy sequence functions, developers can write more efficient and expressive code tailored to specific needs, especially in scenarios requiring extensive or infinite data manipulation.

4.11 Functional Programming Strategies

Functional programming (FP) in Clojure emphasizes the use of functions to process and transform data. Central to FP are a set of strategies that guide the design and implementation of programs, ensuring robustness, maintainability, and clarity. We'll explore several key strategies including immutability, the use of pure functions, function composition, point-free style, and leveraging laziness.

Immutability: One of the foundational principles of functional programming is immutability. In Clojure, data structures are immutable by default, meaning they cannot be changed after creation. Instead of modifying existing structures, new versions of the structures are created with the desired changes. This leads to safer and more predictable programs, as there are no side effects to contend with.

```
(def original-list [1, 2, 3])
(def updated-list (conj original-list 4))
;; original-list remains [1, 2, 3]
;; updated-list is [1, 2, 3, 4]
```

conj is a function that returns a new vector containing the elements of original-list plus the new element, 4. Note that original-list remains unchanged.

Pure Functions: Pure functions are functions where the output value is determined solely by the input values, without observable side effects. They do not modify any state or interact with the outside world. Pure functions are easier to reason about, test, and compose.

```
(defn add [a b]
  (+ a b))
```

```
(defn square [x]
  (* x x))
```

Both add and square are pure functions. Given the same inputs, they will always return the same output without any side effects.

Function Composition: Function composition is the process of combining two or more functions to produce a new function. This new function applies the original functions in sequence. This is facilitated by the comp function in Clojure.

```
(defn add-and-square [a b]
  ((comp square add) a b))

(add-and-square 2 3)
;; Output: 25
```

Here, comp creates a new function that first applies add and then applies square to the result.

Point-Free Style: Point-free (or tacit) programming is a style where functions are defined without mentioning their arguments. This often makes use of function composition and higher-order functions to create concise and readable code.

```
(def add-and-square (comp square add))

(add-and-square 2 3)
;; Output: 25
```

Instead of defining add-and-square with explicit arguments, the function is defined directly using comp.

Leveraging Laziness: Clojure supports lazy sequences, which allow for potentially infinite sequences and efficient, on-demand computation. Laziness is used to defer computations until their results are required, which can conserve memory and increase efficiency.

```
(defn lazy-range [start]
  (lazy-seq (cons start (lazy-range (inc start)))))

(take 5 (lazy-range 0))
;; Output: (0 1 2 3 4)
```

lazy-range produces an infinitely increasing sequence of numbers starting from start. take is used to retrieve the first 5 elements, demonstrating how lazy sequences allow for working with infinite data structures in a finite manner.

The discussed strategies—immutability, pure functions, function composition, point-free style, and leveraging laziness—serve as essential tools in a Clojure programmer's toolkit. They foster the creation of elegant, reliable, and efficient programs. Leveraging these strategies contributes to a deeper understanding and more effective application of functional programming paradigms.

4.12 Using core.async for Concurrency

Concurrency in functional programming is managed efficiently in Clojure through the use of the core.async library. This library allows for asynchronous programming using channels, facilitating concurrent processes without the intricacies and pitfalls of traditional thread-based concurrency. This section will delve into the mechanisms of core.async, covering channels, go blocks, and operations such as >!!, <!!, go-loop, and alts!.

The core component of core.async is the channel, which acts as a conduit between concurrent processes. Channels can be buffered or unbuffered based on the requirement for handling messages.

```
(require '[clojure.core.async :refer :all])
```

Channels can be created using the chan function. The following example demonstrates the creation of an unbuffered channel:

```
(def ch (chan))
```

Buffered channels are instantiated with a specified capacity:

```
(def buffered-ch (chan 10))
```

Sending and receiving messages on channels can be done using the >!! and <!! functions respectively. The >!! function is a blocking put operation, and <!! is a blocking take operation. Below demonstrates usage:

```
(>!! ch "Hello, core.async!")
(def message (<!! ch))
(println message)
```

The above code sends the string "Hello, core.async!" into the channel ch and then retrieves it using the <!! function.

For non-blocking operations, put! and take! should be used:

```
(put! ch "Hello, non-blocking!")
```

```
(take! ch println)
```

To perform asynchronous operations, go blocks are used. The go macro enables the creation of lightweight, asynchronous processes. A go block transforms channel operations into non-blocking operations automatically.

```
(go
  (>! ch "Hello from go block!") ;; Non-blocking put
  (let [msg (<! ch)] ;; Non-blocking take
    (println msg)))
```

Channel operations within a go block are denoted by >! and <!, indicating non-blocking puts and takes respectively.

For iterative operations within a go block, use go-loop:

```
(go-loop [i 0]
  (when (< i 5)
    (>! ch i)
    (recur (inc i))))
```

The alts! function performs an *atomic* "choice" operation between multiple channel operations, dispatching based on which channel operation can proceed first:

```
(go
  (let [[v ch] (alts! [ch1 ch2])]
    (println "Received" v "from" ch)))
```

For example, alts! chooses between ch1 and ch2 and executes the operation for which data is ready first.

The timeout function creates a channel that will close after a specified duration:

```
(go
  (<! (timeout 1000)) ;; Waits for 1000 ms
  (println "1 second elapsed"))
```

Combining channels with timeouts can help manage process coordination effectively.

A more advanced use of core.async involves pipeline, which processes streams of data concurrently through a series of transformations:

```
(defn process [input]
  (* input input))

(defn pipeline-example []
  (let [to (chan)
        from (chan)]
```

```
(pipeline 5 from process to)
(doseq [x (range 10)]
  (>!! to x))
(close! to)
(while true
  (if-let [result (<!! from)]
    (println result)
    (recur)))))
```

In the above example, pipeline manages a transformation function process and applies it to data sent on channel to, with results being outputted on channel from.

Utilizing core.async enables the writing of powerful, concurrent programs in Clojure without delving into the complex details of thread management.

Chapter 5

Advanced Data Structures and Collections

This chapter delves into advanced Clojure data structures and collections, providing an in-depth look at vectors, maps, and sets. It addresses the use of persistent data structures and transients for performance optimization. The chapter covers zippers for tree navigation, sorted collections, and handling nested data. Additionally, it introduces Clojure's data validation using 'spec', efficient string manipulation techniques, and advanced sequence operations.

5.1 Vectors in Depth

Vectors in Clojure are one of the fundamental collection types and are implemented as persistent data structures. A vector is an indexed, sequential collection that provides efficient indexed access (both for reading and writing) and is optimized for append operations.

Vectors can be created using the vector function, the [] syntax, or the vec function.

```
;; Creating vectors
(def v1 (vector 1 2 3))
(def v2 [4 5 6])
(def v3 (vec '(7 8 9)))
```

A common threading macro used with vectors is -», which threads the last value as the first element to the next function call, facilitating a more readable application of transformations.

Accessing Elements in Vectors

Elements in a vector are accessed by their index using the get function or invoking the vector with an index directly.

```
;; Using get function
(get v1 0) ;; => 1

;; Using vector as a function
(v1 1) ;; => 2
```

If an index is requested beyond the bounds of the vector, nil is returned unless a default value is provided:

```
(get v1 10) ;; => nil
(get v1 10 "default") ;; => "default"
```

Updates to vectors can be accomplished using the assoc function which returns a new vector with the specified index updated:

```
;; Updating a vector
(def v4 (assoc v1 1 42))
;; v4 => [1 42 3]
```

Efficiency of Vectors

Clojure vectors offer O(1) time complexity for indexed access and updates in most cases due to their internal implementation using a trie (or tree-like) structure known as a bit-partitioned vector trie. This ensures that operations like nth, assoc, conj, and subvec are highly efficient.

Adding Elements

The conj function adds elements to the end of a vector:

```
(def v5 (conj v1 4))
;; v5 => [1 2 3 4]
```

Removing Elements

Direct removal or modification of elements within vectors is not possible due to their immutable nature. However, subvec can be used to create a new vector out of a subsequence of an existing vector:

```
;; Creating a subvector
(def v6 (subvec v1 0 2))
;; v6 => [1 2]
```

Manipulating Vectors

Besides assoc, various functions like pop, peek, take, drop, and split-at provide efficient ways to manipulate vectors:

```
;; Peeking and popping elements
(peek v2) ;; => 6
(def v7 (pop v2)) ;; => [4 5]

;; Taking and dropping elements
(take 2 v1) ;; => [1 2]
(drop 1 v1) ;; => [2 3]

;; Splitting at a specific index
(split-at 2 v1) ;; => ([1 2] [3])
```

Vector Transformations

Combining vectors, mapping, and reducing are common vector transformations. The map, reduce, and concat functions are largely used for these purposes.

```
;; Mapping over a vector
(map inc v1) ;; => (2 3 4)

;; Reducing a vector
(reduce + v1) ;; => 6

;; Concatenating vectors
(concat v1 v2) ;; => (1 2 3 4 5 6)
```

Performance Considerations

While vectors are efficient for random access and append operations, they are generally not optimized for prepending elements or for concatenation of large vectors due to their need to recreate a significant portion of the internal structure. As an alternative, other data structures like lists or specialized libraries might be more suited to such use cases.

Overall, vectors offer a powerful, flexible method for ordered collections with strong performance characteristics for most operations, primarily due to their persistent data structure implementation in Clojure.

5.2 Maps in Depth

Clojure maps are powerful and essential data structures utilized to store key-value pairs. These maps, also known as hash maps or dictionaries in other programming languages, offer efficient data retrieval based on keys. In Clojure, maps are immutable, allowing safe sharing and manipulation without the risk of unexpected side effects.

Maps can be created using the hash-map function or the literal syntax. For example:

```
(def example-map (hash-map :a 1 :b 2 :c 3))
(def literal-map {:a 1 :b 2 :c 3})
```

Both example-map and literal-map contain the same set of key-value pairs. Clojure maps support a variety of operations, including access, update, and deletion of key-value pairs.

Accessing the value associated with a key can be performed using the get function or the map as a function:

```
(get example-map :a) ; returns 1
(literal-map :b) ; returns 2
```

Updating a map involves the assoc function, which returns a new map with the given key-value pair:

```
(def updated-map (assoc example-map :d 4)) ; {:a 1 :b 2 :c 3 :d 4}
```

To remove an entry from the map, the dissoc function is used:

```
(def reduced-map (dissoc example-map :a)) ; {:b 2 :c 3}
```

Additionally, Clojure maps support checking for the existence of a key using the contains? function:

```
(contains? example-map :a) ; returns true
(contains? example-map :d) ; returns false
```

Combining maps can be achieved with the merge function. This function takes multiple maps as arguments and returns a new map, combining their entries:

```
(def map1 {:a 1 :b 2})
(def map2 {:c 3 :d 4})
(def combined-map (merge map1 map2)) ; {:a 1 :b 2 :c 3 :d 4}
```

Clojure also supports nested maps for more complex data structures. Accessing and updating nested values require additional steps. The get-in function retrieves a value from a nested map structure, and the assoc-in function updates a value within a nested map:

```
(def nested-map {:user {:name "Alice" :address {:city "Wonderland"}}})
(get-in nested-map [:user :address :city]) ; returns "Wonderland"
(def updated-nested-map (assoc-in nested-map [:user :address :city] "Fantasyland")) ; {:
    user {:name "Alice" :address {:city "Fantasyland"}}}
```

To delete a key from a nested map, the update-in function, in conjunction with dissoc, can be employed:

```
(def removed-nested-map (update-in nested-map [:user :address] dissoc :city)) ; {:user {:
    name "Alice" :address {}}}
```

For performance optimization, particularly when working with large maps, Clojure provides transients. A transient version of a map is a mutable variant that allows efficient, in-place modifications:

```
(def transient-map (transient example-map))
(def transient-updated-map (assoc! transient-map :d 4)) ; returns a transient map
(persistent! transient-updated-map) ; returns {:a 1 :b 2 :c 3 :d 4}
```

Transients are particularly useful in scenarios requiring multiple updates before finalizing an immutable structure. The use of assoc!, dissoc!, and persistent! functions ensures high performance by reducing overhead associated with immutability.

Maps in Clojure also play a crucial role in destructuring, an elegant feature for accessing map entries. Destructuring allows binding values directly from a map to variables:

```
(def map-value {:a 1 :b 2 :c 3})
(let [{:keys [a b]} map-value]
  (+ a b)) ; returns 3
```

By leveraging destructuring, code readability and maintainability are significantly enhanced, especially when dealing with nested data structures.

Moreover, Clojure supports sorted maps, which maintain their entries in a sorted order based on the keys. The sorted-map function creates such maps:

```
(def sorted-map (sorted-map :b 2 :c 3 :a 1)) ; {:a 1 :b 2 :c 3}
```

Sorted maps are beneficial when the order of keys is of importance, such as in range queries or when presenting the data in a specific order.

Understanding and effectively utilizing Clojure maps is essential for proficiently managing and manipulating key-value data. The combination of immutable structures, performance optimizations through transients, and the capabilities afforded by nested and sorted maps equip developers with robust tools to handle a wide array of data handling tasks. The above techniques and best practices ensure efficient, readable, and maintainable code within the Clojure language ecosystem.

5.3 Sets in Depth

Clojure sets are collections that contain unique elements, making them essential for operations that require distinct values. Sets in Clojure can be either unordered (hash sets) or ordered (sorted sets). In this section, we will explore the creation, manipulation, and various operations performed using sets, emphasizing their efficiency and use cases in Clojure.

Sets are created using the #{} reader macro or the clojure.core/hash-set and clojure.core/sorted-set functions. A set's uniqueness constraint makes operations such as membership testing and union particularly efficient.

```
;; Create a hash set using reader macro
(def my-hash-set #{1 2 3 4})

;; Create a hash set using hash-set function
(def my-hash-set-alt (hash-set 1 2 3 4))

;; Create a sorted set
(def my-sorted-set (sorted-set 1 3 2 4))
```

Clojure sets support a variety of fundamental operations such as union, intersection, and difference. These operations are facilitated by the functions clojure.set/union, clojure.set/intersection, and clojure.set/difference, respectively.

```
;; Define sets
(def set-a #{1 2 3})
(def set-b #{3 4 5})

;; Perform union
(clojure.set/union set-a set-b)
;; => #{1 2 3 4 5}

;; Perform intersection
(clojure.set/intersection set-a set-b)
;; => #{3}

;; Perform difference
(clojure.set/difference set-a set-b)
;; => #{1 2}
```

One significant advantage of sets is the average constant-time complexity $O(1)$ for membership testing in hash sets. This makes sets particularly suitable for tasks such as filtering duplicates from collections or fast lookups.

```
;; Check membership
(contains? set-a 3)
;; => true
```

```
;; Check non-membership
(contains? set-a 4)
;; => false
```

Sets are also highly compatible with Clojure's rich set of sequence operations. They can be used in conjunction with functions such as map, filter, and reduce.

```
;; Map function over a set
(map inc set-a)
;; => (2 3 4)

;; Filter a set
(filter even? set-a)
;; => (2)

;; Reduce a set
(reduce + set-a)
;; => 6
```

A powerful feature provided by sets is their compatibility with transients. Transient sets offer a mutable version of sets which can significantly optimize performance in scenarios involving numerous modifications. Transients are primarily used in performance-critical code paths.

```
;; Create a transient set
(def transient-set (transient #{1 2 3}))

;; Add elements to the transient set
(def updated-transient-set (conj! transient-set 4 5))

;; Convert back to persistent set
(def persistent-set (persistent! updated-transient-set))

;; Verify changes
persistence-set
;; => #{1 2 3 4 5}
```

Sorted sets, unlike hash sets, maintain elements in a defined order based on a comparator. The default comparator is compare, which sorts elements in natural order. Custom comparators can be used to alter the natural ordering of elements.

```
;; Create a custom comparator for descending order
(def custom-comparator (fn [a b] (compare b a)))

;; Create a sorted set with a custom comparator
(def descending-sorted-set (sorted-set-by custom-comparator 3 1 2 5 4))

;; Verify the order
descending-sorted-set
;; => #{5 4 3 2 1}
```

Another feature of sets includes the ability to convert other collections, such as vectors or lists, into sets. This process removes any duplicate elements in the original collection.

```
;; Convert a vector to a set
(def my-vector [1 2 2 3 3 3 4])
(def my-set (set my-vector))
;; => #{1 2 3 4}
```

The combination of these features makes sets a versatile and powerful data structure within Clojure, suitable for a wide range of applications where uniqueness and efficient operations are required.

5.4 Persistent Data Structures

Persistent data structures in Clojure are foundational to its functional programming paradigm. They ensure immutability and structural sharing, providing efficient means to handle data without the pitfalls of mutable states. This section explores how Clojure achieves persistency through vectors, lists, maps, and sets, and discusses the benefits and implementation details.

A persistent data structure is one that preserves the previous version of itself when modified. Instead of altering the original structure, it yields a new structure with the changes. This guarantee of immutability allows for safer concurrent programming and simpler reasoning about state changes.

Vectors as Persistent Data Structures Clojure's vector is a quintessential example of a persistent data structure. While it provides constant-time access and update operations, it ensures that the original vector remains unchanged upon modification. This is achieved through an underlying tree structure, which ensures that update operations share most of the structure between the old and new vectors.

```
(def original-vector [1 2 3])
(def new-vector (assoc original-vector 1 20))
```

In the snippet above, original-vector retains its state [1 2 3], while new-vector becomes [1 20 3]. This immutability ensures that any references to original-vector remain valid and consistent, avoiding unintended side effects.

Persistent Lists Besides vectors, lists in Clojure are also persistent. Lists support efficient addition and removal of elements from the front. Structural sharing allows lists to represent sequences effectively, enabling safe concurrent modifications.

```
(def original-list '(1 2 3))
(def new-list (conj original-list 0))
```

Here, original-list is (1 2 3), and new-list is (0 1 2 3). The conj function prepends the element to the list, creating a new list while preserving the original.

Persistent Maps and Sets Maps and sets in Clojure also embody persistency. They allow efficient key-based access and uniqueness of elements, respectively. Persistent maps ensure that any addition or removal of key-value pairs results in a new map, whereas sets maintain immutability of their elements.

```
(def original-map {:a 1, :b 2})
(def new-map (assoc original-map :c 3))
```

```
;; original-map remains {:a 1, :b 2}
;; new-map is {:a 1, :b 2, :c 3}
```

In the example, original-map remains intact while new-map includes the new key :c.

```
(def original-set #{1 2 3})
(def new-set (conj original-set 4))
```

```
;; original-set remains #{1 2 3}
;; new-set is #{1 2 3 4}
```

Structural Sharing The efficiency of persistent data structures hinges on structural sharing. When a modification occurs, only the affected parts are copied, and the rest of the structure shares components between the old and new versions. This technique minimizes memory usage and enhances performance.

Consider a vector represented as a balanced tree with branching factor 32. For any change, only the path from the root to the affected leaf node needs updating, and in most cases, this impacts $O(\log_{32} n)$ nodes, where n is the vector's size. This ensures that even large vectors can be copied with minimal overhead.

Implementation Mechanics The underlying implementation of persistent vectors in Clojure utilizes a trie (pronounced "try") data structure, often referred to as a "vector trie" or "bitmap-indexed vector trie".

Here's a detailed breakdown of the vector trie mechanism:

- **Branching Factor**: Each node in the trie can have up to 32 children. This branching factor balances the depth of the tree, maintaining efficient access times.

- **Nodes**: The structure comprises leaf nodes (holding elements) and internal nodes (holding references to other nodes). Shared references between old and new versions of vectors ensure immutability.

- **Update Mechanism**: When an element is updated, a new path is created from the root to the leaf node containing the element. Intermediate nodes along this path are copied and modified accordingly, while untouched nodes are shared between the versions.

```
(def large-vector (vec (range 1000)))
(def updated-vector (assoc large-vector 500 :new-value))
```

In this example, modifying the element at index 500 results in 'updated-vector', sharing much of its structure with 'large-vector' for efficiency.

Persistent maps and sets employ similar principles. Hash array mapped trie (HAMT) structures are common, offering efficient lookups, inserts, and deletions. Such structures ensure that modifications result in minimal copying and maximum sharing.

The power of persistent data structures in Clojure arises from their ability to handle significant modifications efficiently while guaranteeing immutability. This makes them ideal for concurrent applications, where state consistency and thread safety are critical.

Understanding persistent data structures is vital for leveraging Clojure's full potential. Their implementation through structural sharing ensures efficient and reliable data manipulations, fostering a robust environment for functional programming.

5.5 Using Transients for Performance

Transients in Clojure provide a means to temporarily use mutable data structures for performance-critical code paths while maintaining the immutability guarantees of the language when the transient operations are complete. This section will explore the creation and manipulation of transients, the transition from persistent to transient structures, and the implications for performance.

To understand the use of transients, consider the primary persistent data structures in Clojure: vectors, maps, and sets. Each of these structures ensures immutability, meaning that any modifications result in a new data structure rather than altering the original. This immutability, while beneficial for reasoning about code and enabling safe concurrency, can sometimes introduce performance overhead due to the need to create new structures.

Transients offer a solution by allowing temporary mutable states in a controlled manner. The interface to transients in Clojure is clear and straightforward, using a specific set of functions designed to convert between persistent and transient states and to perform efficient modifications.

To work with transients, you first convert a persistent data structure to its transient counterpart using transient. This conversion sets the stage for efficient, mutable operations. Once the necessary modifications are done, you convert the transient structure back to a persistent one using persistent!.

Below is a simple example demonstrating the transition from a persistent vector to a transient one, performing a series of modifications, and converting back to a persistent vector:

```
(def persistent-vector [1 2 3 4 5])
(def transient-vector (transient persistent-vector))
(def modified-transient (assoc! transient-vector 2 33))
(def final-persistent (persistent! modified-transient))
```

In the example:

- persistent-vector is a standard immutable vector.
- transient-vector is created by converting persistent-vector to a transient state.
- modified-transient is the result of mutating transient-vector by associating a new value at index 2.

- final-persistent is the final immutable vector obtained by converting modified-transient back to a persistent vector.

Using transients requires careful management to ensure conversions between persistent and transient states occur correctly. The manipulation functions for transient data structures are postfixed with an exclamation mark (!) to signify their destructive nature. These include functions like assoc!, conj!, dissoc!, and pop!, which parallel their immutable counterparts but operate in a mutable manner for performance gains.

Here is an example of using transients to build a large vector efficiently:

```
(defn build-large-vector
  [n]
  (let [transient-vec (transient [])]
    (loop [i 0, tv transient-vec]
      (if (< i n)
        (recur (inc i) (conj! tv i))
        (persistent! tv)))))
```

In the example, the build-large-vector function constructs a large vector with n elements. This implementation leverages transients for the accumulation of elements:

- An empty transient vector transient-vec is created.
- A loop iterates from 0 to n-1, each time using conj! to add an element to the transient vector.
- After the loop completes, persistent! converts the transient vector back to its persistent form for the final result.

When using transients, it is essential to respect their scope and mutation constraints. Transients should not be passed around or stored in ways that violate their expected lifecycle. Once persistent! has been called on a transient structure, any further operations on the transient will result in an error since the transient is considered "frozen" back to an immutable state.

Here is an example illustrating an error due to improper transient use:

```
(def tv (transient [1 2 3]))
(persistent! tv)
(conj! tv 4)
```

The final conj! on the transient tv after it has been made persistent will result in an error because the transient structure is no longer valid for mutable operations.

The performance benefits of transients come from minimizing the overhead of repeated allocations and copying inherent in persistent data structure manipulations. By batching a series of modifications in a transient state, costly intermediate allocations are avoided, resulting in significant performance gains, especially for large collections.

In employing transients, maturity in understanding Clojure's data manipulation idioms and careful control over transient lifecycles are crucial. This combination allows leveraging their performance benefits without compromising the immutability guarantees foundational to Clojure's concurrency model.

5.6 Zippers for Navigating Trees

Zippers provide an elegant and efficient means of navigating and transforming tree-like data structures. Originating from functional programming paradigms, a zipper consists of two parts: a focus, which represents the current position within the tree, and a context, which maintains information about the path taken from the root to the focus. This allows for a purely functional update mechanism.

To begin with, consider a basic tree structure in Clojure:

```
(def tree
  {:value 1
   :children [{:value 2, :children []}
              {:value 3
               :children [{:value 4, :children []}
                          {:value 5, :children []}]}]})
```

Here, the tree is a nested map where each node contains a :value and potentially a list of :children nodes. To work with zippers in Clojure, the clojure.zip library is used. First, we must transform our tree into a zipper:

```
(require '[clojure.zip :as zip])

(defn tree-zipper [root]
  (zip/zipper
    (fn [node] (seq (:children node))) ; branch?
    (fn [node] (:children node)) ; children
    (fn [node children] (assoc node :children children)) ; make-node
    root))

(def z (tree-zipper tree))
```

In the tree-zipper function, three parameters are required: 1. A function indicating whether the node is a branch. 2. A function to get the children of a node. 3. A function to create a node given the original node and a sequence of children.

The variable z now holds the initial zipper at the root of the tree. Navigation can be done using various clojure.zip functions, such as up, down, left, and right:

```
(def z-down (zip/down z)) ; Move to the first child
(def z-right (zip/right z-down)) ; Move to the right sibling
(def z-up (zip/up z-right)) ; Move back up to the parent
```

To illustrate, z-down moves the focus to the first child of the root, z-right moves the focus to the next sibling, and z-up moves the focus back to the parent node.

Zippers also enable structural editing. For example, if we wish to update the value of the node currently in focus:

```
(def z-updated (zip/edit z-down assoc :value 10))
```

Here, z-updated is a new zipper with the value of the current node changed to 10. Zippers preserve immutability principles by returning new structures rather than modifying the original.

Further, zippers allow the insertion and removal of nodes. To insert a new child node:

```
(def new-child {:value 6, :children []})
(def z-inserted (zip/insert-child z-down new-child))
```

In this snippet, zip/insert-child inserts new-child as a child of the focused node. To remove the current node, use zip/remove:

```
(def z-removed (zip/remove z-right))
```

z-removed will then be a zipper with the current node removed, and the focus will shift appropriately, typically to the node's previous sibling, or up to the parent if no siblings remain.

In more advanced applications, zippers can facilitate complex tree manipulations, such as reordering nodes, selective updates based on conditions, or accumulating results through traversal. The flexibility and power of zippers come from their ability to navigate bi-directionally and to maintain context, which is particularly useful when dealing with deeply nested, hierarchical data structures in a functional programming context.

5.7 Working with Sorted Collections

Clojure provides powerful tools for working with sorted collections, ensuring that elements remain in a specified order. This section examines the creation, manipulation, and characteristics of sorted maps and sets, offering an in-depth understanding of how these structures can optimize performance and maintain order within collections.

Sorted collections in Clojure are backed by composite data structures that maintain efficient insertion, deletion, and lookup operations. Specifically, Clojure uses Red-Black trees for sorted maps and sets, which offer logarithmic time complexity for these operations.

Sorted Sets

Clojure's sorted-set function constructs a sorted set. By default, the elements in a sorted-set are sorted in their natural order (i.e., numeric or lexicographical order).

```
(def sorted-num-set (sorted-set 3 1 4 1 5 9 2 6 5 3 5))
=> #{1 2 3 4 5 6 9}
```

Elements in the sorted set are automatically arranged in ascending order. The sorted nature supports efficient range queries and ordered traversals. Comparison functionality is built on Clojure's compare functions, so ensuring the correct behavior for custom types might require implementing this interface.

sorted-set can also accept a comparator to customize the sort order:

```
(def reverse-set (sorted-set-by #(compare %2 %1) 3 1 4 1 5 9 2 6 5 3 5))
=> #{9 6 5 4 3 2 1}
```

Here, sorted-set-by uses a comparator function to reverse the usual order of elements.

Sorted Maps

Similarly, sorted-map constructs a map where the keys are automatically sorted. Such maps support efficient key-based operations and maintain their entries in a sorted order:

```
(def sorted-str-map (sorted-map "apple" 1 "banana" 2 "grape" 3 "cherry" 4))
=> {"apple" 1, "banana" 2, "cherry" 4, "grape" 3}
```

A sorted-map, like sorted sets, accepts a comparator through the sorted-map-by function for customized key sorting.

```
(def reverse-map (sorted-map-by #(compare %2 %1) "apple" 1 "banana" 2 "grape" 3 "
```

```
  cherry" 4))
=> {"grape" 3, "cherry" 4, "banana" 2, "apple" 1}
```

Operations on Sorted Collections

Sorted collections facilitate various operations that leverage their ordered nature:

- subset: Retrieves a portion of a sorted set within specified bounds.

```
(subseq sorted-num-set >= 2 < 6)
=> (2 3 4 5)
```

- rsubset: Retrieves elements in reverse order within specified bounds.

```
(rsubseq sorted-num-set >= 2 < 6)
=> (5 4 3 2)
```

- first/last: Fetches the first or last element efficiently.

```
(first sorted-num-set)
=> 1
\begin{lstlisting}
\item \texttt{navigating key ranges}: Efficient extraction of map entries
    within key bounds.
\begin{lstlisting}
(subseq sorted-str-map >= "banana" < "grape")
=> (["banana" 2] ["cherry" 4])
```

These operations are optimized internally ensuring the sorted collections remain immutable and thus concurrency-friendly. Additionally, sorted collections preserve the associative operations found in typical sets and maps, such as assoc, dissoc, and membership tests with contains?.

The primary benefit of sorted collections is the combination of order maintenance with a high degree of operation efficiency. This is particularly relevant in scenarios requiring frequent range queries, ordered traversals, or the need to ensure that collection elements align with specific order constraints.

Understanding and effectively utilizing sorted collections in Clojure can lead to significant performance improvements, particularly when handling large datasets or implementing algorithms where sorted order is pivotal.

5.8 Handling Nested Data Structures

When working with nested data structures in Clojure, it is essential to leverage the language's powerful abstractions for managing complex, hierarchical data. Nested data structures often come in forms such as maps within maps, vectors containing other collections, or combinations thereof. Mastering the manipulation of these structures enhances both the expressiveness and performance of Clojure programs.

At the core of handling nested data structures are functions such as get-in, assoc-in, update-in, and merge-with. Each of these functions is designed to perform specific operations on nested data, providing a high level of control and flexibility.

The get-in function is used to retrieve values from nested maps using a sequence of keys. Its usage is straightforward:

```
(def example-nested-map {'a {'b {'c 1}}})

(get-in example-nested-map ['a 'b 'c]) ;; returns 1
```

The assoc-in function is utilized to associate a value in a nested structure, creating intermediate maps as necessary. This is particularly useful for updating deep structures concisely:

```
(def example-nested-map {'a {'b {'c 1}}})

(assoc-in example-nested-map ['a 'b 'c] 42)
;; returns {'a {'b {'c 42}}}

(assoc-in example-nested-map ['a 'b 'd] 99)
;; returns {'a {'b {'c 1 'd 99}}}
```

Updating nested data conditionally is facilitated by the update-in function. This function takes a nested structure, a path, a function, and any additional arguments to apply:

```
(def example-nested-map {'a {'b {'c 1 'd 99}}})

(update-in example-nested-map ['a 'b 'c] inc)
;; returns {'a {'b {'c 2 'd 99}}}
```

Nested structures can also be effectively combined using merge-with. This function is valuable for merging maps and controlling how conflicts are handled through a custom function:

```
(def map-a {'a {'b {'c 1}}})
(def map-b {'a {'b {'d 2} 'e 3}})

(merge-with (fn [x y]
```

```
          (if (map? x)
            (merge-with merge x y)
            y))
        map-a map-b)
;; returns {'a {'b {'c 1 'd 2} 'e 3}}
```

Dealing with nested vectors and maps often involves more complex manipulations, for which Clojure provides functions like mapv and reduce. Consider the following scenario, where we need to increment every number inside a deeply nested structure:

```
(def nested-structure [{:a 1 :b {:c 2}} {:a 3 :b {:c 4 :d [5 6]}}])

(defn increment-values [coll]
  (walk/postwalk (fn [x]
                   (if (number? x)
                     (inc x)
                     x))
                 coll))

(increment-values nested-structure)
;; returns [{:a 2, :b {:c 3}} {:a 4, :b {:c 5, :d [6 7]}}]
```

In the above example, walk/postwalk is a utility that recursively walks the data structure and applies the function to every element, leaving the structure intact. This approach helps in consistently managing any level of nesting within collections.

Additionally, for scenarios where deep updates are frequent and performance-critical, the Specter library provides optimized and highly expressive means for navigating and transforming nested data structures. Specter's transform function simplifies and accelerates complex updates:

```
(require '[com.rpl.specter :as s])

(def nested-structure [{:a 1 :b {:c 2}} {:a 3 :b {:c 4 :d [5 6]}}])

(s/transform [s/ALL :b :d s/ALL] inc nested-structure)
;; returns [{:a 1, :b {:c 2}} {:a 3, :b {:c 4, :d [6 7]}}]
```

Handling nested structures efficiently involves a deep understanding of their composition and the tools provided by the language. Essential functions like get-in, assoc-in, update-in, merge-with, and tools such as Specter are indispensable for mastering nested data manipulation, thus enabling highly readable and maintainable Clojure code.

5.9 Introduction to Clojure Data

Clojure is a functional, modern, and dynamic programming language that is well-suited for working with immutable data structures. This section will cover the fundamental types of data in Clojure and provide you with the basis for understanding more advanced data structures and operations.

Clojure's core data types include numbers, strings, characters, symbols, keywords, lists, vectors, maps, and sets. Each of these data types is designed to be immutable, meaning their state cannot be modified after they are created. This immutability is central to Clojure's design philosophy, promoting safer concurrent programming and simpler reasoning about state.

Numbers: Clojure supports a variety of number types including integers, floating-point numbers, and ratios. Numeric literals are written as in most programming languages:

```
1 ; integer
3.14 ; floating-point number
22/7 ; ratio
```

Operations on numbers are straightforward. The following example showcases basic arithmetic operations:

```
(+ 1 2) ; addition => 3
(- 4 2) ; subtraction => 2
(* 2 3) ; multiplication => 6
(/ 8 4) ; division => 2
```

Strings and Characters: In Clojure, strings are sequences of characters enclosed in double quotes, while characters are prefixed with a backslash:

```
"Hello, World!" ; string
\a ; character
\newline ; newline character
```

String concatenation is achieved using the `str` function:

```
(str "Hello, " "World!") ; => "Hello, World!"
```

Symbols: Symbols are used to refer to variables and functions and are one of the foundational elements of Clojure. They are typically used to name entities:

```
(def my-symbol 'my-symbol) ; defining a symbol
my-symbol ; referencing a symbol
```

Keywords: Keywords are like symbols but have a colon prefix and are typically used as identifiers or to represent enumeration values. Keywords are immutable and interned, meaning that any given keyword is unique in the program:

```
:keyword ; keyword with name "keyword"
:another/namespace ; keyword with namespace "another" and name "namespace"
```

Lists: Lists are ordered collections of elements. They are fundamental to Clojure's structure and are typically used to represent code. Lists are written with elements enclosed in parentheses:

```
(1 2 3) ; list of integers
('a 'b 'c) ; list of symbols
```

To create a list programmatically, you can use the list function:

```
(list 1 2 3) ; => (1 2 3)
```

Vectors: Vectors are similar to lists but provide efficient random access. They are ordered collections enclosed in square brackets:

```
[1 2 3] ; vector of integers
[\'a \'b \'c] ; vector of symbols
```

Vectors can be created using the vector function:

```
(vector 1 2 3) ; => [1 2 3]
```

Maps: Maps are collections of key-value pairs. They are enclosed in curly braces, with keys and values alternating. Keys can be any Clojure data type, but are often keywords or strings:

```
{:a 1, :b 2, :c 3} ; map with keyword keys
{"a" 1, "b" 2} ; map with string keys
```

Maps can also be created with the hash-map function:

```
(hash-map :a 1 :b 2 :c 3) ; => {:a 1 :b 2 :c 3}
```

Sets: Sets are collections of unique elements. They are enclosed in #{}, and can be created with the set function. Sets inherently disallow duplicates:

```
#{1 2 3} ; set of integers
(set [1 2 3 1 2]) ; => #{1 2 3}
```

conj can be used to add elements to a set:

```
(conj #{1 2} 3) ; => #{1 2 3}
```

These core data types form the foundation of data modeling in Clojure. By utilizing these immutable data structures, Clojure ensures that programs are robust, maintainable, and inherently thread-safe. Future sections will build on this knowledge, introducing more advanced data structures and techniques, providing you with the tools necessary to master data manipulation in Clojure.

5.10 Using Spec for Data Validation

Clojure's spec library is a powerful tool for data validation and function argument checking. It allows developers to define specifications for the function parameters, return values, and data structures, ensuring that the data adheres to expected constraints and formats. This section provides an in-depth exploration of spec, starting with the basics and progressing to more advanced usage.

spec is part of the clojure.spec.alpha namespace. To use spec, you need to require it in your namespace as follows:

```
(ns my-namespace
  (:require [clojure.spec.alpha :as s]))
```

Defining Basic Specs

The simplest form of spec is defining constraints for basic data types. For instance, we can create a spec for integers and strings as follows:

```
(s/def ::integer-int int?)
(s/def ::string-str string?)
```

This example defines a spec named ::integer-int that validates whether a value is an integer, and ::string-str that checks if a value is a string. The double colon (::) creates namespaced keywords, which are unique within the namespace.

The valdiity of the data can be checked using the s/valid? function:

```
(s/valid? ::integer-int 5) ; Returns true
(s/valid? ::integer-int "hello") ; Returns false
(s/valid? ::string-str "hello") ; Returns true
(s/valid? ::string-str 5) ; Returns false
```

Composing Complex Specs

Spec also allows composing more complex predicates. For example, to define a positive integer spec:

```
(s/def ::positive-int (s/and int? pos?))
```

In this case, s/and combines multiple predicates. The pos? predicate checks whether a number is positive.

Defining Specs for Collections

To validate collections, spec provides functions like s/coll-of and s/map-of. Here is an example of a vector of integers:

```
(s/def ::vector-of-ints (s/coll-of int? :kind vector?))
```

Similarly, you can define a spec for a map with specific keys:

```
(s/def ::person (s/keys :req-un [::name ::age]))
(s/def ::name string?)
(s/def ::age pos-int?)
```

The s/keys function defines a spec for a map that must contain name and age keys. The :req-un option specifies that the keys are unqualified.

Spec for Function Arguments

Using spec, one can also validate function arguments and return values. The fdef macro helps define specifications for functions:

```
(defn add [x y]
  (+ x y))

(s/fdef add
  :args (s/tuple int? int?)
  :ret int?)
```

In this example, the (fdef add) defines a spec for the add function. The :args key specifies that add takes a tuple of two integers as arguments, and the :ret key indicates that it returns an integer.

Using spec for Conform and Explanations

The s/conform function is used to check if a value conforms to a spec and returns the conformed value or :clojure.spec.alpha/invalid. If the data does not conform to the spec, s/explain provides detailed error information:

```
(s/conform ::positive-int 42) ; Returns 42
(s/conform ::positive-int -1) ; Returns :clojure.spec.alpha/invalid

(s/explain ::positive-int -1)
; Output:
; val: -1 fails spec: :my-namespace/positive-int
```

```
; predicate: pos?
```

Integrating Spec with Instrumentation

Instrumentation is used to enforce function specifications at runtime. The timbre library can be used to enable instrumentations:

```
(require '[clojure.spec.test.alpha :as stest])
(stest/instrument 'add)
```

With instrumentation, calling the add function with invalid arguments will trigger an error.

```
(add 1 "a")
; Output:
; clojure.lang.ExceptionInfo: Call to #'my-namespace/add did not conform to spec.
```

Utilizing Specs for Failure Reporting and Testing

Finally, with spec, automated testing can be significantly enhanced by validating properties and invariants:

```
(stest/check 'add)
```

This will generate test cases based on specs and check if the function behaves correctly based on those automatically generated cases.

In practical applications, spec can greatly enhance code reliability and maintainability by ensuring data integrity at multiple system boundaries. When combined with thorough testing and validation practices, it provides a robust framework for building cohesive and error-resistant Clojure applications.

5.11 Efficient String Manipulation

Clojure provides a robust set of built-in functions for string manipulation, leveraging the power of Java's extensive String API while adhering to functional programming principles. Understanding and applying these functions efficiently is crucial for optimizing the performance and readability of your Clojure code.

At the core of Clojure's string manipulation capabilities is the clojure.string namespace, which imports and extends Java's String functionalities with a more idiomatic Clojure approach. Below we will explore some key functions and patterns for effective string manipulation.

clojure.string contains functions for splitting, joining, uppercasing, lowercasing, trimming, and replacing substrings among others. These functions are designed to provide concise and readable string operations in a functional style.

```
(require '[clojure.string :as str])
```

Splitting Strings

The str/split function is used to divide a string into substrings based on a delimiter. It returns a vector of these substrings.

```
(def example-string "Clojure is a powerful, functional language")

(def split-result (str/split example-string #" "))
```

```
=> ["Clojure" "is" "a" "powerful," "functional" "language"]
```

The delimiter is defined using a regular expression. In scenarios requiring more nuanced control over splitting, such as limiting the number of splits, an additional parameter can be specified:

```
(def limited-split-result (str/split example-string #" " 3))
```

```
=> ["Clojure" "is" "a powerful, functional language"]
```

Joining Strings

Conversely, str/join enables the combination of elements in a collection into a single string, using a specified separator.

```
(def words-vec ["Clojure" "is" "fun"])

(def joined-string (str/join " " words-vec))
```

```
=> "Clojure is fun"
```

For efficiency, use str/join instead of manual concatenation using loops, especially when dealing with large collections.

Case Transformation

Case conversion functions str/upper-case and str/lower-case convert all characters in a string to uppercase or lowercase, respectively.

```
(def upper "clojure")
(def lower "CLOJURE")

(def upper-result (str/upper-case upper))
(def lower-result (str/lower-case lower))
```

```
=> "CLOJURE"
=> "clojure"
```

Trimming

Removing leading and trailing whitespace is performed using str/trim. For removing only leading or trailing spaces, str/triml and str/trimr are available.

```
(def untrimmed " Clojure ")

(def trimmed (str/trim untrimmed))
```

=> "Clojure"

Replacing Substrings

Replacing occurrences of substrings within a string is simplified using str/replace. Basic usage involves specifying the target and replacement strings.

```
(def original "Clojure is fun")

(def replaced (str/replace original "fun" "powerful"))
```

=> "Clojure is powerful"

For more complex replacements, regular expressions can be employed:

```
(def regex-replaced (str/replace original #"\bis\b" "is indeed"))
```

=> "Clojure is indeed fun"

Efficient String Concatenation

Concatenating strings in a loop can be inefficient due to the immutable nature of String objects. Use StringBuilder for efficient concatenation in performance-critical sections.

```
(let [sb (StringBuilder.)]
  (doseq [word ["Clojure" "is" "efficient"]]
    (.append sb word " "))
  (.toString sb))
```

=> "Clojure is efficient "

While StringBuilder is an imperative tool, it can be wrapped in a functional style if needed. For most everyday tasks, Clojure's native string functions provide sufficient efficiency and readability.

Regular Expressions

With clojure.string functions relying on regular expressions, it is beneficial to understand their syntax and capabilities. Matching patterns, capturing groups, and leveraging specialized constructs enhance the power and flexibility of string manipulation.

For instance, extracting parts of a string using re-find:

```
(def email "user@example.com")

(def domain (second (re-find #"@(.*)" email)))
```

```
=> "example.com"
```

By recursively applying these principles, efficient and readable string manipulation practices can be achieved without sacrificing performance. This is essential in data processing, text analysis, and various other domains where strings are intensively handled.

5.12 Advanced Sequence Operations

This section delves into advanced sequence operations in Clojure, exploring sophisticated techniques for manipulating and interacting with sequences. We build upon foundational knowledge, addressing efficient and expressive ways to handle sequence data.

One of the core operations is map, which applies a function to each item in a sequence. Consider the following example, which doubles each number in a sequence:

```
(def numbers [1 2 3 4 5])
(def doubled (map #(* 2 %) numbers))
```

Evaluating doubled yields:

```
(2 4 6 8 10)
```

To filter sequences, we use filter. For instance, to extract even numbers:

```
(def evens (filter even? numbers))
```

Evaluating evens yields:

```
(2 4)
```

More complex operations often use reduce, which accumulates values. For example, summing a list of numbers:

```
(def sum (reduce + numbers))
```

Evaluating sum yields:

15

To understand reduce, consider applying a function repeatedly. Here's an implementation that concatenates strings:

```
(def words ["hello" "world"])
(def sentence (reduce str words))
```

Evaluating sentence yields:

"helloworld"

Using reductions, we can track intermediate reduce results:

```
(def sums (reductions + numbers))
```

Evaluating sums yields:

(1 3 6 10 15)

Sequence transformations like mapcat concatenate results of map, flattening nested sequences:

```
(def nested [[1 2] [3 4] [5]])
(def flat (mapcat identity nested))
```

Evaluating flat yields:

(1 2 3 4 5)

For lazy sequences, Clojure leverages lazy-seq, creating sequences that compute elements on demand. Here's an infinite Fibonacci generator:

```
(defn fib
  ([]
   (fib 0 1))
  ([a b]
   (lazy-seq
     (cons a (fib b (+ a b))))))
(def fibs (fib))
(take 10 fibs)
```

Executing the above yields:

(0 1 1 2 3 5 8 13 21 34)

Extending sequence capabilities, partition divides sequences into subsequences. To partition into triplets:

```
(def triplets (partition 3 numbers))
```

Evaluating triplets yields:

((1 2 3) (4 5))

Alternatively, partition-all includes shorter sub-sequences for unmatched elements:

```
(def triplets-all (partition-all 3 numbers))
```

Evaluating triplets-all yields:

((1 2 3) (4 5))

For windowing operations, partition-by splits sequences based on a predicate. Grouping numbers by evenness:

```
(def grouped-by-even (partition-by even? numbers))
```

Evaluating grouped-by-even yields:

((1) (2) (3) (4) (5))

Using iterate, we generate infinite sequences derivatively. Adding one repeatedly:

```
(def ones (iterate inc 0))
(take 10 ones)
```

Evaluating ones yields:

(0 1 2 3 4 5 6 7 8 9)

The comprehension syntax for allows complex sequence building with nested loops and filters:

```
(def squares (for [x numbers :when (even? x)] (* x x)))
```

Evaluating squares yields:

(4 16)

For more specific cases, take-while and drop-while selectively take or drop elements based on a predicate. Taking elements before hitting a number greater than three:

```
(def taken (take-while #(<= % 3) numbers))
```

Evaluating taken yields:

(1 2 3)

Applying drop-while discards initial elements until the predicate fails:

```
(def dropped (drop-while #(<= % 3) numbers))
```

Evaluating dropped yields:

```
(4 5)
```

Combining these advanced sequence operations empowers efficient manipulation of Clojure collections, offering expressive yet performant data handling strategies.

Chapter 6

State and Concurrency in Clojure

This chapter examines the principles of state and concurrency in Clojure, focusing on managing state with atoms, refs and Software Transactional Memory (STM), agents, and dynamic scope with vars. It explores concurrency primitives, state coordination with watches and validators, and the use of 'core.async' channels. Key topics include concurrency patterns, handling side effects in concurrent programs, and testing and debugging concurrent applications.

6.1 Understanding State and Identity

State and identity are fundamental concepts in any programming language dealing with mutable data. In Clojure, these concepts are treated with specific constructs and philosophies that promote immutability and functional programming principles. Understanding these concepts is crucial for effectively managing mutable state and ensuring safe concurrency.

Identity in Clojure refers to an entity that holds a reference to a value. For example, when you create a variable in a traditional programming language, you are creating an identity that can refer to various values over time. Clojure separates the notion of identity from the mutable state, leading to cleaner and more predictable code.

State refers to the value to which an identity points at any given moment in time. While the state can change, each change creates a new immutable value. This separation provides significant advantages in concurrent programming, reducing issues related to mutable shared state.

Vars in Clojure provide a mechanism to define an identity with an associated value that can change. Unlike other references which maintain a single value over time, vars can be dynamically rebound.

For example, consider the following Clojure code to define a var:

```
(def my-var 42)
```

Here, my-var is an identity referring to the value 42. If you change the state of my-var, it will refer to a new value:

```
(def my-var "new value")
```

However, the original value (42) remains immutable and can still be referenced if needed. This immutability is the cornerstone of Clojure's approach to managing state.

In Clojure, the need for managing state within concurrent programs introduces the challenge of ensuring thread safety. This requires a careful approach to avoid race conditions and deadlocks. Clojure provides several constructs to manage state that adhere to its philosophy of functional programming and immutability:

- Atoms - Use for managing synchronous, independent state changes.
- Refs - Use for coordinated, synchronous state changes across multiple identities.
- Agents - Use for managing asynchronous, independent state changes.
- Vars - Use for binding and rebinding within a dynamic scope.

Understanding state in Clojure also involves distinguishing between value and reference. A value is an immutable piece of data, whereas a reference is a construct that points to a value and can be updated. For example, when working with atoms:

```
(def my-atom (atom 0))
```

Here, my-atom is a reference to the value 0. The state can be updated:

```
(swap! my-atom inc) ; increments the value by 1
```

The swap! function safely applies a function to the current value of the atom and updates the state, ensuring atomicity.

Additionally, Clojure's design ensures that functions are first-class citizens, which means they can be passed around and manipulated like any other data. This property is particularly useful in the context of state and identity. For instance, modifying state in an atom:

```
(def counter (atom 0))

(defn increment [atm]
  (swap! atm inc))

(increment counter)
```

Here, increment is a function that can be applied to any atom. This approach leverages Clojure's functional programming paradigm to manage state transitions coherently.

Clojure's design aims for software transactional memory (STM) and concurrency primitives in ensuring safe and efficient state changes. Understanding state in Clojure, therefore, necessitates a comprehension of these constructs and the underlying philosophy of immutability.

By treating state changes as a series of immutable values and leveraging references like atoms, refs, agents, and vars, you can achieve more predictable and robust concurrent applications. The principles of state and identity in Clojure pave the way for building concurrent programs with minimal side effects and enhanced maintainability.

6.2 Managing State with Atoms

In Clojure, atoms are a core abstraction for managing state. Atoms provide a way to maintain and manage shared, mutable state in a thread-safe manner. Atoms ensure that changes to the state are atomic and visible to all threads immediately after the update. This section explores how to define atoms, perform atomic updates, and utilize validators and watches to manage state effectively.

Atoms in Clojure are defined using the atom function. An atom is created by passing an initial value to this function. For example:

```
(def my-atom (atom 0))
```

In this example, my-atom is an atom initialized with the value 0. To retrieve the current value of an atom, use the deref function or the shorthand @ operator:

```
@my-atom ; Dereference to obtain the current value
```

Atoms are updated using the swap! and reset! functions. The swap! function applies a function to the current value of the atom and sets the atom to the new value. The update is atomic, ensuring thread safety. For instance, to increment the value of my-atom by 1:

```
(swap! my-atom inc)
```

The function passed to swap! can also accept additional arguments. For example, to add a specific value to the current value of my-atom:

```
(swap! my-atom + 5)
```

The reset! function sets the atom to a new value directly:

```
(reset! my-atom 10)
```

While reset! is simpler, it should be used with caution as it does not provide the same level of atomicity as swap!. Specifically, swap! retries until the function can be applied successfully, whereas reset! merely sets the new value, potentially clashing with other concurrent updates.

Validators are functions attached to atoms to ensure that any change to the atom satisfies certain criteria. When a new value is set, the validator is invoked, and if it returns false or throws an exception, the update is rejected. Validators are defined using the :validator keyword:

```
(def my-validated-atom (atom 0 :validator pos?))
```

Here, pos? ensures that only positive values can be stored in my-validated-atom. Attempts to set a negative value will result in an error:

```
(reset! my-validated-atom -5)
;; IllegalStateException Invalid reference state
```

Watches provide a mechanism to observe changes to an atom. A watch is a function that is called whenever the atom's value changes, receiving the key, the atom itself, the old value, and the new value. Watches are added using the add-watch function:

```
(defn watch-fn [key atom old-state new-state]
  (println "Atom changed from" old-state "to" new-state))
(add-watch my-atom :watch-key watch-fn)
```

When my-atom is updated, watch-fn prints the old and new values:

```
(swap! my-atom inc)
;; Atom changed from 10 to 11
```

Watches can be removed using the remove-watch function:

```
(remove-watch my-atom :watch-key)
```

Atoms facilitate safe, mutable state management in concurrent programs by ensuring atomic updates and providing mechanisms for validation and observation. By appropriately utilizing swap! for atomic operations, reset! for straightforward updates, validators to enforce constraints, and watches to observe changes, developers can effectively manage shared state in Clojure applications.

6.3 Managing State with Refs and Software Transactional Memory (STM)

Refs in Clojure provide a way to manage coordinated, synchronous updates to shared state. They are ideally used in scenarios requiring atomicity across multiple shared references and are best suited within the Software Transactional Memory (STM) system that Clojure provides. This section delves into the mechanics of refs, the STM model, and how these concepts interweave to offer a robust mechanism for state management in concurrent applications.

Refs are created using the ref function. To define a ref, wrap an initial state in the ref function as shown:

```
(def counter (ref 0))
```

The state within a ref can only be modified within a transaction, ensuring atomic and coordinated updates. Transactions are initiated using the dosync macro which creates a transactional context where ref states can be safely altered. The primary functions to alter states within transactions are ref-set and alter.

ref-set sets the state of the ref to a new value unconditionally:

```
(dosync
  (ref-set counter 1))
```

Conversely, alter takes a ref, a function, and arguments to apply the function to the current state of the ref:

```
(dosync
  (alter counter inc))
```

The true power of refs emerges through coordinated updates across multiple refs within a single transaction. The STM system ensures isolation and consistency, preventing race conditions and ensuring all changes succeed or none do. Consider managing a simple bank account with refs for the balance:

```
(def account1 (ref 100))
(def account2 (ref 200))

(defn transfer [from to amount]
  (dosync
    (alter from - amount)
    (alter to + amount)))
```

Here, the transfer function ensures that funds are moved atomically between accounts. If any part of the transaction fails, the state reverts to its prior form, reflecting the ACID (Atomicity, Consistency, Isolation, Durability) properties crucial for database transactions.

Clojure's STM also supports retry mechanism which is critical in the presence of contention. When a transaction detects a conflict due to concurrent updates, it automatically retries until it succeeds. Below is an example detailing the withdrawal operation reinforcing the automatic retry feature:

```
(defn withdraw [account amount]
  (dosync
    (let [balance @account]
      (when (>= balance amount)
        (alter account - amount)))))
```

Notice the use of @ to dereference and read the current value of a ref within the transaction. By leveraging STM, we ensure that concurrent withdrawal or transfer operations operate correctly without interleaving issues.

Clojure provides additional features to support STM such as ensure, commute, and validator. The ensure function can be employed to establish read locks, preventing write contention while allowing multiple reads:

```
(defn read-balance [account]
  (dosync
    (ensure account)
    @account))
```

The commute function optimizes for commutative operations where the order of execution does not affect the outcome, thus reducing contention. For example:

```
(defn safe-deposit [account amount]
  (dosync
    (commute account + amount)))
```

Validators add another layer of integrity by ensuring state adheres to defined constraints immediately after a transaction commits:

```
(defn non-negative? [balance]
  (>= balance 0))

(def secure-account (ref 0 :validator non-negative?))
```

Attempting to alter secure-account to a negative value would result in a transaction failure, thus enforcing the non-negative balance requirement.

Through the cohesive blend of refs and STM, Clojure offers powerful semantics for managing shared state with high reliability and expressive power, allowing developers to build robust concurrent applications with ease. Understanding and effectively utilizing these constructs is pivotal for mastering state management in Clojure.

6.4 Managing State with Agents

Agents in Clojure are used to manage state in a way that allows safe concurrent modifications. They are suited for managing independent, asynchronous, and potentially long-running state changes. Unlike atoms and refs, agents provide a mechanism whereby changes to state can propagate without blocking the main thread, using a dedicated thread pool to handle updates asynchronously.

Clojure agents are created using the agent function. Once an agent is created, states are updated using the send or send-off functions, which schedule actions to be applied to the agent's state. These actions are applied sequentially; however, they are computed asynchronously which means the caller can continue processing without waiting for these actions to complete.

```
(def counter (agent 0)) ; Creating an agent with an initial state of 0

(send counter inc) ; Incrementing the agent's state asynchronously

@counter ; Dereferencing the agent to get its current value
```

In the example above, the counter agent is initialized with a value of 0. The send function schedules the inc function to be applied to the agent's state. The @counter syntax dereferences the agent, yielding its current state.

send vs send-off: - send is used for actions that are CPU-bound. It uses a fixed-size thread pool. - send-off is used for actions that may block, such as I/O operations, and uses a separate, unbounded thread pool to prevent starvation of CPU-bound tasks.

```
(send-off counter (fn [state] (Thread/sleep 1000) (inc state))) ; Performing a blocking
    operation
```

In this example, the state increment is delayed by one second, simulated by Thread/sleep. The send-off function ensures that this blocking operation does not exhaust the thread pool reserved for send operations.

Error Handling in Agents: Clojure agents provide mechanisms to handle errors that occur during state updates. If an action applied to an agent throws an exception, the agent becomes ̈failedänd will not apply any further actions until it is fixed. The agent-error function retrieves the error, and the restart-agent function can reset the agent's state:

```
(def error-prone-agent (agent 0))

(send error-prone-agent (fn [_] (/ 1 0))) ; An action that will fail

(agent-error error-prone-agent) ; Retrieve the error

(restart-agent error-prone-agent 0) ; Restart the agent with initial state of 0
```

Agents also support the utilization of watchers, similar to atoms and refs, allowing for the invocation of functions when the agent's state changes. The add-watch function attaches a watcher to an agent:

```
(def monitored-agent (agent 0))

(add-watch monitored-agent :watch-key
  (fn [key agent old-value new-value]
    (println "The agent's state changed from" old-value "to" new-value)))

(send monitored-agent inc) ; Update the state, triggering the watch
```

In this example, whenever the monitored-agent's state changes, the watcher function prints the old and new states to the console.

Agents can also invoke functions periodically using the set-agent-send-executor! and set-agent-send-off-executor! functions, allowing for customized executor services that can leverage advanced concurrency facilities provided by the java.util.concurrent package. This provides fine control over how state transitions are executed, ensuring robust handling of asynchronous state management in concurrent applications.

```
(import '[java.util.concurrent Executors])

(def custom-executor (Executors/newFixedThreadPool 4))
(set-agent-send-executor! custom-executor)

(def periodic-agent (agent 0))

(send periodic-agent (fn [state]
  (println "State is:" state) (inc state)))
```

This example demonstrates creating a custom executor service with a fixed thread pool and assigning it to handle send operations for agents. The agent's state transition function is then executed on the specified custom executor.

Agents are a powerful tool in Clojure for managing state in concurrent applications, allowing for non-blocking, independent, and asynchronous state modifications. They simplify the design of complex concurrent workflows, ensuring that state is managed safely and efficiently across multiple threads.

6.5 Managing State with Vars and Dynamic Scope

Vars in Clojure offer a robust mechanism for managing state with dynamic scope. Vars are mutable references that can be dynamically rebound, which makes them suitable for representing thread-local, dynamic states. They are primarily defined using def and can be dynamically rebound using binding. This flexibility provides significant utility in specific scenarios, particularly in multi-threaded environments.

Defining and Accessing Vars: Typically, Vars are declared using the def keyword. This keyword associates a symbol with a value, effectively creating a global binding that can be referenced throughout the program.

```
(def my-var 42)
(println my-var) ; outputs: 42
```

In this instance, my-var is bound to the value 42, which can then be accessed from any point in the application. The value of a Var can be changed using the alter-var-root function, although this practice is generally discouraged due to potential side effects stemming from global state mutation.

Dynamic Rebinding with Binding: The binding macro allows the creation of thread-local bindings for Vars. These bindings are localized to the dynamic scope of the block in which the binding is executed. This feature is extremely beneficial for maintaining thread-local states, enabling functions to operate independently and concurrently without interfering with each other.

```
(def \texttt{^:dynamic} *app-context* "production")

(defn print-context []
  (println *app-context*))

(print-context) ; outputs: production

(binding [*app-context* "development"]
  (print-context)) ; outputs: development

(print-context) ; outputs: production
```

Here, *app-context* is a dynamically scoped Var, signified by the ^:dynamic metadata. The binding macro temporarily rebinds *app-context* to "development" within its scope. Outside this scope, the Var returns to its original definition, showcasing the power of dynamic scoping.

Situations Where Dynamic Vars Are Ideal: Dynamic Vars excel in scenarios where state needs to be temporarily overridden. A classic use case is in configuring application environments (e.g., changing from production to development settings within specific blocks of code) or managing resources that should vary per request in a web application.

Potential Pitfalls: Despite their advantages, the misuse of dynamic Vars can introduce hard-to-debug side effects and non-deterministic behavior, particularly in concurrent applications. Therefore, their use should be judicious and well-controlled. Employing best practices like limiting their scope and utilizing immutability whenever possible can mitigate these risks.

Using Vars with Callbacks and Events: When dealing with callbacks or events that may execute in different threads, dynamic scope becomes particularly useful. For instance, handling user sessions in a web application often requires dynamic bindings to maintain session-specific information across various callbacks. Here is a hypothetical web server example demonstrating this principle:

```
(require '[ring.adapter.jetty :refer [run-jetty]])
(require '[ring.middleware.params :refer [wrap-params]])

(def \texttt{^:dynamic} *current-user* nil)

(defn handler [request]
  (binding [*current-user* (:user request)]
    (process-request)))

(defn process-request []
  (println "Processing request for:" *current-user*)
  {:status 200
  :headers {"Content-Type" "text/plain"}
   :body (str "Hello, " *current-user*)})

(run-jetty (wrap-params handler) {:port 3000})
```

In this scenario, each HTTP request binds *current-user* to the associated user of the request. The function process-request then processes the request with the context of the *current-user*. Such an approach ensures that user context is maintained accurately and is thread-local.

Interaction with Other Concurrency Constructs: Vars can also operate in conjunction with other concurrency primitives like atoms, refs, and agents. While vars manage localized state, atoms, refs, and agents manage shared and coordinated mutable state across threads. For example, combining dynamic scope with atoms can be used to maintain thread-local adjustments to shared, thread-safe configurations.

```
(def \texttt{^:dynamic} *config* {:log-level "info"})
(def config-atom (atom *config*))

(defn update-config [key val]
  (binding [*config* (assoc *config* key val)]
    (swap! config-atom merge *config*)))
```

Here, the dynamic var *config* temporarily overrides its state for the thread, and the shared config-atom is updated through a coordinated state mechanism by atomically merging the temporary *config* with the global configuration.

The use of vars in combination with dynamic scope thus provides the flexibility to manage thread-local states effectively while interacting seamlessly with Clojure's concurrency primitives. This capability significantly enhances the robustness, maintainability, and efficiency of concurrent applications.

6.6 Concurrency Primitives in Clojure

Concurrency and parallelism are critical aspects of modern computing, enabling programs to perform multiple tasks simultaneously and efficiently. Clojure, being a functional programming language with immutable data structures, provides several concurrency primitives that ensure safe and efficient concurrent programming. This section delves into these primitives, explaining their purpose and usage.

Atoms, Refs, Agents, and Vars are the primary concurrency primitives in Clojure. These abstractions manage mutable state while preserving the benefits of functional programming. Detailed understanding of these primitives is essential for writing robust concurrent applications in Clojure.

Atoms: The simplest concurrency primitive in Clojure is the atom. Atoms provide a way to manage state changes in a thread-safe manner without locking. They support atomic operations, which means updates are indivisible and occur without interference from other threads.

The atom is created using the atom function:

```
(def counter (atom 0))
```

Here, counter is an atom initialized to 0. To change the state of an atom, the swap! function is used, which applies a function to the current state atomically:

```
(swap! counter inc)
(swap! counter + 5)
```

The reset! function is used to set the atom to a new value directly:

```
(reset! counter 0)
```

Atoms are ideal for managing independent, synchronous state changes, ensuring visibility of changes across threads without blocking.

Refs and Software Transactional Memory (STM): Clojure's refs and Software Transactional Memory (STM) provide a more sophisticated mechanism for managing shared state. Refs ensure that multiple related state changes are consistent and isolated. STM allows safe and atomic modifications across multiple refs using transactions.

A ref is created using the ref function:

```
(def shared-state (ref {}))
```

To alter the state of a ref, state changes must be enclosed in a dosync block, ensuring they are executed atomically:

```
(dosync
  (alter shared-state assoc :key "value"))
```

The ref primitive supports coordinated changes to multiple refs, ensuring their consistency.

Agents: Agents in Clojure are designed for managing asynchronous state changes. Unlike atoms and refs, agents do not block the calling thread. Instead, they schedule state changes to be performed independently.

An agent is created using the agent function:

```
(def my-agent (agent 0))
```

State changes are sent to the agent using the send or send-off functions:

```
(send my-agent inc)
(send my-agent + 5)
```

The state changes are processed asynchronously, and the calling thread continues execution without waiting for the changes to complete.

Vars and Dynamic Scope: Vars in Clojure provide a mechanism for dynamic scoping and thread-local state. Vars can be rebound on a per-thread basis, offering a way to manage state that is specific to a thread's context.

A var is created using the def function:

```
(def ^:dynamic *my-var* 0)
```

To rebind a var dynamically within a thread, the binding macro is used:

```
(binding [*my-var* 10]
  (println *my-var*)) ; Prints 10
```

Outside the binding form, the var retains its original value.

Understanding these concurrency primitives is crucial for leveraging Clojure's capabilities to write efficient and safe concurrent programs.

Each primitive offers distinct advantages based on the requirements of the program's state management and concurrency model.

To demonstrate, consider a scenario involving multiple threads updating a shared counter. Using atoms ensures simple and efficient updates without additional coordination mechanisms, making them suitable for independent state changes. For coordinated updates involving multiple state variables, refs and STM provide the required atomicity and consistency. When dealing with asynchronous or potentially long-running tasks, agents offer non-blocking updates. Lastly, vars enable maintaining thread-local context, which is essential for dynamic scoping.

6.7 Coordinating State with Watches

Clojure provides a powerful mechanism called watches to observe and react to state changes. Watches offer a way to set up callbacks that trigger when an atomic reference's state is modified. This is particularly useful for coordinating state between different parts of an application or for implementing reactive programming patterns.

A watch is essentially a key-value pair where the key is a unique identifier and the value is a callback function. The callback function is executed when the state changes, receiving four arguments: the reference being watched, the old state, the new state, and the key of the watch. This design allows for flexibility in monitoring and reacting to state transitions in a Clojure program.

To better understand how watches function, consider the following example where we monitor an atom's state:

```
(def my-atom (atom 0))

(defn state-changed [ref old-state new-state]
  (println "State changed from" old-state "to" new-state))

(add-watch my-atom :state-watcher state-changed)

(swap! my-atom inc)
```

In this example, we first define an atom called my-atom initialized to 0. We then define a function state-changed that takes three parameters: the reference ref, the old state old-state, and the new state new-state. This function prints a message whenever the state changes.

We attach the watch to my-atom using the add-watch function. The arguments are the atom, a unique key :state-watcher to identify the watch, and the callback function state-changed. When we modify the state of my-atom using swap!, the callback function is executed automatically, and we see the following output:

```
State changed from 0 to 1
```

This output indicates that the watch successfully monitored the state transition from 0 to 1. Watches are not limited to atoms; they can also be used with other reference types such as refs and agents.

To remove a watch, the remove-watch function is used. This function takes the reference and the key of the watch to be removed:

```
(remove-watch my-atom :state-watcher)
```

It is crucial to understand that the watch function runs synchronously in the same thread that changes the state. This means it should be used carefully to prevent blocking operations in the main execution thread. Watches should not perform lengthy computations, network calls, or any side effects that could introduce latency or deadlocks.

The following example demonstrates attaching multiple watches to the same reference. This can be useful in scenarios where different functionalities need to react independently to the same state transition.

```
(defn log-change [ref old-state new-state]
  (println "Logging change:" old-state "->" new-state))

(defn validate-change [ref old-state new-state]
  (when (< new-state 0)
    (println "Negative state is not allowed")
    (reset! ref old-state)))

(add-watch my-atom :logger log-change)
(add-watch my-atom :validator validate-change)

(swap! my-atom dec)
```

In this case, we add two watches: :logger and :validator. The log-change function logs the state transition, while the validate-change function ensures that the state does not become negative. If a negative state is detected, the function resets the atom to its previous state and prints a warning message:

```
Logging change: 1 -> 0
Logging change: 0 -> -1
Negative state is not allowed
```

By coordinating state changes with watches, developers can build more reactive and resilient applications. It's a powerful tool for managing state transitions, ensuring data integrity, and enforcing business rules.

Watches in Clojure provide an efficient and flexible mechanism for observing and responding to state changes. By attaching callback functions to reference types, developers can coordinate state between different parts of an application, validate state transitions, and implement reactive programming patterns. This allows for streamlined state management and improved control over an application's behavior and workflow.

6.8 Coordinating State with Validators

Validators in Clojure provide a mechanism for ensuring that certain conditions or invariants hold when the state changes. Validators are functions that take a single argument, the proposed new state, and return true if the new state is acceptable or false otherwise. Validators can be associated with atoms, refs, and agents.

In Clojure, you can associate a validator function to maintain the state coherence automatically every time a state change is attempted. If the validator function returns false, the state change is aborted and an exception is thrown. This allows for a robust mechanism to enforce rules and invariants critical to the application.

Atoms can have validators set using the :validator key in their options map. Let's examine a basic example of using a validator with an atom.

```
(defn positive-number-validator [new-value]
  (pos? new-value))

(def my-atom (atom 0 :validator positive-number-validator))

;; This will fail
(swap! my-atom dec)
;; This will succeed
(swap! my-atom inc)
```

In this example, the positive-number-validator function checks whether a given number is positive. When an attempt is made to decrement the value inside my-atom, the operation fails because the validator function returns false, ensuring the state never becomes non-positive.

For refs, validators can be set similarly, as they also support the :validator key when they are constructed.

```
(defn non-empty-string-validator [new-value]
  (and (string? new-value) (not (empty? new-value))))

(def my-ref (ref "" :validator non-empty-string-validator))
```

```
;; This will fail
(dosync (ref-set my-ref ""))
;; This will succeed
(dosync (ref-set my-ref "valid"))
```

The non-empty-string-validator ensures that the new state for my-ref is both a string and not empty. Any attempt to set an invalid state inside a dosync transaction will be aborted.

Validators are also applicable to agents. When creating an agent, the :validator keyword can be used to enforce constraints. Here's an example:

```
(defn even-number-validator [new-value]
  (even? new-value))

(def my-agent (agent 2 :validator even-number-validator))

;; This will fail
(send my-agent inc)
;; This will succeed
(send my-agent + 2)
```

In this illustration, the even-number-validator ensures that the number stored in my-agent remains even. As a result, the attempt to increment the value fails while adding two succeeds.

When setting validators, it is crucial to design them carefully to avoid overly restrictive or unnecessary restrictions that might hinder the application's functionality. Validators should ideally be pure functions without side effects, as they may be called multiple times and should consistently produce the same result for the given input state.

Moreover, when dealing with complex state transitions or validations, it might be beneficial to encapsulate the validation logic in well-tested and reusable functions. Here is an example of a more complex validator:

```
(defn complex-validator [new-state]
  (and (map? new-state)
       (contains? new-state :required-key)
       (> (count (keys new-state)) 3)))

(def my-complex-atom (atom {:required-key "value" :other-key 1} :validator complex-
      validator))

;; This will fail
(swap! my-complex-atom dissoc :required-key)
;; This will succeed
(swap! my-complex-atom assoc :additional-key 2)
```

In this validator, complex-validator ensures that the state of the atom is always a map, contains a specific key (:required-key), and has more than three keys. Such complex validators are advantageous for enforcing intricate application-level invariants.

Validators are instrumental for enforcing business logic at the state level, reducing error propagation and simplifying debugging. By providing a declarative way to assert correctness, they streamline maintaining the state invariants that are central to application integrity.

Thus, validators form an integral part of state coordination in Clojure, ensuring robust and predictable state transitions across concurrent programming paradigms.

6.9 Using core.async Channels

The core.async library in Clojure provides powerful tools for managing concurrency using channels and processes. Built around Communicating Sequential Processes (CSP), the library allows for decoupled asynchronous operations via channels, where data can be communicated without shared state.

Channels are at the heart of core.async. They provide a medium for communications between different threads or processes, offering an effective mechanism for concurrency without common pitfalls such as race conditions or locking issues. In this section, we will explore the use of channels, focusing on their creation, operations to put and take data, and how different types of channels can be utilized to solve concurrency problems.

Creation of Channels

A channel can be created using the chan function.

```
(require '[clojure.core.async :refer [chan]])

(def c (chan))
```

Channels can be both buffered and unbuffered. An unbuffered channel will block both the sender and receiver until a corresponding receive or send operation completes. Buffered channels, on the other hand, can hold multiple items, controlled by the buffer size.

```
(def c (chan 10)) ;; buffered channel with a capacity of 10
```

Putting and Taking Data

The primary operations on channels are >!! and <!!, used to put and

take data synchronously.

```
(require '[clojure.core.async :refer [>!! <!!]])

(>!! c "hello") ;; puts "hello" into the channel
(def result (<!! c)) ;; takes the value from the channel
```

For non-blocking operations, one can use >! and <! within a go block.

```
(require '[clojure.core.async :refer [go >! <!]])

(go
  (>! c "hello"))
(go
  (let [result (<! c)]
    (println result))) ;; prints "hello"
```

This go block represents an asynchronous computation. It performs the operations specified within it without blocking the current thread, leveraging lightweight threads known as go blocks.

Closing Channels

Channels can be explicitly closed using the close! function.

```
(require '[clojure.core.async :refer [close!]])

(close! c)
```

Upon closure, no more data can be put onto the channel. However, any pending and subsequent take operations will continue to retrieve items until the channel is empty, after which they will return nil.

Channel Buffers

Buffers control the capacity and behavior of channels. The common buffer types include fixed buffers, dropping buffers, and sliding buffers.

```
(require '[clojure.core.async :refer [fixed-buffer dropping-buffer sliding-buffer]])

(def fixed-c (chan (fixed-buffer 2)))
(def dropping-c (chan (dropping-buffer 2)))
(def sliding-c (chan (sliding-buffer 2)))
```

- fixed-buffer: Channels with a fixed buffer store a limited number of items and block when full.
- dropping-buffer: These channels drop the newest item when the buffer is full.
- sliding-buffer: Channels with sliding buffers will drop the oldest item when full.

Alts Operations

The alts! operation provides a way to perform non-deterministic choice, attempting multiple channel operations and proceeding with the first successful one.

```
(require '[clojure.core.async :refer [alts!]])

(go
  (let [[v ch] (alts! [c1 c2 c3])]
    (println "Got" v "from" ch)))
```

This example will wait for any of the channels in [c1 c2 c3] to have a value available and then print the first obtained value and the respective channel from which the value was taken.

Pipelines

core.async also supports building pipelines of transformations over data streams using pipeline, pipeline-async, and pipeline-blocking.

```
(require '[clojure.core.async :refer [pipeline chan]])

(defn process [in-chan]
  (let [out-chan (chan)]
    (pipeline 10 out-chan some-xform in-chan)
    out-chan))
```

The pipeline function provides a mechanism to transform data passing through channels efficiently.

Channels and their operations form a versatile foundation for building concurrent programs in Clojure, enabling elegant solutions to complex concurrency challenges through straightforward composition and effective communication paradigms.

6.10 Concurrency Patterns and Practices

Effective concurrency management in Clojure requires an understanding of various patterns and the best practices for applying them. In this section, we explore essential concurrency patterns and provide practical advice on how to implement them in Clojure.

core.async simplifies many concurrency scenarios by allowing communication over channels. Channels act as conduits for passing messages between different parts of your application, enabling coordination without direct reference or locking.

```
(ns async-patterns
  (:require [clojure.core.async :refer :all]))

(let [ch (chan)]
  (go
    (>! ch 42))
  (go
    (println "Received:" (<! ch))))
```

The go blocks are lightweight threads managed by Clojure's runtime. This pattern avoids the complexity of managing traditional threads and is non-blocking, making full use of available processors without locking up resources.

Actors, implemented via agents, encapsulate state and provide a simple yet powerful model for concurrency. Agents ensure that updates to their state happen sequentially by dispatching actions asynchronously.

```
(def counter (agent 0))

(send counter inc)
(send counter (fn [v] (* v 2)))

(await-for 1000 counter)
(println "Counter value:" @counter)
```

Agents process updates to their state via actions, ensuring thread-safe mutations. The use of await-for guarantees the agent completes its pending actions within the specified timeout, thus allowing the program to ascertain the final state of counter.

Software Transactional Memory (STM) enables composing multiple state changes atomically. Refs are modified within transactions, ensuring that either all changes succeed or none do, which simplifies reasoning about state.

```
(defn transfer [from to amount]
  (dosync
    (alter from - amount)
    (alter to + amount)))
```

The dosync macro initiates a transaction, ensuring that the balance changes in both accounts occur together. If any part of the transaction fails, no changes are committed, maintaining consistent state.

For cases where mutable shared state is necessary, atoms provide an excellent mechanism. Atoms ensure safe concurrent updates through compare-and-swap (CAS) operations, allowing multiple threads to safely modify a shared value.

```
(def counter (atom 0))
```

```
(swap! counter inc)
(println "Counter:" @counter)
```

The swap! function ensures that updates to counter are atomic and consistent. Utilizing atoms for independent states that do not require complex or coordinated updates is suitable.

Selective mutation for global state, managed with vars, leverages dynamic scoping to make temporary state changes.

```
(def ^:dynamic *conn* nil)

(defn make-connection []
  (binding [*conn* {:db "sample"}]
    (println "Connection:" *conn*)))
```

The binding macro temporarily changes the value of *conn* within its scope, reverting to the previous state upon exit. This pattern is useful for resource management and testing.

Channel-based communication simplifies producer-consumer scenarios, decoupling the producer and consumer computations.

```
(let [ch (chan)]
  (go
    (>! ch (some-computation))
    (close! ch))
  (go
    (while true
      (if-let [result (<! ch)]
        (println "Result:" result)
        (do
          (println "Channel closed.")
          (break))))))
```

In this example, the producer computation is asynchronous and once done, the channel is closed. The consumer loop processes messages until it detects the closed channel. This pattern abstracts the complexities of thread management and synchronization.

Applying these concurrency patterns requires adhering to certain practices to ensure correctness and performance. Avoiding shared mutable state, favoring immutability, and limiting side effects within transactions are fundamental. Making judicious use of locks and ensuring minimal transactional scope further enhance performance.

Handling side effects separately from the core logic, typically by communicating results through channels, results in more predictable and testable code. Testing concurrent code demands thorough and, often, invariant-based approaches to verify state consistency under various concurrent operations.

These patterns and practices cultivate robust concurrent applications in Clojure, leveraging functional programming paradigms synergistically with concurrency primitives.

6.11 Handling Side Effects in Concurrent Programs

In concurrent programming, side effects can introduce significant complexity, as they often affect shared state, which may lead to nondeterministic behaviors. Clojure provides various constructs and idioms to manage side effects effectively, ensuring that programs remain predictable and maintainable.

Side effects occur when a function alters some state outside its local environment, such as modifying a global variable, performing I/O operations, or changing the content of a data structure. In a purely functional paradigm, all functions are deterministic and free of side effects. However, real-world applications necessitate side effects for tasks such as reading from databases, handling user input, and writing to files.

Clojure's approach to handling side effects in concurrent programs involves isolating mutable state and employing synchronization mechanisms to ensure safe and consistent state changes. Key constructs for managing side effects include atoms, refs, agents, and the use of core.async channels.

Atoms provide a mechanism for managing independent, synchronous state changes. When an atom's state is updated, it ensures atomic updates via the compare-and-swap (CAS) operation. This guarantees that state transitions occur safely and predictably, even in a concurrent setting.

The basic usage of an atom is demonstrated below:

```
(def counter (atom 0))

; Atomically incrementing the counter
(swap! counter inc)
```

The swap! function employs a CAS operation to ensure the atomicity of the update.

Refs and Software Transactional Memory (STM) are designed for managing coordinated, synchronous state changes across multiple variables. STM allows transactions to be composed, ensuring that either all changes within a transaction are applied or none are, thereby preventing inconsistent state.

Example of using refs in STM:

```
(def balance (ref 1000))
(def interest-rate (ref 0.05))

(dosync
  (alter balance + (* @balance @interest-rate)))
```

In this code, the dosync block ensures that the operations on balance and interest-rate are executed atomically.

Agents provide a mechanism for managing independent, asynchronous state changes. Agents update their state in response to actions submitted asynchronously, which execute in a thread pool separate from the agent's main thread.

An example demonstrating the use of agents:

```
(def log-agent (agent []))

; Asynchronously add a new log entry
(send log-agent conj "New log entry")
```

The send function dispatches the conj action to the log-agent, ensuring that the log list is safely updated.

core.async channels provide a powerful abstraction for handling concurrency primitives and side effects by facilitating communication between concurrent processes through message passing. Channels help avoid shared mutable state by transferring data between threads safely.

Example of using core.async channels:

```
(require '[clojure.core.async :refer [>! <!! go chan]])

(def messages (chan))

; Sender goroutine
(go (>! messages "Hello, World!"))

; Receiver goroutine
(go (println (<! messages)))
```

Here, the chan function creates a channel, and the go blocks allow for asynchronous message passing, ensuring side effects are handled properly across different threads.

Effective handling of side effects in concurrent programs necessitates a careful design to ensure predictable execution:

- **Minimize shared state**: Encapsulate mutable state within localized contexts where possible.
- **Use immutable data structures**: Leverage Clojure's persistent data structures to avoid unintentional modifications.
- **Favor higher-level abstractions**: Make use of atoms, refs, agents, and channels to manage state changes predictably.
- **Implement thorough error handling**: Anticipate and manage exceptions or errors that could arise from side effects during concurrent operations.

Holistically, when designing concurrent programs in Clojure, careful consideration must be paid to the introduction and management of side effects, ensuring that the principles of immutability and coordinated state changes are adhered to, thus maintaining the integrity and predictability of the system.

6.12 Testing and Debugging Concurrent Applications

Concurrent applications, by their very nature, present unique challenges in terms of testing and debugging. In Clojure, the functional paradigm combined with immutable data structures simplifies some of these aspects, but a deep understanding of concurrency issues remains essential.

Multithreading introduces a level of non-determinism that can manifest as race conditions, deadlocks, or other synchronization issues. Effective testing and debugging approaches in Clojure require a strategic framework to ensure robustness and reliability of concurrent applications. The following sections outline essential techniques and tools for testing and debugging in Clojure.

Unit Testing of Concurrent Code

Concurrent code can be unit tested similarly to sequential code, but additional considerations are needed to ensure that the code correctly handles concurrency. One effective approach is to use the clojure.test library, which is a part of Clojure's standard library. This involves creating tests that check not only the correctness of individual functions but also their behavior under concurrent execution.

```
(ns my-app.core-test
  (:require [clojure.test :refer :all]
            [my-app.core :refer :all]))

(deftest test-concurrent-function
  (let [results (atom [])
        n-threads 10
        tasks (repeatedly n-threads #(future (swap! results conj (some-function))))]
    (doseq [t tasks] @t)
    (is (= n-threads (count @results)))))
```

In the above test, some-function is executed concurrently in multiple threads. The results are collected in an atom to ensure thread-safe mutation. The test checks that the correct number of results is produced, implicitly testing the function's thread safety.

Handling Race Conditions

A race condition occurs when the outcome of a program depends on the relative timing of threads. Detecting race conditions programmatically can be challenging. One approach is to use randomized or controlled scheduling to explore different interleavings of concurrent operations.

```
(deftest test-for-race-condition
  (let [counter (atom 0)
        n-threads 4
        increments 1000
        tasks (repeatedly n-threads
                          #(future (dotimes [_ increments]
                                     (swap! counter inc))))]
    (doseq [t tasks] @t)
    (is (= (* n-threads increments) @counter))))
```

This test checks that the counter atom is incremented the expected number of times when accessed by multiple threads. If the increment operations are correctly synchronized, the final count should match the expected value.

Deadlock Detection

Deadlocks can arise when two or more threads maintain a circular wait for resources held by each other. Avoiding deadlocks involves careful design and testing. One common deadlock scenario in Clojure involves the incorrect use of refs and Software Transactional Memory (STM).

```
(defn transfer [from-account to-account amount]
  (dosync
    (alter from-account - amount)
```

```
    (alter to-account + amount)))

(deftest test-deadlock-avoidance
  (let [acc1 (ref 100)
        acc2 (ref 100)]
    (future (transfer acc1 acc2 10))
    (future (transfer acc2 acc1 20))
    (Thread/sleep 1000) ;; Waiting for transactions to complete
    (is (= 90 @acc1))
    (is (= 110 @acc2))))
```

dosync ensures that data integrity is maintained by the STM system, preventing deadlocks through careful ordering of resource acquisition.

Using core.async for Concurrency Testing

The core.async library provides channels and operations to handle asynchronous programming. Testing core.async channels requires simulating communication between multiple processes.

```
(ns my-app.async-test
  (:require [clojure.test :refer :all]
            [clojure.core.async :refer :all]))

(deftest test-async-communication
  (let [ch (chan)]
    (go (>! ch 42))
    (is (= 42 (<!! ch)))))
```

In this test, a value is sent to the channel ch using a go block, and the <!! function is used to receive and assert the value.

Logging and Analysis

Effective debugging of concurrent applications often requires logging to trace execution flow and understand the interactions between threads. Clojure's logging libraries, such as clojure.tools.logging, provide mechanisms to log from within different threads.

```
(ns my-app.logging
  (:require [clojure.tools.logging :as log]))

(defn logged-task [id]
  (log/info "Starting task" id)
  (Thread/sleep (rand-int 1000))
  (log/info "Completing task" id))

(defn concurrent-tasks []
  (let [tasks (map #(future (logged-task %)) (range 5))]
    (doseq [t tasks] @t)))
```

Running concurrent-tasks will log messages indicating the start and completion of each task, making it easier to diagnose issues related to execution order and timing.

Testing and debugging concurrent applications in Clojure entails employing specific strategies to ensure correctness and reliability. By combining unit testing, concurrency-specific tests, deadlock avoidance techniques, core.async usage, and comprehensive logging, developers can build robust concurrent systems.

Chapter 7

Macros and Metaprogramming

This chapter introduces the concepts of macros and metaprogramming in Clojure, including the basics of writing simple macros and using ‘quote‘, ‘unquote‘, and ‘syntax-quote‘ with auto-gensym. It covers macro hygiene, code generation techniques, and the creation of domain-specific languages (DSLs). Advanced topics include debugging and testing macros, performance considerations, and real-world examples to demonstrate practical applications of macros in Clojure.

7.1 Introduction to Macros

In the Clojure programming language, macros are a powerful tool that allows for the manipulation and generation of code at compile time. Macros enable developers to introduce new syntactic constructs in a manner that would be difficult or impossible to achieve with standard functions. This section explores the definition, usage, and underlying concepts of macros in Clojure.

A macro in Clojure is defined using the defmacro form. The primary difference between a macro and a function is that macros operate on unevaluated code: they receive Clojure forms as arguments and return new forms that subsequently get evaluated. This capability allows macros to perform code transformations during compilation, thereby enabling metaprogramming.

Consider the following simple macro definition:

```
(defmacro unless [condition & body]
  `(if (not ~condition)
     (do ~@body)))

; Usage
(unless false
  (println "This will print."))
```

When this macro is expanded, the unless macro transforms into an if expression that checks the negation of the condition. If the condition fails, it executes the body expressions. This macro provides a succinct way to express conditions where code execution depends on a false condition.

Macros operate at the syntactic level and thus interact directly with Clojure's reader. When the Clojure compiler encounters a macro call, it invokes the macro and evaluates its result, allowing macros to generate and manipulate code. Because macros manipulate syntactical constructs, they require an understanding of quoting mechanisms such as quote, unquote, and syntax-quote.

The key benefits macros offer include:

- **Code Reusability and Abstraction**: Macros can encapsulate repetitive code patterns, improving both reusability and readability.

- **Custom Control Structures**: Developers can create new control structures tailored to specific needs that are not provided by the language's core libraries.

- **Domain-Specific Languages (DSLs)**: Macros can be used to create expressive DSLs within Clojure, facilitating the creation of specialized languages for particular problem domains.

However, macros introduce complexities that require careful consideration:

- **Complex Debugging**: Debugging macros can be more challenging than debugging regular code because code is transformed before it is executed.

- **Macro Hygiene**: Ensuring that macros do not unintentionally interfere with the surrounding code environment is crucial. This involves careful handling of symbol capture and namespace pollution.

- **Performance Overhead**: While macros run at compile time, they can introduce performance overhead if not designed efficiently.

A fundamental concept that underpins macros in Clojure is the distinction between compile-time and runtime. Macros expand at compile-time, meaning their primary purpose is to reshape code before it gets runtime execution. An understanding of this distinction is crucial for designing effective and efficient macros.

Let us examine another example that demonstrates macro hygiene:

```
(defmacro with-resource [resource & body]
  `(let [r# ~resource]
     (try
       ~@body
       (finally
         (.close r#)))))

; Usage
(with-resource (java.io.StringReader. "sample text")
  (println (read-line r#)))
```

In this with-resource macro: - let binds the resource to a unique symbol r#, generated using auto-gensym. - try block ensures that body executes, and the resource is closed via finally.

The ‘, , and @ constructs are used within the macro body for unquoting, ensuring that resource variables are appropriately expanded. The r# symbol is automatically generated to avoid naming conflicts—demonstrating macro hygiene by preventing symbol capture issues.

Studying macros also involves inspecting their expanded forms to understand how the transformation occurs. This can be achieved using the macroexpand function:

```
(macroexpand '(unless false (println "This will print.")))
```

```
(if (not false)
  (do (println "This will print.")))
```

The expanded code reveals that the unless macro translates into a standard if statement. This insight is instrumental in debugging and ensuring that macros perform as expected.

Ultimately, macros provide a robust platform for advancing the capabilities of Clojure, enabling powerful abstractions and customizations to enhance the language's expressiveness and utility.

7.2 Writing Simple Macros

Macros in Clojure provide a powerful mechanism for metaprogramming, allowing you to extend the language by writing code that generates other code. This section describes the process of writing simple macros, building on the fundamental concepts already introduced. We will explore practical examples to understand macro definition and usage better.

Macros operate at the syntactic level, meaning they manipulate the structure of the code before it gets evaluated. To define a macro, we use the defmacro construct, which is analogous to defn but functions on unevaluated code.

defmacro takes a name, an argument list, and a body, just like defn, but the body of a macro is not executed immediately. Instead, the body should return code that will be executed later. Here is a simple example to illustrate the basic structure and functionality of a macro:

```
(defmacro when-not [test & body]
  `(if (not ~test)
     (do ~@body)))
```

In this example, the macro when-not takes a test expression and a body of code. The macro expands into an if expression where the test is negated using not. If the test returns false, the body is executed within a do block.

In the macro, note the usage of backquote (‘), unquote ( ), and unquote-splicing (@):

* ‘ (backquote): It allows us to create a quoted list that can contain unquoted elements. * (unquote): It allows evaluated insertion of code within the backquoted expression. * @ (unquote-splicing): It is used for injecting and splicing sequence elements into a list.

To see the macro in action, consider the following usage:

```
(when-not (= 1 2)
  (println "1 is not equal to 2"))
```

When this macro is expanded, it transforms into:

```
(if (not (= 1 2))
  (do (println "1 is not equal to 2")))
```

This shows how the macro expansion works and manifests the structure generated by the macro.

Another example of a simple macro is unless, which acts as the logical opposite of when:

```
(defmacro unless [test & body]
  `(if (not ~test)
     (do ~@body)))
```

Here, unless will execute the body only if the test condition is false. It is functionally similar to when-not, providing an alternative syntax.

Next, consider macro expansion, which can be visualized using macroexpand or macroexpand-1. The macroexpand function fully expands a macro, providing the final code, while macroexpand-1 performs a single step of expansion:

```
(macroexpand '(when-not (= 1 2)
                (println "1 is not equal to 2")))

(macroexpand-1 '(when-not (= 1 2)
                  (println "1 is not equal to 2")))
```

The results will be:

```
(if (not (= 1 2)) (do (println "1 is not equal to 2")))

(if (not (= 1 2)) (do (println "1 is not equal to 2")))
```

Both functions would yield the same output in this simple case, demonstrating the concept of macro expansion.

Macros need proper handling to avoid unexpected behaviors. One common issue is variable capture, where symbols in the macro's body might unintentionally refer to variables outside its scope. This is due to the macro's substitution procedure, which can lead to naming conflicts. To mitigate this, Clojure provides the auto-gensym feature, which appends a unique suffix to symbols to ensure no collision occurs.

Consider an enhanced version of when-not that uses auto-gensym to avoid variable capture:

```
(defmacro safe-when-not [test & body]
  `(let [temp# ~test]
     (if (not temp#)
       (do ~@body))))
```

Here, the temporary variable temp# is generated with a unique suffix each time safe-when-not is called. This ensures the macro's internal variables do not interfere with those outside its scope.

Simple macros illustrate the fundamental principles of macro writing and expansion in Clojure. By understanding these basic constructs, you can begin to leverage macros for more complex metaprogramming tasks, allowing for flexible, readable, and maintainable code.

7.3 Using quote and unquote

In Clojure, the quote and unquote constructs are fundamental for controlling the evaluation of code, particularly within macros. These constructs enable the programmer to manage when expressions are evaluated, which is critical for macro expansion.

The quote construct prevents the evaluation of an expression. It returns the expression as it is, without executing or interpreting it. This can be particularly useful when you need to handle code as data. The quote operator can be used in its long form or in its shorthand form using a single quotation mark (').

```
(quote (+ 1 2)) ; Use of the full quote form
'(+ 1 2) ; Use of the shorthand form
```

In both cases, the output is the list $(+ 1\ 2)$, not the result of the addition.

```
(+ 1 2)
```

The unquote construct, denoted by the tilde character (), is used within a quoted expression to indicate that a particular part of the expression should be evaluated. This is instrumental in macros for inserting evaluated expressions into a quoted template.

Consider the following example where we use quote and unquote together:

```
(def x 10)
`(+ 1 ~x) ; Using syntax quote and unquote
```

Here, the backtick () is the syntax quote, which is an extended form of the quote that assists with code generation. Inside this syntax-quoted expression, the $\tilde{x}$ unquote evaluates the variable x.

The output of this expression would be:

```
(+ 1 10)
```

Thus, the unquote ensures the value of x is substituted into the resulting code.

Nested usage of quote and unquote allows complex macro transformations where different levels of code abstraction are necessary. For example:

```
(def x 10)
(quote `(list '+ 1 ~x))
```

In this case, `(list '+ 1 x̃) is syntax-quoted but embedded in another quoted expression, so the output remains a quoted form that contains an unquote.

```
(list 'quote (list 'list ''+ 1 10))
```

Moreover, unquote-splicing denoted by @ is a specialized form of unquote for inserting multiple elements into a list. If another list ys contains elements that need to be included in another list directly:

```
(def ys '(2 3 4))
`(1 ~@ys 5) ; Using unquote-splicing
```

This will expand to:

```
(1 2 3 4 5)
```

Here, all elements of ys are spliced into the resulting list.

Understanding the interplay of quote, unquote, and unquote-splicing is essential for writing effective macros in Clojure. It enables the precise control over the code generation process, ensuring that parts of the code are evaluated exactly when needed, and others remain unevaluated for later use.

The following example demonstrates a practical use-case in macros:

```
(defmacro with-logging [expr]
  `(do
     (println "Evaluating:" '~expr)
     (let [result# ~expr]
       (println "Result:" result#)
       result#)))

(with-logging (+ 1 2))
```

In this macro, with-logging, the quote prevents expr from being evaluated in the println statement, allowing the raw expression to be printed. The syntax quote` combined with unquote allows the actual evaluation of expr in the macro body. The unique # suffix ensures the hygienic generation of a temporary variable.

When evaluated:

```
Evaluating: (+ 1 2)
Result: 3
```

This example illustrates the practical aspect of using quote and unquote to construct macros that manipulate evaluation order and generate code dynamically.

7.4 Syntax-quote and Auto-gensym

In Clojure, the syntax-quote, denoted by the backtick (`), is a powerful tool for writing macros that need to generate code in a precise and controlled manner. One of the key benefits of using syntax-quote is that it provides a straightforward way to handle variable capture issues through auto-gensym.

Let's start by understanding the basic use of syntax-quote. When you enclose a form in a syntax-quote, Clojure automatically resolves the symbols within the context of the current namespace. Additionally, syntax-quote allows the inclusion of unquoted forms via the unquote operator, denoted by the tilde (~).

```
(def x 10)
(def y 20)

`(+ x y) ; => (clojure.core/+ user/x user/y)
```

In the example above, you can see that the syntax-quoted form translates the symbols x and y to their fully qualified names, user/x and user/y. This ensures that the symbols refer to the correct bindings in the current namespace.

Next, we explore the unquote operator. Unquote allows you to evaluate specific expressions within a syntax-quoted form. This is particularly useful when you want to include dynamic content in the generated code.

```
(def a 5)

`(+ ~a 3) ; => (clojure.core/+ 5 3)
```

Here, the unquote operator forces the evaluation of a, replacing it with its value (5) in the generated code.

The auto-gensym feature of syntax-quote is designed to avoid variable capture, which can occur when macros inadvertently bind to symbols that are already in use in the code where the macro is expanded. Auto-gensym is triggered by appending # to a symbol name within a syntax-quoted form. This ensures that each such symbol is replaced by a unique generated symbol.

Consider the following example:

```
(defmacro gen-sym-example []
  `(let [x\# 42]
     (println x\#)))
```

In this macro gen-sym-example, the symbol x# is given a unique identifier each time the macro is expanded, preventing any accidental collision with existing bindings.

To illustrate this further, let's introduce a user-defined function that makes use of auto-gensym in a more complex macro:

```
(defmacro demo-auto-gensym [expr]
  `(let [temp\# (do ~expr)]
     (println "The result is:" temp\#)))

(demo-auto-gensym (+ 1 2))
```

When demo-auto-gensym is expanded, temp# is replaced with a unique symbol. This substitution ensures that the temporary variable will not clash with any other binding named temp.

Evaluating the macro:

```
The result is: 3
```

In practical scenarios, auto-gensym can be particularly beneficial for generating dynamically scoped bindings within macros, ensuring robustness and avoiding subtle bugs.

Consider using both syntax-quote and auto-gensym when developing macros that manipulate bindings dynamically. These features enhance the macro's readability and maintainability while preventing unintended interactions with the surrounding code.

Understanding and leveraging syntax-quote and auto-gensym is a vital step toward mastering Clojure's metaprogramming capabilities. Proper use of these tools allows for cleaner, more reliable macro definitions, facilitating the development of sophisticated and flexible code transformations.

7.5 Macro Hygiene and Avoiding Pitfalls

Macro hygiene is an essential concept in the development of macros, ensuring that macros not only expand correctly but also do not inadvertently interfere with the surrounding code. In Clojure, macros operate at the syntactic level of code transformations, hence it is crucial to understand potential pitfalls that may arise during their implementation. This section delves into the importance of macro hygiene and provides strategies to avoid common pitfalls, ensuring robust and maintainable macros.

A key aspect of macro hygiene is the management of variable bindings to prevent unintentional clashes between variable names within the macro and those in the macro's invocation context. This issue is known as *name collision*. Consider a basic example with a macro that introduces a local variable:

```
(defmacro example-macro []
  `(let [x 10]
     (println "Inside macro, x:" x)))
```

When the example-macro is expanded within a code block which also uses a variable named x, it can result in unintended behavior:

```
(def x 5)
(example-macro)
(println "Outside macro, x:" x)
```

Execution of the above code yields:

```
Inside macro, x: 10
Outside macro, x: 5
```

In this scenario, no conflict arises since the x within the macro is locally scoped to the let block. However, if the same x name were to be reused outside the macro by mistake, it would lead to unexpected results. This is where *auto-gensym* (automatic generation of unique symbols) becomes vital.

The syntax-quote (`) in conjunction with the unquote ( ) and auto-gensym (appending #) mechanisms can mitigate such risks. The following modification employs auto-gensym for hygienic macro expansion:

```
(defmacro safe-macro []
  `(let [x# 10]
     (println "Inside macro, x:" x#)))
```

In this version, x is transformed into a unique symbol (x#), ensuring it does not clash with any variables outside the macro. When expanded and executed:

```
(def y 5)
(safe-macro)
(println "Outside macro, y:" y)
```

The output remains the same:

```
Inside macro, x: 10
Outside macro, y: 5
```

Apart from name collisions, another pitfall is improper capture and usage of free variables—variables that are not locally bound within a macro but are assumed to be supplied by the macro's context. Consider a macro embedding a free variable:

```
(defmacro unsafe-free-var []
  `(println "Using free variable a:" a))
```

Using this macro without defining a will cause an error. A more robust approach is to explicitly declare dependencies and use arguments:

```
(defmacro safe-free-var [a]
  `(println "Using provided variable a:" ~a))
```

This pattern ensures that the required variable is unambiguously supplied during macro invocation:

```
(safe-free-var 20)
```

The execution output now correctly displays:

```
Using provided variable a: 20
```

Additionally, another common pitfall involves unintentional multiple evaluations of an expression within a macro. Consider the following problematic macro:

```
(defmacro repeat-print [n]
  `(do (println "hello")
       (dotimes [_# ~n]
         (println "world"))))
```

Every invocation of repeat-print re-evaluates n, leading to possible incorrect behavior or performance concerns if n involves complex computation. Instead, it is safer to bind the computation once within the macro and reference this bound value:

```
(defmacro safe-repeat-print [n]
  `(let [times# ~n]
```

```
    (do (println "hello")
      (dotimes [_# times#]
        (println "world")))))
```

Here, times# captures the evaluated result of n, ensuring it is computed only once. Such precautions help maintain expression semantics and performance, essential in constructing reliable macros.

Throughout macros' development, strive for hygiene through thoughtful use of unique symbols and mindful handling of free variables, balancing clarity with robustness. Employ the pattern of transforming potential conflicts into unique entities and controlling environments and evaluations precisely. These practices foster the creation of macros that integrate seamlessly into diverse codebases, enhancing reliability and maintainability.

7.6 Metaprogramming Concepts

Metaprogramming involves writing programs that generate or manipulate other programs or themselves. In Clojure, metaprogramming's power is exemplified through macros, which allow the transformation and generation of code at compile time. This section explores the foundational concepts central to metaprogramming in Clojure, emphasizing macro usage and their implications for code flexibility and reduction in boilerplate.

1. Macros as Code Transformers

Macromatics in Clojure revolve around the principle of code-as-data. The Clojure philosophy and its underlying structure, based on Lisp, use S-expression (symbolic expression) lists, making code inherently data manipulatable by programs.

Macros in Clojure can be seen as code transformers. They take forms of code as input, often represented as data structures like lists, vectors, and maps and transform them into other valid code forms. Consider the following example:

```
(defmacro unless [condition & body]
  `(if (not ~condition)
     (do ~@body)))
```

In this example, the unless macro takes a condition and a variable number of forms (body). It then outputs a transformed piece of code that uses an if clause to evaluate the negated condition, followed by executing the body if the condition is false.

2. Homoiconicity

Clojure shares the homoiconic nature of Lisp, meaning that code and data have the same representation. This property allows manipulation of code with the same constructs used to process data. When a macro receives its arguments, it gets them in an unevaluated form, so the macro can interpret or transform the code before it gets executed. The following illustrates how a macro leverages homoiconicity:

```
(defmacro demo-macro [arg]
  `(println "The argument was:" ~arg))

(demo-macro (* 2 3))
```

Upon expansion by the macro system, demo-macro replaces (* 2 3) with its result, producing:

```
(println "The argument was:" (* 2 3))
```

This concept ensures any code generation or manipulation is seamlessly integrated into the usual development flow.

3. Macro Expansion Process

Understanding macro expansion is imperative in metaprogramming. During macro expansion, the Clojure compiler recursively expands macros within a form until no further macros remain to be expanded. The expansion process can be visualized through the following steps:

- The compiler identifies macros in the source code.
- Each identified macro is expanded by calling the macro with its arguments.
- The resulting code from the macro replaces the original macro call.
- This process continues until a macro-free code form results.

4. Avoiding Macro Pitfalls with Hygiene

A critical aspect of macros is maintaining referential transparency and preventing unintended symbol capture, known as hygiene. A common pitfall in macros is name collision, where macro-generated symbols inadvertently shadow vars from the macro's invocation context. This problem is mitigated using gensym to create unique symbols automatically. Consider the following macro:

```
(defmacro safe-divide [numerator denominator]
  (let [result-sym (gensym "result")]
    `(let [~result-sym ~denominator]
       (if (zero? ~result-sym)
         (throw (Exception. "Division by zero"))
         (/ ~numerator ~result-sym)))))
```

Here, gensym generates a unique symbol for the denominator computation, ensuring that no name collision occurs within the macro expansion.

5. Leveraging Metaprogramming for Code Generation

Metaprogramming excels in reducing boilerplate code and creating domain-specific abstractions. Functions and macros together allow complex programmatic generation of repetitive, structured code. For instance, consider the automatic generation of accessor functions:

```
(defmacro create-accessors [struct & fields]
  `(do ~@(map (fn [f]
                `(defn ~(symbol (str "get-" (name f))) [s]
                   (get s ~f)))
              fields)))

(create-accessors person :name :age :address)
```

This macro generates accessor functions such as get-name, get-age, and get-address for a person structure, exemplifying efficient and concise code generation.

6. Contextual Adaptations with Metaprogramming

The adaptability of macros permits their flexible application across varied contexts and domains. Macros can adapt their expansions based on the surrounding code environment, enabling contextual optimizations and customizations. For instance:

```
(defmacro log [msg]
  (if (resolve 'debug)
    `(println "DEBUG:" ~msg)
    `(println "INFO:" ~msg)))

(def debug true)

(log "Initial setup complete.")
```

Here, the log macro alters its behavior based on the presence of a debug flag, demonstrating how macros can render context-aware code transformations efficiently.

Understanding these fundamental metaprogramming concepts is essential for mastering macro development and leveraging the full capabilities of Clojure. The interplay between macros, code-as-data, hygiene techniques, and context-sensitive expansions empowers developers to write succinct, powerful, and highly adaptable code.

7.7 Defining Domain Specific Languages (DSLs)

A Domain Specific Language (DSL) is a specialized mini-language tailored to a specific application domain. DSLs are contrasted with general-purpose programming languages (GPLs), which are broadly applicable across various domains. The goal of a DSL is to increase productivity, readability, and maintainability by providing syntax and semantics closely aligned with a particular domain's concepts and requirements. In Clojure, macros are an invaluable tool for creating powerful DSLs, enabling developers to extend the language with domain-specific constructs.

To define a DSL in Clojure, we leverage macros to introduce new syntax or simplify complex code patterns. A typical approach is to first identify repetitive patterns within the domain and abstract them into macro definitions. This abstraction allows domain experts to express solutions in a more natural and concise manner.

Example: Simple DSL for Database Queries

Consider a scenario where we need to interact with a database frequently. We can create a macro-based DSL to streamline the creation of SQL queries. The following example demonstrates a simple DSL for building SQL SELECT statements:

```
(defmacro select
  [table & clauses]
  `(str "SELECT * FROM " ~table " WHERE "
       (string/join " AND " (map (fn [[k v]] (str k " = '" ~v "'")) (partition 2 '~clauses
            )))))
```

Here, the select macro takes a table name and an arbitrary number of column-value pairs as arguments. The macro constructs a SELECT SQL statement by combining these clauses with AND conditions.

```
(select "users" :id 1 :name "Alice")
```

This invocation expands to the following SQL query string:

```
"SELECT * FROM users WHERE id = '1' AND name = 'Alice'"
```

Such a DSL not only simplifies the construction of SQL queries but also makes the code more readable and less error-prone. However, creating effective DSLs involves more than just syntax wrapping. Below, we delve into some principles and advanced techniques to design robust DSLs in Clojure.

Principles of DSL Design

When designing a DSL, consider the following essential principles:

- **Clarity:** The DSL should be intuitive for domain experts. Its constructs must map naturally to domain concepts and avoid exposing unnecessary implementation details.
- **Expressiveness:** Ensure that the DSL can concisely represent the required domain operations. Strive for a balance between simplicity and completeness.
- **Consistency:** Maintain uniformity in the DSL's syntax and semantics. Consistent naming conventions and patterns help users predict and learn the language more easily.
- **Safety:** Design the DSL to prevent common errors. Include safeguards where possible to catch mistakes early, such as invalid input or incorrect usage of constructs.

Advanced Techniques for DSLs

DSLs can benefit significantly from advanced macro features and techniques. These include:

1. Hygiene Preservation:

When expanding macros, ensure that you do not inadvertently capture names or clash with existing bindings. Clojure's syntax-quote (') and auto-gensym (using #) features help prevent such issues.

```
(defmacro safe-let [bindings & body]
  ;; Ensure unique symbols to avoid name clashes
  `(let ~(vec (mapcat (fn [[sym val]] [(gensym (name sym)) val]) (partition 2 bindings)))
     ~@body))
```

This safe-let macro guards against variable name collisions by using auto-generated symbols for bindings.

2. Composability:

Design DSL constructs to be easily combined. This often involves creating macros that expand into other macros or functions, fostering reuse and modularity.

```
(defmacro where [clauses]
  (str "WHERE " (string/join " AND " (map (fn [[k v]] (str k " = '" v "'")) (partition
      2 clauses)))))

(defmacro select [table & clauses]
  `(str "SELECT * FROM " ~table " " (where ~clauses)))
```

By breaking down the select macro into smaller components like where, we enhance the DSL's modularity and reusability.

3. Error Handling:

Incorporate error checking and validation within macros to guide users and provide meaningful feedback. This improves the DSL's robustness and user experience.

```
(defmacro assert-params [param-name pred]
  `(when-not ~(list pred param-name)
     (throw (IllegalArgumentException. (str "Invalid parameter: " ~param-name)))))
```

```
(defmacro select [table & clauses]
  `(do
     (assert-params ~table string?)
     (str "SELECT * FROM " ~table " " (where ~clauses))))
```

Here, the assert-params macro ensures that the table name provided to select is a string, aiding the user in identifying mistakes early.

Through careful design and advanced metaprogramming techniques, Clojure DSLs can significantly enhance domain-specific implementations, making them more readable, maintainable, and efficient. The flexibility and power of macros are pivotal in achieving these objectives, enabling the creation of expressive and robust DSLs tailored to specific problem domains.

7.8 Using Macros for Code Generation

In Clojure, macros are powerful tools for code generation. They allow developers to analyze and transform code at compile time, producing new code that will subsequently be executed. This capability is particularly useful for generating repetitive code patterns, abstracting common idioms, and constructing domain-specific languages (DSLs).

The essence of macro-based code generation lies in understanding how macros manipulate the abstract syntax tree (AST) of the code. A macro receives the unevaluated code as its argument, processes this code to produce a new code structure, and finally emits the transformed code to be evaluated in place of the original macro call.

Macros are written using the defmacro construct. In order to generate new code forms, one typically makes extensive use of quote, unquote, and syntax-quote – constructs covered in previous sections. Below, we will delve into practical examples of using macros for code generation, demonstrating their efficacy in creating more efficient and maintainable code.

```
(defmacro inc-and-return [x]
  `(let [result# (inc ~x)]
     result#))
```

In the above macro, syntax-quote (backtick) is used to quote the code template. unquote (tilde) is employed to insert the value of x into the template. The auto-gensym mechanism ensures that the variable result# is uniquely named, thus preventing collisions with other variables in the surrounding code.

To understand how this macro generates code, consider the following usage:

```
(inc-and-return 5)
```

After macro expansion, the code becomes:

```
(let [result__1234 (inc 5)]
  result__1234)
```

This demonstrates how macros can automate the generation of variegated code patterns. Next, consider a more complex example involving a macro that generates a series of functions based on a template:

```
(defmacro define-operations [name operations]
  `(do
     ~@(for [[op-symbol op-fn] operations]
         `(defn ~(symbol (str name "-" op-symbol)) [a b]
            (~op-fn a b)))))
```

This macro, define-operations, generates a collection of function definitions. The do construct allows for multiple expressions to be executed in sequence. The for loop iterates over each operation, dynamically generating function names by concatenating the name with the op-symbol. The @ unquotes and splices the list of generated expressions into the do block.

Using the define-operations macro, one can define a suite of arithmetic operations succinctly:

```
(define-operations my-math
  [['add +]
   ['subtract -]
   ['multiply *]
   ['divide /]])
```

This invocation results in the generation of the following function definitions:

```
(defn my-math-add [a b] (+ a b))
(defn my-math-subtract [a b] (- a b))
(defn my-math-multiply [a b] (* a b))
(defn my-math-divide [a b] (/ a b))
```

Here, each function follows a consistent naming pattern and leverages the corresponding arithmetic operator. This exemplifies how macros facilitate the generation of systematic and consistent code, significantly reducing boilerplate.

Beyond simple patterns, macros can also be employed to generate more sophisticated code constructs such as entire data structures, classes, or even small DSLs. The fundamental advantage lies in the abstraction of common patterns, making the codebase more concise and maintainable.

Consider an example where a macro generates helper functions for a given data structure:

```
(defmacro defstruct-helpers [struct-name fields]
  `(do
     ~@(for [field fields]
         `(defn ~(symbol (str struct-name "-get-" field)) [m]
            (get m ~(keyword field))))
     ~@(for [field fields]
         `(defn ~(symbol (str struct-name "-set-" field)) [m value]
            (assoc m ~(keyword field) value)))))
```

Using this macro, defining getter and setter functions for a sample struct becomes trivial:

```
(defstruct-helpers person [:name :age :email])
```

This generates:

```
(defn person-get-name [m] (get m :name))
(defn person-get-age [m] (get m :age))
(defn person-get-email [m] (get m :email))
(defn person-set-name [m value] (assoc m :name value))
(defn person-set-age [m value] (assoc m :age value))
(defn person-set-email [m value] (assoc m :email value))
```

Macros like these abstract and encapsulate repetitive coding patterns, enhancing both productivity and code quality. By leveraging macros for code generation, developers can devise robust, maintainable, and clean abstractions that encapsulate complex code transformations into simple, reusable templates. This approach not only streamlines the coding process but also ensures consistency across the codebase.

7.9 Debugging and Testing Macros

Debugging and testing macros are critical to ensuring that they behave as expected and do not introduce subtle bugs into the program. Macros, unlike functions, operate on code rather than data, making their debugging and testing more complex. In this section, we will explore various techniques to debug and test macros effectively in Clojure.

Clojure provides several tools and practices that can aid in the debugging and testing of macros. Among these are the macroexpand functions, unit testing frameworks like clojure.test, and considerations for writing self-contained and predictable macros.

Macro Expansion:

To understand what code a macro generates, use the expansion functions macroexpand-1 and macroexpand. These functions take a macro expression and return the expanded code. The macroexpand-1 function performs a single expansion step, while macroexpand fully expands the macro recursively.

```
(defmacro unless [condition & body]
  `(if (not ~condition) (do ~@body)))

(macroexpand-1 '(unless false (println "Hello, World!")))
```

The output of the above expansion would be:

```
(if (not false) (do (println "Hello, World!")))
```

Understanding the expanded form helps identify mistakes that may not be apparent when writing the macro. For more complex macros, consider multiple levels of expansion to ensure correctness.

Assistive Functions for Macro Debugging:

Sometimes, it's helpful to include print statements or other forms of logging within the macro definition. However, this approach can be intrusive. Instead, you can use intermediate functions within the macro that generate intermediate representations. Clojure's gen-class and deftype constructs can be particularly useful for this.

```
(defn debug-macro [code]
```

```
  (println "Debugging macro:")
  (println code)
  code)

(defmacro debug-unless [condition & body]
  (debug-macro `(if (not ~condition) (do ~@body))))
```

When debug-unless is invoked, it will print the intermediate code representation, aiding the understanding of the macro's behavior.

Unit Testing Macros:

Unit tests for macros should cover various cases, including edge cases and potential misuse. Clojure's built-in clojure.test framework can be used to write tests for macros. Ensure that macro tests not only check the generated code but also the runtime behavior.

```
(ns my-macros-test
  (:require [clojure.test :refer :all]
            [my-macros :refer :all]))

(deftest test-unless
  (testing "unless macro"
    (is (= (macroexpand-1 '(unless false (println "It works!")))
           '(if (not false) (do (println "It works!")))))
    (is (= (macroexpand-1 '(unless true (println "It shouldn't print")))
           '(if (not true) (do (println "It shouldn't print")))))))
```

In this snippet, the test-unless unit test verifies both the expansion of the unless macro and its expected behavior. This covers the macro's correctness from both a syntax and logical perspective, ensuring it behaves correctly under varying conditions.

Best Practices:

Several best practices can make debugging and testing macros more manageable:

- *Keep Macros Simple:* Limit the complexity of each macro. Simple macros are easier to debug and test.
- *Use Intermediate Functions:* Break down macro transformations into intermediate functions. This modular approach allows for isolated testing of each transformation stage.
- *Avoid Side Effects:* Ensure macros are free from unexpected side effects. This makes prediction and reasoning about macro behavior easier.
- *Document Macro Intent:* Clear documentation helps future maintainers understand the macro's purpose and correct usage. This

can prevent misuse and simplify debugging.

Macro Hygiene:

Ensuring macro hygiene is vital. Macro hygiene refers to avoiding name collisions between macro-introduced variables and user-defined variables. Using syntax-quote (‘) and auto-gensym (suffixing symbols with #) ensures unique and collision-free symbols.

```
(defmacro hygienic-unless [condition & body]
  `(let [cond# ~condition]
     (if (not cond#) (do ~@body))))
```

The use of cond# guarantees that the introduced symbol does not interfere with any user-defined symbols named cond.

Writing Self-contained Macros:

Macros should be self-contained, meaning they do not depend on external context or state. This isolation simplifies debugging and promotes reliable behavior. For example, avoid relying on dynamic variables or external state. Instead, pass all necessary information as arguments to the macro.

```
(defmacro with-temp-file [file-path & body]
  `(let [file# (java.io.File/createTempFile ~file-path "tmp")]
     (try
       ~@body
       (finally
         (.delete file#)))))
```

This macro ensures that temporary files are correctly handled within the macro's scope without external dependencies.

Effective debugging and testing are inseparable from macro development. Employing expansion functions, unit testing, and best practices ensures that macros perform as intended, both syntactically and logically. These efforts contribute to writing robust, maintainable, and error-free macro code in Clojure.

7.10 Advanced Macro Techniques

In this section, we delve deeper into sophisticated strategies for macro creation and manipulation in Clojure, focusing on advanced techniques that promote flexibility, power, and maintainability. Building on previous sections, we explore pattern matching within macros, creating recursive macros, and handling macro expansions cleanly.

Pattern Matching in Macros

Pattern matching is an advanced technique that can simplify the creation of macros significantly. By matching against specific forms in macro definitions, you can rewrite or transform input expressions more effectively.

Using a library like clojure.pattern allows you to integrate pattern matching features within your macros. Consider the following example, which demonstrates a pattern-matching macro that handles simple arithmetic operations:

```
(defmacro match-arith [expr]
  (clojure.match/match [expr]
    [('+ ?a ?b)] '(+ ~a ~b)
    [('- ?a ?b)] '(- ~a ~b)
    [('* ?a ?b)] '(* ~a ~b)
    [('/ ?a ?b)] '(/ ~a ~b)
    :else (throw (IllegalArgumentException. "Unsupported operation"))))
```

In this macro, the match function inspects the provided expression and matches it against predefined arithmetic patterns. The matched pattern's variables (denoted by ?a and ?b) are then unquoted and reinserted into the corresponding arithmetic operation.

Creating Recursive Macros

Recursive macros can pose significant challenges, but they offer immense power by enabling repeated transformations until a desired condition is met. A common application of recursive macros is in the expansion of nested data structures.

Consider the example below, which recursively transforms nested lists into vectors:

```
(defmacro list-to-vec [lst]
  (if (seq? lst)
    (let [items (map (fn [item]
                       (if (seq? item)
                         '(list-to-vec ~item)
                         item)) lst)]
      '[(~@items)])
    lst))
```

In this macro, the list-to-vec function checks whether lst is a sequence. If so, it recursively maps each item within the sequence, transforming any nested lists into vectors. This results in completely vectorized structures.

Handling Macro Expansions Cleanly

Managing the expansion process of macros cleanly can prevent excessive complexity and ensure robust code generation. One technique is to separate the logic for transformation from the logic for construction.

```
(defmacro clean-expand [args]
  (let [transformed-args (transform-args args)]
    `(do
       ~@transformed-args)))

(defn transform-args [args]
  (map (fn [arg]
         ;; Define transformation logic here
         `(println "Processing" ~arg))
       args))
```

Here, the clean-expand macro separates the transformation logic into a dedicated function, transform-args. This approach allows for cleaner, more maintainable code by delegating the transformation to an auxiliary function.

transform-args applies a specific transformation—in this case, wrapping each argument with a println statement. The do block in the clean-expand macro ensures that all transformed expressions are processed sequentially.

Utilizing Multi-phase Expansion

Multi-phase expansion is a technique used to perform macro transformations in successive stages. It is particularly useful when the desired output requires multiple passes of transformation to achieve the final form.

Consider the following example that demonstrates a two-phase expansion:

```
(defmacro phase-expand [expr]
  (let [phase1 (phase1-transform expr)
        phase2 (phase2-transform phase1)]
    phase2))

(defn phase1-transform [expr]
  `(+ ~expr 1))

defn phase2-transform [expr]
  `(* ~expr 2))
```

In this example, phase-expand first applies phase1-transform to the input expression, incrementing it by one. The resulting expression is then passed to phase2-transform, which multiplies it by two. This multi-phase approach allows for modular and incremental transformations.

Context-sensitive Macros

Context-sensitive macros can behave differently based on the context in which they are expanded. By accessing the macro expansion environment, you can create more dynamic and adaptable macros.

The example below shows a context-sensitive macro that behaves differently based on the presence of a specific metadata tag:

```
(defmacro context-sensitive [expr]
  (if (-> expr meta :special)
    `(println "Special processing for" ~expr)
    `(println "Regular processing for" ~expr)))
```

By utilizing Clojure's support for metadata, the context-sensitive macro checks whether the given expression has a :special metadata tag. If the tag is present, it proceeds with a "special" processing routine. Otherwise, it performs a "regular" processing routine.

Integrating these advanced techniques in macro creation can greatly enhance your ability to write flexible and powerful macros, allowing greater control over DSLs and easing complex code generation tasks in Clojure.

7.11 Performance Considerations with Macros

When employing macros in Clojure, it is imperative to consider the potential performance implications, both positive and negative. This section delves into various performance aspects associated with macros, examining both their compile-time efficiencies and runtime impacts.

First, we must distinguish between compile-time and runtime performance. Macros primarily operate at compile-time. They transform code before it is executed, potentially optimizing the resulting executable code. By generating more efficient code, macros can enhance performance. However, improper use may also introduce inefficiencies or debugging difficulties.

Compile-time Overhead:

Macros add complexity at compile-time due to the necessity of code generation and transformation. By design, Clojure macros produce more concise and reusable code, but they require the compiler to perform additional work to expand these macros into executable code.

Consider the following comparison between a manually expanded function and its macro counterpart:

```
(defmacro square [x]
  `(* ~x ~x))

;; Using the macro
(square 5)
```

The macro square transforms the input into an expression equivalent to (* 5 5) during compilation. Macro expansion entails additional steps that consume time and resources, thereby introducing a non-negligible compile-time overhead. Profiling and measuring compile-time are needed for macros heavily used within a project.

Runtime Efficiency:

Although macros introduce overhead during compilation, they can significantly enhance runtime efficiency by eliminating repetitive tasks and minimizing function calls. Instead of executing function calls, expanded macros perform the required operations directly.

Consider the following non-macro version for comparison:

```
(defn square-fn [x]
  (* x x))

;; Using the function
(square-fn 5)
```

A function call, such as square-fn, typically incurs a runtime cost due to the call stack operations. By contrast, the macro-integrated code – already expanded to a direct multiplication operation – eliminates this function call overhead.

Inlining and Loop Unrolling:

Macros can facilitate inlining and loop unrolling, essential techniques for performance optimization. Loop unrolling, in particular, reduces the overhead of managing loop control structures by expanding them into a sequence of direct instructions.

```
(defmacro simple-loop [n & body]
  `(dotimes [i# ~n]
     ~@body))

;; Expanding the loop at compile-time
(simple-loop 3
  (println "Iteration" i))
```

Here, simple-loop macro expands into a straightforward dotimes loop, ensuring efficient iteration. However, excessive macro expansion can result in code bloat, adversely affecting the performance. Thus, balance is key.

Code Bloatedness:

Generating large swaths of inline code via macros can lead to increased memory consumption and cache inefficiencies. Each instantiation of a macro generates a new segment of compiled bytecode, potentially inflating the final executable size. This issue, known as code bloat, can degrade performance by increasing instruction cache misses and memory usage.

It is beneficial to profile the application to determine if macros are the source of code bloat. Tools such as Criterium can be utilized for precise measurement of memory usage and execution efficiency.

```
(require '[criterium.core :as crit])

(crit/quick-bench (square 5))
```

Using Criterium for benchmarking informs whether the macro optimization justifies the trade-off in code size.

Recursion and Tail-Call Optimization:

Clojure macros can be used to implement patterns such as recursion efficiently. A notable macro technique involves enabling tail-call optimization (TCO), providing syntactic constructs analogous to tail-recursive function calls.

```
(defmacro tail-rec [name args & body]
  `(loop [~@(interleave args args)]
     (if-let [[result# ~@(butlast body)] (do ~@body)]
       result#
       (recur ~@(first body)))))
```

In this example, tail-rec implements a form of TCO using loop/recur. Such constructs can replace conventional recursion with iterative looping, providing significant performance benefits.

Macro-generated Functions and Inline Expansion:

Another performance consideration is the generation of functions within macros. When macros generate functions that are frequently called, the ease of inlining by the Just-In-Time (JIT) compiler can influence runtime performance.

Explicitly marking functions for inlining ensures that the JIT compiler recognizes them for optimization. However, one must caution against generating functions that cannot be inlined efficiently, as this may counteract the intended performance benefits.

Hence, the judicious use of macro-generated functions and awareness of the underlying execution context are critical in maximizing performance.

Pragmatically evaluating these compile-time and runtime aspects, and balancing efficiency with maintainability, is essential for proficient macro utilization in Clojure.

7.12 Real-world Examples of Macros

Macros are a powerful feature in Clojure used for metaprogramming, allowing developers to write code that generates and transforms other code. Here, we explore some practical examples to demonstrate the use of macros in real-world scenarios. These examples will build on concepts from previous sections and illustrate how macros can be effectively utilized in various contexts.

Example 1: Logging Macro

One common use of macros is to create logging utilities that can be employed throughout an application. This example demonstrates how to create a log macro that conditionally includes logging statements based on a global logging level.

```
(def logging-level :info)

(defmacro log [level & message]
  `(when (>= (get {:trace 0 :debug 1 :info 2 :warn 3 :error 4} ~logging-level)
             (get {:trace 0 :debug 1 :info 2 :warn 3 :error 4} ~level))
     (println ~(str "[" (name level) "]") ~@message)))
```

Usage of the log macro:

```
(log :debug "This is a debug message.")
(log :info "This is an info message.")
(log :warn "This is a warning message.")
```

When the logging-level is set to :info, the output would be:

```
[info] This is an info message.
[warn] This is a warning message.
```

Example 2: Benchmarking Macro

Another useful macro can be designed for benchmarking the execution time of code snippets. This macro, named benchmark, evaluates a given expression and prints the time taken to execute it.

```
(defmacro benchmark [expr]
```

```
`(let [start# (System/nanoTime)
       result# ~expr
       end# (System/nanoTime)]
   (println "Execution time:" (/ (- end# start#) 1e6) "ms")
   result#))
```

Using the benchmark macro:

```
(benchmark (Thread/sleep 1000))
```

The output will display the execution time in milliseconds:

```
Execution time: 1000.123456 ms
```

Example 3: DSL for SQL Queries

Creating Domain-Specific Languages (DSLs) is a compelling application for macros. Consider a macro select that allows defining SQL queries in a more Clojure-like syntax.

```
(defmacro select [columns table & where-clause]
  `(str "SELECT " (clojure.string/join ", " (map name '~columns))
        " FROM " (name '~table)
        (when ~@where-clause (str " WHERE " ~@(interpose " AND " (map
          (fn [[col op val]]
            (str (name col) " " op " " val)) (partition 3 where-clause)))))))
```

Using the select macro for query generation:

```
(select [name age] users [age ">=" 30 location "=" "NY"])
```

The resulting output SQL query string will be:

```
"SELECT name, age FROM users WHERE age >= 30 AND location = NY"
```

Example 4: Data Transformation Macros

Macros can also be used for data transformation tasks. This example illustrates a macro, transform-map, that transforms a map by applying a series of functions to its keys and/or values.

```
(defmacro transform-map [mappings m]
  `(reduce (fn [acc# [k# v#]]
             (assoc acc#
                    (~(first mappings) k#)
                    (~(second mappings) v#)))
           {} ~m))
```

Using the transform-map macro to apply transformations:

```
(transform-map [keyword str] {"a" 1, "b" 2, "c" 3})
```

The transformed map will be:

{:a "1", :b "2", :c "3"}

Example 5: Testing Macros

Macros can be leveraged to simplify repetitive testing patterns. Here, a deftestmacro is created to define multiple test cases with a single macro invocation.

```
(defmacro deftestmacro [name & tests]
  `(deftest ~name
     (doseq [[desc# test-fn#] '~tests]
       (testing desc#
         (test-fn#)))))
```

Define a set of tests using deftestmacro:

```
(deftestmacro simple-tests
  ["Test addition" #(is (= 4 (+ 2 2)))]
  ["Test multiplication" #(is (= 9 (* 3 3)))]
  ["Test subtraction" #(is (= 0 (- 5 5)))])
```

In these illustrations, macros exhibit their ability to enhance code convenience, readability, and maintenance by abstracting recurring patterns.

Chapter 8

Interoperability with Java

This chapter covers the interoperability between Clojure and Java, detailing how to call Java methods from Clojure, import Java classes and packages, and create Java objects. It includes working with Java collections, handling Java exceptions, and using Java libraries in Clojure projects. The chapter also explores extending Java classes and interfaces, integrating Java with the Clojure REPL, compiling Clojure code for Java interop, addressing performance considerations, and troubleshooting common issues with real-world examples.

8.1 Calling Java Methods from Clojure

One of the significant advantages of Clojure is its seamless interoperability with Java, allowing developers to leverage the extensive Java ecosystem. By calling Java methods directly from Clojure, we can utilize existing Java libraries and frameworks, facilitating the reuse of robust, well-tested Java code within Clojure applications.

To call Java methods from Clojure, we first need to understand how Clojure interacts with Java objects and methods. In Clojure, the dot operator (.) is used to call methods on Java objects or to access fields. Let's explore this with practical examples.

To execute an instance method on a Java object, we use the following syntax:

```
(.methodName instance args...)
```

For instance, to call the toUpperCase method on a Java String object:

```
(def my-string "hello world")
(.toUpperCase my-string)
```

The foregoing code snippet produces the output "HELLO WORLD" by invoking the toUpperCase method on the string my-string.

Alternatively, a more idiomatic way in Clojure is to use the threading macro (->) to enhance readability:

```
(-> my-string .toUpperCase)
```

To call static methods in Java, the syntax is slightly different. We use the Classname/staticMethod form:

```
(Classname/staticMethod args...)
```

For example, to call the static valueOf method from the Integer class:

```
(Integer/valueOf "42")
```

This code converts the string '"42"' to the integer 42 using the static method valueOf of the Integer class.

Another essential aspect is working with Java constructors to create new Java objects. The new special form is used for this purpose:

```
(new Classname args...)
```

To construct a new ArrayList, we can write:

```
(def my-list (new java.util.ArrayList))
```

Clojure provides a concise alternative to the new special form using class names directly:

```
(def my-list (java.util.ArrayList.))
```

When interacting with Java methods that accept or return primitive types, Clojure handles the conversion seamlessly. The following example demonstrates calling a method that accepts an integer and returns an integer:

```
(def number (Integer. 10))
(.intValue number)
```

The method intValue returns the primitive int representation of the Integer object.

For methods returning arrays or collections, Clojure provides seamless conversion to its native data structures. Consider the following example, invoking the split method on a String, which returns a Java array of strings:

```
(def parts (.split my-string " "))
(vec parts)
```

Here, the Java array parts is converted to a Clojure vector using the vec function.

Next, we examine method overloading, where multiple methods have the same name but differ in parameters. Clojure will automatically select the correct method based on the argument types passed:

```
(def my-number "42")
(Math/abs (Integer/parseInt my-number)) ; Calls abs(int) method
(Math/abs -42.0) ; Calls abs(double) method
```

In the snippet above, calling Math/abs with an integer selects the abs(int) method, while passing a double selects the abs(double) method seamlessly.

Calling methods that throw exceptions requires special handling since Java exceptions are checked, meaning that they must be caught or declared in Java. In Clojure, exceptions are handled using the try/catch constructs:

```
(try
  (do
    (some-java-method-that-may-throw-exception))
  (catch java.lang.Exception e
    (println "Caught exception:" (.getMessage e))))
```

In this example, if some-java-method-that-may-throw-exception throws an exception, it is caught by the catch block, and the exception message is printed.

Wrappers can be written to encapsulate common Java method calls, improving code readability and maintenance. Here's how you can wrap a method call:

```
(defn string-reverse [s]
  (.reverse (StringBuilder. s)))
```

Calling (string-reverse "hello") will return "olleh".

Understanding how Clojure interoperates with Java allows for powerful integration and code reuse, reducing the need to reimplement existing functionalities. By mastering method calling conventions and the nuances of Clojure-Java interop, developers can effectively harness the full potential of both ecosystems.

8.2 Importing Java Classes and Packages

Clojure's flexibility and powerful interoperation capabilities with Java allow seamless integration between the two languages. Understanding how to import Java classes and packages in Clojure is fundamental to leveraging the vast ecosystem of Java libraries and tools. This section elucidates various approaches and methods for importing Java classes and packages, as well as nuanced details about their usage within Clojure code.

Clojure provides the import form for bringing Java classes into the current namespace, similar to Java's import statement. The basic syntax for importing a Java class is as follows:

```
(import 'java.util.Date)
```

This imports the Date class from the java.util package, making it accessible in the Clojure code. Note that single quotes are used to reference the class name.

Once imported, the Java class can be used to create new instances or call static methods. Creating an instance of the Date class is straightforward:

```
(def today (java.util.Date.))
```

The Date. is the constructor invocation for the Date class.

When multiple classes from the same package are required, it is practical to import them in a single import statement. Clojure supports a vector of class names within the import form:

```
(import '[java.util Date Calendar TimeZone])
```

This imports the Date, Calendar, and TimeZone classes from the java.util package.

For convenience, Clojure also offers the :import keyword within the ns macro to include imports directly while defining a namespace. This approach is highly recommended for organizing code in larger projects. An example namespace definition with multiple imports looks like this:

```
(ns my.project.core
  (:import [java.util Date Calendar TimeZone]
           [java.io File IOException]))
```

The :import keyword can import classes from multiple packages, each specified within a vector.

In some scenarios, a Java class might contain nested or inner classes, requiring a slightly different import syntax. For example, the Map.Entry nested class within java.util is imported as:

```
(import 'java.util.Map$Entry)
```

The dollar sign ($) is used to denote the nested class.

The ns macro's ability to import packages by grouping related classes supports better code organization and readability. Consider the following expanded namespace declaration:

```
(ns my.project.utils
  (:require [clojure.string :as str])
  (:import [java.util HashMap ArrayList]
           [java.time LocalDateTime ZoneId]
           [java.nio.file Files Paths]))
```

This declares dependencies on both Clojure and Java libraries, differentiating between Clojure's :require and Java's :import, ensuring clear separation.

Working with Java classes in Clojure sometimes involves dealing with Java interfaces. Clojure handles this seamlessly as well. For instance, to work with the Runnable interface, it can be imported and used as:

```
(import 'java.lang.Runnable)

(defn run-task []
  (proxy [Runnable] []
    (run []
      ;; Task implementation
      (println "Task is running."))))
```

The proxy macro creates an instance of Runnable that provides an implementation of the run method.

Additionally, importing Java enumerations follows the same principle. Consider the DayOfWeek enum from the java.time package:

```
(import 'java.time.DayOfWeek)
```

```
;; Using the enumeration
(def monday DayOfWeek/MONDAY)
(println "The first day of the week is:" monday)
```

In this case, DayOfWeek/MONDAY accesses the MONDAY constant from the DayOfWeek enumeration.

In Clojure, it is possible to avoid redundant import statements by using fully qualified class names directly in the code. For example:

```
(def now (java.time.LocalDateTime/now))
```

However, using fully qualified names extensively can lead to verbose and less readable code. Utilizing the import form or the :import keyword within the ns macro is recommended for improved code clarity and maintainability.

Effective utilization of Java imports in a Clojure project not only enhances code readability and organization but also facilitates leveraging a comprehensive range of existing Java libraries and frameworks. Such integration empowers developers to capitalize on the strengths of both languages efficiently.

8.3 Creating Java Objects in Clojure

In this section, we delve into the intricacies of creating Java objects within the Clojure programming environment. The ability to instantiate Java objects from within Clojure is fundamental for leveraging Java's extensive libraries and frameworks. This operation extends the capabilities of Clojure, allowing for more versatile and robust application development.

Clojure provides direct support for Java interop through a set of well-defined constructs. To create an instance of a Java class, the new keyword or its shorthand . (dot) can be employed. Below, we discuss these methods in detail and provide examples to illustrate their usage.

Using the new Keyword

The new keyword in Clojure is used to create a new instance of a Java class. The general syntax for using new is straightforward:

```
(new ClassName argument-list)
```

Here, ClassName represents the fully qualified name of the Java class, and argument-list contains the constructor arguments. Consider the following example where we create an instance of the java.util.Date class:

```
(def date (new java.util.Date))
```

This statement constructs a new Date object representing the current date and time. For Java classes requiring multiple arguments in the constructor, provide the arguments within the parentheses as shown:

```
(def point (new java.awt.Point 10 20))
```

In this example, a Point object is instantiated with x and y coordinates set to 10 and 20, respectively.

Using the Dot Shorthand

Clojure also supports a shorthand notation for object instantiation using the dot . notation. This shorthand is more concise and widely used in idiomatic Clojure code:

```
(ClassName. argument-list)
```

The following example demonstrates the creation of a java.util.Date object using this shorthand:

```
(def date (java.util.Date.))
```

Similarly, for the java.awt.Point:

```
(def point (java.awt.Point. 10 20))
```

Both methods pictured above are functionally identical, and the choice between them typically depends on personal or project style preferences.

Instantiating Inner Classes

Java inner classes can be instantiated from Clojure using a two-step process. Create an instance of the outer class first, followed by the inner class instantiation. Consider a typical scenario with an outer class Outer and an inner class Inner:

```
(def outer (new Outer))
```

```
(def inner (new Outer$Inner outer))
```

This syntax leverages the dollar sign $ to denote the nested relationship. The outer class instance is passed as an argument to the inner class constructor.

Using Factory Methods

Many Java classes provide factory methods for object creation. These static methods offer an alternative to direct constructor calls and can be seamlessly utilized in Clojure. A common example is the java.util.Calendar class:

```
(def calendar (java.util.Calendar/getInstance))
```

Here, getInstance is a static method that returns an instance of Calendar configured with the current date and time.

Handling Arrays

Creating arrays in Java from Clojure involves the java.lang.reflect.Array class. This class provides static methods for creating and manipulating Java arrays. Construct a new array as follows:

```
(def int-array (java.lang.reflect.Array/newInstance Integer/TYPE 5))
```

This code snippet creates an integer array of size 5. Populate the array using Clojure's aset function:

```
(aset int-array 0 42)
(aset int-array 1 7)
(aset int-array 2 13)
```

You can then access the elements using the aget function:

```
(aget int-array 0)
```

This retrieves the first element of the array, which is 42 in this example.

By mastering these techniques for creating Java objects in Clojure, developers can effectively harness the rich ecosystem of Java while benefiting from the expressive power of Clojure. Each method and class instantiation strategy offers unique advantages, enabling the construction of sophisticated applications with ease and precision.

8.4 Working with Java Collections

When leveraging the interoperability between Clojure and Java, understanding how to work with Java collections seamlessly from within Clojure is crucial. This section elucidates the methods to create, manipulate, and utilize Java collections such as ArrayList, HashSet, and HashMap in Clojure.

Clojure provides direct and straightforward mechanisms to interact with Java collections, allowing for smooth integration and transition between Clojure's immutable data structures and Java's mutable collections.

Creating Java Collections

Creating instances of Java collections in Clojure is done using the new keyword or invoking constructor methods directly.

```
;; Creating an ArrayList
(def array-list (new java.util.ArrayList))

;; Alternatively
(def array-list (java.util.ArrayList.))
```

Adding Elements to Java Collections

To add elements to Java collections, you can use the methods provided by the respective Java classes.

```
;; Adding elements to ArrayList
(.add array-list "Element 1")
(.add array-list "Element 2")

;; Check the contents of array-list
(array-list)
```

The output will display the elements added to the ArrayList.

```
["Element 1", "Element 2"]
```

Interacting with Java Collections using Clojure Functions

Clojure provides functions to interact with Java collections. For instance, to access an element:

```
;; Accessing an element by index
(.get array-list 0) ;; Returns "Element 1"
```

You can also use the Clojure seq function to obtain a sequence from Java collections, enabling the use of Clojure's higher-order functions.

```
;; Getting a sequence from array-list
(seq array-list)

;; Using higher-order function 'map' on Java collection
(map println (seq array-list))
```

Removing Elements from Java Collections

Removing elements from Java collections is facilitated through methods such as remove.

```
;; Remove "Element 1" from array-list
(.remove array-list "Element 1")

;; Check the contents of array-list
(array-list)
```

The resulting output after removal:

```
["Element 2"]
```

Working with Other Java Collections

Other Java collections, such as HashSet and HashMap, can be manipulated similarly.

```
;; Create and manipulate a HashSet
(def hash-set (java.util.HashSet.))
(.add hash-set "Element A")
(.add hash-set "Element B")
(seq hash-set) ;; Iterate over elements

;; Create and manipulate a HashMap
(def hash-map (java.util.HashMap.))
(.put hash-map "Key1" "Value1")
(.put hash-map "Key2" "Value2")
(.get hash-map "Key1") ;; Access value for a key
(seq hash-map) ;; Get entry set as a sequence
```

Interacting with these collections in Clojure makes it possible to leverage the strengths of Java's comprehensive APIs while writing idiomatic Clojure code.

Conversion between Clojure and Java Collections

At times, it becomes necessary to convert between Clojure's persistent data structures and Java collections. Clojure's into function simplifies this conversion.

```
;; Convert a Clojure vector to Java ArrayList
(def clojure-vector [1 2 3])
(def java-array-list (into (java.util.ArrayList.) clojure-vector))

;; Convert a Java ArrayList back to a Clojure vector
(def converted-vector (vec java-array-list))
```

Similarly, conversion can be performed with other collections, ensuring that data can move efficiently between the immutable and mutable worlds.

Mastering the interplay between Clojure and Java collections is essential for effective interoperability. By combining these techniques, developers can maximize the utility of both languages, crafting robust and efficient applications.

8.5 Handling Java Exceptions in Clojure

Understanding how to handle exceptions when interoperating with Java is crucial for building robust Clojure applications. Java has a well-defined exception handling mechanism that Clojure can leverage, ensuring that code is resilient and error-resistant.

Clojure provides means to catch Java exceptions using the try-catch construct, which is syntactically similar to Java's own exception handling paradigm. This construct allows the interception of exceptions, enabling the programmer to execute alternative code or rethrow exceptions as necessary.

The basic structure of exception handling in Clojure involves the try block, within which potentially problematic code is placed. If an exception occurs within this block, execution is immediately transferred to the catch block. Clojure also allows for a finally block, which is executed regardless of whether an exception was thrown.

Here is a basic example of how to handle exceptions in Clojure:

```
(try
  ;; Code that may throw an exception
  (Integer/parseInt "NotANumber")
  (catch NumberFormatException e
```

```
    ;; Handling code
    (println "Caught NumberFormatException: " (.getMessage e)))
  (finally
    ;; Code that will always run
    (println "This will always execute")))
```

In this example, the try block attempts to parse a non-numeric string, which raises a NumberFormatException. The catch block catches this specific exception and prints an error message. Finally, the finally block prints a message indicating its execution.

Clojure's catch clauses are more flexible than Java's because you can distinguish between exceptions by their types:

```
(try
  ;; Triggering a potential IOException
  (slurp "non\_existent\_file.txt")
  (catch java.io.FileNotFoundException e
    (println "File not found: " (.getMessage e)))
  (catch java.io.IOException e
    (println "IOException: " (.getMessage e)))
  (catch Exception e
    (println "General exception: " (.getMessage e))))
```

This example shows multiple catch clauses, each tailored to handle different types of exceptions. The slurp function attempts to read from a non-existent file, potentially causing an IOException. If the file is not found, the specific FileNotFoundException is caught, and an appropriate message is printed. Any other IOException is caught by the next catch clause, and a general Exception is handled by the final catch block.

Handling multiple exceptions in this manner provides fine-grained control over error handling logic, allowing developers to write precise and meaningful responses to various failure modes.

Java's checked exceptions dictate that certain operations must be enclosed in try-catch blocks. This rule does not directly apply to Clojure, but it is advisable to address these exceptions to prevent runtime errors from propagating and causing application crashes.

One key aspect of handling exceptions is deciding whether to catch and handle an exception at the current level or to propagate it up the call stack. Clojure's throw function can rethrow exceptions, maintaining the stack trace:

```
(try
  ;; Code that may cause an exception
  (Integer/parseInt "InvalidNumber")
  (catch NumberFormatException e
    ;; Re-throw exception
```

```
    (throw e)))
```

In this case, the NumberFormatException is caught and immediately rethrown, allowing it to be handled further up the call stack.

Integrating Clojure's exception handling seamlessly with Java code is essential when invoking Java methods that throw exceptions. Here's an example involving a method from a custom Java class:

```
// Java Class Example
public class ExceptionHandlingExample {
    public void throwException() throws Exception {
        throw new Exception("Java Exception");
    }
}
```

To handle this in Clojure:

```
; Import the Java class
(import 'ExceptionHandlingExample)

; Create an instance of the class
(def example (ExceptionHandlingExample.))

; Handle exceptions
(try
  (.throwException example)
  (catch Exception e
    (println "Caught Java exception: " (.getMessage e))))
```

In this scenario, the ExceptionHandlingExample Java class contains a method that throws a generic Exception. The Clojure code imports the class, instantiates it, and attempts to invoke the method within a try-catch block. The exception is caught, and an error message is printed.

When handling Java exceptions in Clojure, it is essential to:

- Understand the types of exceptions that Java methods can throw.
- Appropriately catch and handle specific exception types.
- Consider whether to handle or propagate exceptions.
- Leverage Clojure's flexibility to write concise, maintainable error handling code.

8.6 Using Java Libraries in Clojure Projects

Interoperability between Clojure and Java is one of the key features that makes Clojure a powerful language, particularly in leveraging the vast ecosystem of Java libraries. This section provides a comprehensive overview of the techniques and practices for integrating Java libraries into Clojure projects, ensuring that you can fully utilize existing Java resources.

To utilize Java libraries within a Clojure project, you need to include the necessary Java dependencies in your project's configuration file, interact with Java classes and methods, and handle common interop scenarios. We will walk through each of these aspects in detail.

Adding Java Dependencies

In Clojure, project dependencies, including Java libraries, are managed using the project configuration file, typically project.clj for projects using Leiningen or deps.edn for those using the Clojure CLI tools.

For Leiningen, dependencies are specified in the :dependencies vector. Here's an example configuration to include the Apache Commons IO library:

```
(defproject clojure-java-example "0.1.0-SNAPSHOT"
  :dependencies [[org.clojure/clojure "1.10.3"]
                 [commons-io/commons-io "2.8.0"]])
```

For the Clojure CLI tools, dependencies are added in the :deps map within the deps.edn file:

```
{:deps {org.clojure/clojure {:mvn/version "1.10.3"}
        commons-io/commons-io {:mvn/version "2.8.0"}}}
```

Once the dependencies are declared, they will be automatically fetched and made available on the classpath.

Importing Java Classes

To use Java classes in Clojure, you typically import them using the import form or the :import keyword within the ns declaration. Here's how you can import classes from the Commons IO library:

```
(ns clojure-java-example.core
  (:import [org.apache.commons.io FileUtils]))
```

Alternatively, you can import the class directly within your code using the import function:

```
(import 'org.apache.commons.io.FileUtils)
```

Using Java Methods

Clojure provides seamless access to Java methods via the dot operator (.). For static methods, use the forward slash (/). Here is an example that utilizes methods from the Commons IO's FileUtils class to read the contents of a file:

```
(ns clojure-java-example.core
  (:import [java.io File]
           [org.apache.commons.io FileUtils]))

(defn read-file [file-path]
  (let [file (File. file-path)]
    (.readFileToString FileUtils file "UTF-8")))
```

In this example, the File. instantiates a new File object, and the readFileToString method from FileUtils reads the contents of the specified file.

Handling Java Collections

Although Clojure has its own set of immutable collections, you will often need to work with mutable Java collections. When interfacing with Java, be aware of the differences between Clojure's and Java's collection types. For instance, converting between a Clojure list and a Java ArrayList might be necessary:

```
(ns clojure-java-example.core
  (:import [java.util ArrayList]
           [clojure.java.api Clojure]))

(defn clojure-list-to-java-arraylist [clj-list]
  (ArrayList. clj-list))

(defn java-arraylist-to-clojure-list [java-list]
  (into [] java-list))
```

The ArrayList. constructor wraps a Clojure list in a Java ArrayList, and the into function converts a Java ArrayList back into a Clojure vector.

Example: Utilizing a Java Library

To exemplify the usage of Java libraries in a practical scenario, let's consider using the Apache Commons Math library to perform mathematical operations. First, add the dependency in the project.clj or deps.edn:

```
[org.apache.commons/commons-math3 "3.6.1"]
```

Next, import the necessary classes and use them to calculate the cosine of a value:

```
(ns clojure-java-example.core
  (:import [org.apache.commons.math3.analysis.function Cos]))

(defn calculate-cosine [x]
  (let [cos (Cos.)]
    (.value cos x)))
```

In this example, an instance of Cos is created and the value method is called to compute the cosine of x.

Understanding how to effectively incorporate and utilize Java libraries in Clojure substantially extends the functionality available to your projects. The interop capabilities provide seamless integration, allowing you to leverage existing Java infrastructure and libraries, thus augmenting the capabilities of your Clojure programs.

8.7 Extending Java Classes and Interfaces

In Clojure, it is possible to extend Java classes and implement Java interfaces, which allows seamless integration and the extension of existing Java libraries. This capability is crucial for harnessing Java's extensive ecosystem while maintaining the flexibility and expressiveness of Clojure. Understanding how to extend Java classes and implement interfaces in Clojure can significantly enhance your ability to integrate Clojure within a Java-based application architecture.

To extend a Java class in Clojure, you use the gen-class function in conjunction with specific directives. The gen-class function generates a Java class that can be compiled and run as if it were a standard Java class. The primary directives include specifying the class name, the superclass, and any interfaces that the new class implements. Let's consider an example to illustrate this process.

First, create a Java interface and class that we will extend in Clojure:

```
public interface Greeter {
    void greet(String name);
}

public class BaseGreeter {
    public void baseGreeting() {
        System.out.println("Hello from BaseGreeter");
    }
}
```

Next, we extend this class and implement the Greeter interface in Clojure. Create a Clojure namespace and use the ns macro to include the necessary Clojure core libraries along with the gen-class directive.

```
(ns myproject.extender
  (:gen-class
    :name myproject.CustomGreeter
    :extends myproject.BaseGreeter
    :implements [myproject.Greeter]
    :methods [[greet [String] void]]))

(defn -greet [this name]
  (println (str "Hello, " name ", from CustomGreeter!")))

(defn -baseGreeting [this]
  (println "Custom greeting from CustomGreeter"))
```

In the above code:

- The namespace myproject.extender is defined.
- The :gen-class directive specifies the class name (myproject.CustomGreeter), the superclass (myproject.BaseGreeter), and the implemented interface (myproject.Greeter).
- The :methods directive lists a method, greet, which takes a String as a parameter and returns void, corresponding to the method in the Greeter interface.
- The -greet function provides the implementation for the greet method from the Greeter interface.
- The -baseGreeting function overrides the baseGreeting method from the BaseGreeter superclass.

Compile the Clojure code to generate the corresponding Java class files using the 'compile' function or a build tool like Leiningen or Maven. This step translates the Clojure code into Java bytecode. Using Leiningen, the command would be:

```
lein compile
```

To demonstrate the usage, write a simple Java program that instantiates and interacts with the CustomGreeter class:

```
public class Main {
    public static void main(String[] args) {
        myproject.CustomGreeter greeter = new myproject.CustomGreeter();
        greeter.greet("World");
        greeter.baseGreeting();
```

```
    }
}
```

The output when the Java program is executed will be:

```
Hello, World, from CustomGreeter!
Custom greeting from CustomGreeter
```

It showcases the interoperability by calling methods implemented in Clojure from a Java context.

Another powerful feature is handling constructor overloading. By default, the auto-generated class has a default constructor. To specify multiple constructors, include the :constructors option in the gen-class directive:

```
(ns myproject.extender
  (:gen-class
    :name myproject.AdvancedGreeter
    :extends myproject.BaseGreeter
    :implements [myproject.Greeter]
    :constructors {[String] []}
    :methods [[greet [String] void]]))

(defn -init [greeting]
  [[] greeting])

(defn -greet [this name]
  (let [greeting (.-greeting this)]
    (println (str greeting ", " name ", from AdvancedGreeter!"))))

(defn -baseGreeting [this]
  (println "Custom greeting from AdvancedGreeter"))
```

The :constructors option indicates that the AdvancedGreeter class has a single constructor taking one String parameter. The -init function initializes the new instance. Accessing instance variables in Clojure is accomplished with the .-variable syntax. The resulting Java program can use this overloaded constructor as follows:

```
public class Main {
    public static void main(String[] args) {
        myproject.AdvancedGreeter greeter = new myproject.AdvancedGreeter("Hey
            there");
        greeter.greet("World");
        greeter.baseGreeting();
    }
}
```

Compiling and running this program will produce:

```
Hey there, World, from AdvancedGreeter!
Custom greeting from AdvancedGreeter
```

This shows how constructor arguments can be managed and utilized within Clojure-extended Java classes. Extending Java classes and implementing interfaces in Clojure provides a robust mechanism to intertwine Clojure's functional paradigm with Java's object-oriented architecture, thus enabling sophisticated and efficient applications.

8.8 Integrating Java with Clojure REPL

The Clojure Read-Eval-Print Loop (REPL) is an interactive environment that allows developers to enter expressions, evaluate them, and see the results immediately. This dynamic and iterative mode of development is one of the core strengths of Clojure. When working with Java from the Clojure REPL, it is essential to seamlessly integrate Java classes and methods. This integration allows for leveraging the extensive Java ecosystem directly within the development workflow.

To begin, ensure that the Java Development Kit (JDK) is properly installed and configured on your system. Having the JDK set up correctly is crucial because Clojure relies on Java for execution. Additionally, your classpath should include the necessary Java libraries to be accessible from the REPL.

To illustrate the integration, consider the following steps:

```
;; Start the Clojure REPL
lein repl
```

This command initializes the REPL using Leiningen, a popular Clojure build automation tool. Once the REPL is running, Java classes and methods can be accessed directly.

To import a Java class, the import function is used:

```
(import 'java.util.Date)
```

This imports the java.util.Date class, making it available for instantiation and usage. To create an instance of this class, use the new keyword:

```
(def current-date (new java.util.Date))
;; Alternatively, using the dot-notation for constructor
(def current-date (java.util.Date.))
```

This code initializes current-date with the current date and time. The dot-notation is a shorthand for calling constructors and methods. To invoke a method on an object, use the following syntax:

```
(.toString current-date)
```

This calls the toString method on the current-date object, converting the date to its string representation. The output in the REPL will show the formatted date string:

```
"Fri Sep 23 09:18:25 PDT 2023"
```

For static methods or fields, the syntax does not require an instance of the class. Instead, use the class name followed by a forward slash:

```
(java.lang.Math/sqrt 16)
```

This code calculates the square root of 16 using the static sqrt method from the Math class. The result:

```
4.0
```

It is also possible to import multiple classes at once. The import statement can take a list of classes to bring into the current namespace:

```
(import '(java.util Date Calendar TimeZone))
```

In this example, Date, Calendar, and TimeZone from the java.util package are imported. Each imported class can be instantiated or used in method calls immediately.

To further illustrate this integration, consider a scenario where you want to work with Java collections. Clojure provides seamless interaction with Java's collection framework.

```
(import '(java.util ArrayList))

(def my-list (ArrayList.))
(.add my-list "Clojure")
(.add my-list "Java")

;; Use clojure interoperability to convert Java collection to a Clojure sequence
(def clojure-seq (seq my-list))
(clojure.pprint/pprint clojure-seq)
```

The ArrayList instance, my-list, is populated with two strings: "Clojure" and "Java". The seq function converts the Java collection into a Clojure sequence, which is then printed using pprint. The output:

```
("Clojure" "Java")
```

This integration is especially powerful when using Java libraries not natively available in Clojure. For instance, if using the java.nio.file package to perform file operations, import the required classes:

```
(import '(java.nio.file Files Paths))
(def file-path (Paths/get "example.txt" (into-array [""])))
```

```
;; Read all lines from file
(def all-lines (Files/readAllLines file-path))
(map println all-lines)
```

This script performs file I/O operations, demonstrating that Java's rich standard library is fully accessible from within the Clojure REPL.

When working on complex projects, encapsulating Java interop logic within functions or macros helps maintain readability and reusability. Moreover, the interop syntax, involving extensive use of dots and slashes, can be abstracted to enhance clarity.

Integration with build tools like Leiningen and Maven further streamlines this process. Specifying dependencies in project files ensures the required Java libraries are available. For example, adding dependencies in project.clj for a Leiningen project:

```
(defproject my-clojure-project "0.1.0-SNAPSHOT"
  :dependencies [[org.clojure/clojure "1.10.1"]
                 [org.apache.commons/commons-lang3 "3.12.0"]])
```

Includes the commons-lang3 library, which can be used as follows:

```
(import 'org.apache.commons.lang3.StringUtils)
(StringUtils/abbreviate "Integrating Java with Clojure REPL" 20)
```

The StringUtils/abbreviate method truncates the string, ensuring it fits the specified length.

Troubleshooting Java interop issues is crucial for efficient development. Common issues include classpath problems, missing dependencies, and incompatible method signatures. Utilizing Clojure's error messages, stack traces, and REPL-driven debugging practices can help swiftly resolve these issues. Enhanced REPL environments like CIDER for Emacs or IntelliJ with Cursive can further augment this debugging process.

Ensuring smooth interoperability between Clojure and Java within the REPL facilitates real-time experimentation, rapid prototyping, and a streamlined development workflow.

8.9 Compiling Clojure Code for Java Interoperability

Compiling Clojure code for Java interoperability involves translating Clojure source code into Java bytecode, which can then be executed on the Java Virtual Machine (JVM). This process is essential for integrating Clojure with Java, allowing Clojure programs to seamlessly interact with Java libraries, classes, and objects. This section will provide a detailed examination of the steps and tools required for this compilation process, as well as best practices to ensure effective and efficient interoperability.

To begin with, the Clojure code must be written in such a way that it can be easily compiled. This includes careful structuring of namespaces, proper handling of dependencies, and following idiomatic Clojure practices that align well with Java conventions.

```
(ns my.clojure.namespace
  (:import [java.util ArrayList]))

(defn create-java-arraylist []
  (let [list (ArrayList.)]
    (doto list
      (.add "Clojure")
      (.add "Java")
      (.add "Interoperability"))))
```

In this example, the ns macro is used to define a namespace and import the ArrayList class from the Java java.util package. The function create-java-arraylist demonstrates creating and manipulating a Java ArrayList using Clojure.

Clojure code can be compiled using the lein tool, which automates many tasks associated with Clojure development, including dependency management, project setup, and compilation. To compile a Clojure project, include the necessary dependencies and plugins in the project.clj file:

```
(defproject my-clojure-project "0.1.0-SNAPSHOT"
  :dependencies [[org.clojure/clojure "1.10.3"]]
  :plugins [[lein-cljsbuild "1.1.7"]]
  :cljsbuild {
    :builds [{
      :source-paths ["src"]
      :compiler {
        :output-to "target/main.js"
        :optimizations :whitespace
        :pretty-print true}}]})
```

In the above project.clj file, dependencies and plugins are defined. The lein-cljsbuild plugin is specifically used for compiling ClojureScript, but similar settings can be adapted for traditional Clojure projects compiled to Java bytecode.

To compile the project, the following lein commands can be used:

```
$ lein javac
$ lein compile
```

The lein javac command compiles Java source files if any are part of the project, while the lein compile command compiles the Clojure source files, generating Java bytecode that can be executed on the JVM.

It is crucial to organize the directory structure of the Clojure project to align with the conventional Java project layout. The source files should be placed under the src directory, and compiled classes should be located in the target/classes directory. This organization facilitates easier integration with Java tools and libraries:

```
my-clojure-project/
  src/
    my/clojure/namespace.clj
  target/
    classes/
      my/clojure/namespace.class
```

After compilation, the generated bytecode can be inspected or invoked using standard Java tools such as javap:

```
$ javap -p target/classes/my/clojure/namespace.class
```

Properly compiled Clojure code can be packaged into JAR files for distribution or deployment:

```
$ lein jar
```

The resulting JAR file can be included in Java projects and utilized like any other Java library. This file contains all the compiled Clojure classes, resources, and dependencies, enabling seamless Java-Clojure interoperability.

Here are some additional tips to ensure the compilation process is smooth and error-free:

- Ensure all Java dependencies are explicitly declared in the project.clj file.
- Use the AOT (Ahead-of-Time) compilation for namespaces requiring early compilation by specifying :aot in project.clj.

```
:aot [my.clojure.namespace]
```

- Regularly clean up the project directory to remove outdated compiled classes and avoid conflicts:

  ```
  $ lein clean
  ```

- Utilize profile configuration in project.clj to manage different environments and dependencies.

By adhering to these practices, developers can ensure their Clojure code is efficiently compiled into Java bytecode, facilitating robust and effective interoperability with Java components. This enables leveraging the strengths of both the Clojure and Java ecosystems in a cohesive manner.

8.10 Performance Considerations with Java Interop

Efficient performance is a central concern when integrating Clojure with Java, especially in high-stake applications. This section delves into various performance aspects entailing method calls, data structures, exception handling, and compilation strategies. The aim is to ensure that your Clojure code interoperates with Java seamlessly without sacrificing efficiency.

Firstly, it is important to understand that calling Java methods from Clojure can introduce overhead. Each method call requires the Clojure runtime to perform reflection, which is inherently slower than static method calls. To mitigate this, it is advisable to use the import and proxy mechanisms judiciously to avoid repeated reflection. When calling a Java method frequently within a Clojure loop, consider caching the result of reflective calls using Clojure's memoize function. Below is an example:

```
(def my-method (memoize #(.someJavaMethod (JavaClass.))))
```

Where someJavaMethod is the method being repeatedly called on JavaClass. This minimizes the overhead by storing the result of expensive operations and reusing them without repeated reflective calls.

Moreover, it is crucial to pay attention to data structures. Java's native collections such as ArrayList, HashMap, etc., provide performance benefits in scenarios that demand frequent updates and random access. In contrast, Clojure's persistent data structures can incur higher costs due to their immutability constraints. When numerous updates are required, consider using transient collections which offer a mutable yet controlled performance boost before ultimately converting them back to persistent structures. Here's an illustration of using transient collections:

```
(let [t-coll (transient [1 2 3])]
  (persistent! (conj! t-coll 4 5 6)))
```

The above code creates a transient collection t-coll, modifies it, and then converts it back to an immutable state with persistent!. This approach can significantly enhance performance during intensive update operations.

Handling exceptions also incurs performance penalties. Java's exception handling mechanism can be expensive if exceptions are thrown frequently. A prudent strategy is to structure the code in such a way that exceptions are used primarily for truly exceptional conditions rather than for flow control or handling predictable events. An example is shown below:

```
(defn safe-divide [num denom]
  (try
    (/ num denom)
    (catch ArithmeticException e
      (println "Cannot divide by zero!")
      nil)))
```

The above code handles exceptions but should be used judiciously to avoid frequent performance hits.

A critical aspect of improving performance in Clojure-Java integration is optimizing garbage collection (GC). Clojure's functional paradigm encourages a high rate of object creation, leading to potential GC bottlenecks. Java's garbage collectors, such as G1GC or ZGC, can be fine-tuned to minimize pause times and handle large heaps efficiently. Configuring the JVM with appropriate GC settings can significantly improve the performance of a Clojure application interacting extensively with Java.

JVM settings can be tailored by adding flags in the Clojure project configuration file (e.g., project.clj):

```
:jvm-opts ["-Xms1g" "-Xmx2g" "-XX:+UseG1GC"]
```

This configuration allocates initial and maximum heap sizes and specifies the use of the G1 garbage collector. Fine-tuning these parameters based on profiling results can lead to more predictable and lower-latency operations.

Another performance consideration is the direct compilation of Clojure code to Java bytecode using :gen-class or :proxy constructs. The :gen-class utility generates optimal bytecode and can replace reflection-heavy code with statically-compiled method calls, significantly enhancing runtime performance.

```
(ns example.core
  (:gen-class))
```

By annotating the namespace with :gen-class, the Clojure compiler generates a fully-fledged Java-compatible class, reducing the need for runtime interpretation and reflection.

Lastly, leveraging Clojure's built-in type hints can preempt reflection and foster performance gains. Type hints explicitly inform the compiler about the types of objects, facilitating the generation of more efficient bytecode. Example usage includes:

```
(defn example-fn [^String s ^int n]
  (println (.toUpperCase s) (+ n 10)))
```

Here, Ŝtring and înt are type hints that reduce the overhead associated with dynamic type checking. Utilizing type hints consistently where applicable ensures that your code remains performant and idiomatic.

By strategically employing these techniques, you can mitigate performance bottlenecks and achieve efficient interoperability between Clojure and Java, ensuring that both languages' strengths are fully harnessed in your projects.

8.11 Debugging Java Interop Issues

Debugging Java interoperability issues when working with Clojure requires a systematic approach. These issues primarily arise from the complex interactions between the dynamic features of Clojure and the static typing of Java. Understanding the common problems and employing appropriate debugging techniques is essential for effective problem resolution.

When debugging, it is important to identify whether the issue originates from the Clojure code, the Java code, or the interaction between the two. The following strategies and tools can assist in isolating and diagnosing these issues:

Common Issues and Solutions

One of the frequent issues is ClassNotFoundException. This occurs when Clojure cannot locate a Java class at runtime. The solution typically involves verifying the classpath configuration. Ensure that the JAR files or compiled classes are correctly included in the classpath.

Another common error is NoSuchMethodException. This happens when Clojure code attempts to invoke a method that does not exist. This can be caused by spelling mistakes, incorrect method signatures, or accessing methods not available in the specified class version. Double-check the method names and signatures, and ensure compatibility with the Java class version.

Complex data type conversions between Clojure and Java can also lead to ClassCastException. Clojure's dynamic typing can sometimes lead to unexpected type coercions. Using the correct Java type explicitly and leveraging Clojure's proxy and reify features can mitigate type mismatch issues.

Diagnostic Tools and Techniques

Logging is an invaluable tool for debugging Java interop issues. By adding comprehensive logging statements in both Clojure and Java code, one can track the execution flow and data transformations. The clojure.tools.logging library provides a straightforward way to integrate logging into Clojure applications.

```
(require '[clojure.tools.logging :as log])

(defn example-function []
  (log/info "Starting example-function")
  (try
    ;; Java interop code
    (catch Exception e
      (log/error e "Error in example-function"))))
```

Using an IDE that supports both Clojure and Java development, such as IntelliJ IDEA with the Cursive plugin, can significantly enhance debugging capabilities. These IDEs often include interactive debuggers, allowing step-by-step execution and variable inspection.

Java Debugger Integration

The Java Debugger (JDB) can be used to debug Clojure code that interoperates with Java. Configuring Clojure to run within the Java Debugger involves modifying the JVM options to enable debugging and specifying the appropriate transport and port. For example:

```
java -agentlib:jdwp=transport=dt_socket,server=y,suspend=n,address=*:5005 -jar
    target/myapp.jar
```

Once the JVM is running in debug mode, an IDE or command-line JDB can connect to the specified port to allow debugging sessions.

Analyzing Stack Traces

When an exception occurs, the stack trace provides valuable information about the source of the problem. Understanding and analyzing stack traces can pinpoint the location in the code where the error originates. A typical stack trace includes the exception type, message, and the call hierarchy. Here is an example of analyzing a stack trace in Clojure:

```
Exception in thread "main" java.lang.NoSuchMethodException: MyClass.nonExistentMethod()
  at java.base/java.lang.Class.getMethod(Class.java:2108)
  at clojure.lang.Reflector.invokeMatchingMethod(Reflector.java:167)
  at clojure.lang.Reflector.invokeInstanceMethod(Reflector.java:102)
  at my-ns.core/my-function(core.clj:10)
  ...
```

Identify the specific lines in the Clojure and Java code corresponding to the stack trace entries. The line numbers and method names indicate where the problem occurs, facilitating targeted investigation and resolution.

Unit Testing

Unit tests are essential for ensuring the correctness of Clojure code that interacts with Java. Writing comprehensive tests using frameworks like clojure.test or midje allows for early detection of issues arising from Java interop. Consider the following example:

```
(ns my-ns.core-test
  (:require [clojure.test :refer :all]
            [my-ns.core :refer :all]))

(deftest test-java-interop
  (testing "Testing Java method call"
    (is (= expected-value (java-method-call)))))

(run-tests)
```

These tests can be run frequently during development to catch issues early and ensure that changes in code maintain expected behavior.

Debugging Java interop issues in Clojure necessitates a multifaceted approach, incorporating logging, stack trace analysis, debugging tools, and comprehensive unit testing. These strategies collectively aid in effectively diagnosing and resolving interoperability challenges, ensuring robust integration between Clojure and Java components.

8.12 Real-world Examples of Java Interop

Understanding theory is important, but applying that knowledge to practical, real-world examples solidifies learning. Here, we discuss three detailed examples that leverage Java interoperability within Clojure: creating a graphical user interface (GUI) using Java's Swing library, manipulating data using Apache POI for Excel, and using Java's networking capabilities to create a simple web server.

Example 1: Creating a GUI with Java Swing

Java's Swing library provides a robust framework for building graphical user interfaces. The following example demonstrates how to create a basic window with a button that displays a message when clicked.

```
(ns gui-example
  (:import (javax.swing JFrame JButton JOptionPane)))

(defn create-gui []
  (let [frame (JFrame. "Clojure GUI Example")
        button (JButton. "Click Me")]
    (.addActionListener button
                        (proxy [java.awt.event.ActionListener] []
                          (actionPerformed [e]
                            (JOptionPane/showMessageDialog frame "Button Clicked!"))))

    (.add (.getContentPane frame) button)
    (.setSize frame 300 200)
    (.setDefaultCloseOperation frame JFrame/EXIT_ON_CLOSE)
    (.setVisible frame true)))

(create-gui)
```

The code snippet above:

- Imports the necessary Swing classes: JFrame, JButton, and JOptionPane.
- Defines a function create-gui that sets up the GUI.
- The JFrame object represents the main window.
- The JButton object represents a button.
- Adds an action listener to the button using a Java proxy to handle button clicks, triggering the display of a message dialog.
- Adds the button to the frame's content pane.
- Sets the frame size, default close operation, and visibility.

- Calls the create-gui function to display the window.

Executing the above code will display a window with a button. Clicking the button triggers a dialog box with the message "Button Clicked!".

Example 2: Manipulating Excel Files with Apache POI

Apache POI provides comprehensive support for manipulating Microsoft Office documents. The following example demonstrates reading an Excel file and printing the content of the first sheet.

```
(ns excel-example
  (:import (org.apache.poi.ss.usermodel WorkbookFactory)))

(defn print-excel-content [file-path]
  (let [workbook (WorkbookFactory/create (java.io.FileInputStream. file-path))
        sheet (.getSheetAt workbook 0)]
    (doseq [row (.iterator sheet)]
      (doseq [cell (.iterator row)]
        (print (.toString cell))
        (print "\t"))
      (println))))

(print-excel-content "example.xlsx")
```

The code snippet above:

- Imports the WorkbookFactory class from the org.apache.poi.ss.usermodel package.
- Defines a function print-excel-content that takes a file path as an argument.
- Uses WorkbookFactory/create to open the specified Excel file.
- Retrieves the first sheet of the workbook.
- Iterates over rows and cells of the sheet, printing the cell values.
- Calls the print-excel-content function with the path to an Excel file.

This will print the contents of the first sheet to the console, with cell values separated by tabs.

Example 3: Creating a Simple Web Server with Java Networking

Java boasts a comprehensive networking library. The following example shows how to create a simple web server that responds with "Hello, World!"

```
(ns web-server-example
  (:import (java.net ServerSocket Socket)
           (java.io PrintWriter InputStreamReader BufferedReader)))

(defn start-server []
  (with-open [server-socket (ServerSocket. 8080)]
    (println "Server started on port 8080")
    (while true
      (let [client-socket (.accept server-socket)
            out (PrintWriter. (.getOutputStream client-socket) true)
            in (BufferedReader. (InputStreamReader. (.getInputStream client-socket)))]
        (try
          (println "Client connected")
          (.println out "HTTP/1.1 200 OK")
          (.println out "Content-Type: text/plain")
          (.println out "Connection: close")
          (.println out "")
          (.println out "Hello, World!")
          (.flush out)
          (finally
            (.close client-socket)))))))

(start-server)
```

The code snippet above:

- Imports the necessary classes: ServerSocket, Socket, PrintWriter, InputStreamReader, and BufferedReader.
- Defines a function start-server.
- The ServerSocket object is created on port 8080.
- Enters an infinite loop to accept client connections.
- For each connection, reads the input and writes the HTTP response "Hello, World!".
- Uses a with-open block to automatically close the ServerSocket.
- Encloses actions inside a try block to ensure the client socket is closed after serving the response.
- Calls the start-server function, starting the server.

When the above code is executed, it starts a web server that listens on port 8080 and responds with "Hello, World!" to every request.

Through these examples, practitioners can explore Java interoperability features in Clojure, enhancing their ability to integrate Clojure with Java libraries effectively for practical applications.

Chapter 9

Clojure Development Tools and Workflow

This chapter provides an overview of essential development tools and workflows for Clojure programming. It includes setting up the development environment, using Leiningen for project management, and exploring popular editors and IDEs such as Emacs and IntelliJ IDEA with Cursive. Key topics include REPL-driven development, running tests, debugging and profiling code, version control, dependency management, and continuous integration and deployment strategies. Best practices for an efficient Clojure development workflow are also discussed.

9.1 Introduction to Clojure Development Tools

Clojure development relies on an array of tools designed to streamline the coding, testing, and deployment process. Understanding these tools is crucial for efficient and effective development. This section lays the foundation for mastering the essential tools needed for Clojure development, providing a comprehensive look at their functionalities and applications.

Leiningen is the de facto build automation and project management tool for Clojure. Leiningen simplifies the setup and management of Clojure projects, handling dependencies, testing, packaging, and deploying applications. A typical Leiningen project is defined by a project.clj file that specifies project dependencies and configurations. Here's a sample project.clj file:

```
(defproject sample-project "0.1.0-SNAPSHOT"
  :description "A sample Clojure project"
  :url "http://example.com/sample-project"
  :license {:name "Eclipse Public License"
            :url "http://www.eclipse.org/legal/epl-v10.html"}
  :dependencies [[org.clojure/clojure "1.10.3"]]
  :main ^:skip-aot sample-project.core
  :target-path "target/%s"
  :profiles {:uberjar {:aot :all}})
```

Leiningen is highly customizable and supports plugins that extend its functionality. For example, the lein-ring plugin facilitates web development by handling server tasks. Installation of Leiningen is simple and involves executing a script file that can be downloaded from https://leiningen.org/.

Clojure REPL (Read-Eval-Print Loop) is an interactive programming environment that provides instant feedback for code expressions. The REPL is a vital tool for testing hypotheses, debugging, and exploring the language. Using the REPL in conjunction with a robust editor enhances productivity. Here's an example of using the REPL for basic arithmetic operations:

```
user=> (+ 1 2 3)
6
user=> (* 2 3 4)
24
user=> (map inc [1 2 3 4])
(2 3 4 5)
```

Editors and IDEs play a significant role in Clojure development by providing syntax highlighting, code completion, and error checking. Popular choices include Emacs with CIDER (Clojure Interactive Development Environment that Rocks) and IntelliJ IDEA with the Cursive plugin. Both tools offer powerful integrations with the REPL, allowing developers to evaluate code fragments directly within the editor.

Emacs and CIDER offer a powerful, extensible environment tailored for Clojure. CIDER integrates seamlessly with the REPL, offering features such as autocompletion, code navigation, and inline documentation. Configuring Emacs to work with Clojure requires installing the cider and clojure-mode packages. Here are the essential Emacs configuration steps:

```
; Add MELPA to your packages repositories
```

```
(require 'package)
(add-to-list 'package-archives
             '("melpa" . "https://melpa.org/packages/") t)
(package-initialize)

; Bootstrap `use-package`
(unless (package-installed-p 'use-package)
  (package-refresh-contents)
  (package-install 'use-package))

; Install clojure-mode and cider
(use-package clojure-mode
  :ensure t)
(use-package cider
  :ensure t)
```

IntelliJ IDEA and Cursive provide an integrated development environment with advanced functionalities like code refactoring, debugging, and sophisticated project navigation. Cursive brings many of the powerful features of IntelliJ IDEA to Clojure development, including a built-in REPL, which can be launched by following these steps:

```
1. Open IntelliJ IDEA and create or open a Clojure project.
2. Ensure the Cursive plugin is installed and enabled.
3. Navigate to 'Run' > 'Run...' and select '+Run Configuration'.
4. Choose 'Clojure REPL' and configure the necessary settings.
5. Click 'OK' and start the REPL by selecting 'Run'.
```

Version Control Systems (VCS) like Git are indispensable for tracking changes, collaborating with team members, and maintaining project history. Git, coupled with platforms such as GitHub, provides a robust framework for version control:

```
$ git init
Initialized empty Git repository in /path/to/repo/.git/

$ git add .
$ git commit -m "Initial commit"
[master (root-commit) d1e8f29] Initial commit
 1 file changed, 1 insertion(+)
 create mode 100644 README.md
```

Effective Clojure development also leverages Continuous Integration (CI) and Continuous Deployment (CD) practices, which automate the building, testing, and deployment of applications. Tools like Travis CI, CircleCI, and Jenkins integrate with GitHub to provide these capabilities. A .travis.yml file for a Clojure project might look like this:

```
language: clojure
lein: leiningen-2.9.6
script:
  - lein test
```

This configuration ensures that tests are run automatically for each commit, facilitating early detection of issues and maintaining code quality. By understanding and utilizing these development tools, developers can significantly improve their workflow, resulting in more efficient and effective Clojure programming.

9.2 Setting Up Your Development Environment

To effectively develop in Clojure, the first step is setting up a robust and efficient development environment. This process encompasses installing the necessary software, configuring the tools, and ensuring they all work seamlessly together. The essential components include the Java Development Kit (JDK), Leiningen for project management, and a compatible editor or Integrated Development Environment (IDE).

1. Installing Java Development Kit (JDK)

Clojure runs on the Java Virtual Machine (JVM), requiring a proper installation of the JDK. Follow these steps to install the JDK:

- Visit the official Oracle JDK download page or an alternative like OpenJDK.
- Download the JDK suited for your operating system (Windows, macOS, or Linux).
- Follow the installation instructions provided on the JDK download page to complete the setup.
- Verify the installation by opening a terminal window and executing the following command:

```
java -version
```

The output should display the installed version of the JDK, confirming the successful installation:

```
java version "1.8.0_231"
Java(TM) SE Runtime Environment (build 1.8.0_231-b11)
Java HotSpot(TM) 64-Bit Server VM (build 25.231-b11, mixed mode)
```

2. Installing Leiningen

Leiningen is a build automation and dependency management tool for Clojure. It simplifies project creation, management, and running the Clojure code. To install Leiningen:

- Download the Leiningen script from the official website. For Unix-based systems, you can download and install it using the terminal:

```
wget https://raw.githubusercontent.com/technomancy/leiningen/stable/bin/lein
chmod +x lein
sudo mv lein /usr/local/bin/
```

- For Windows, download the lein.bat script and place it in a directory included in your system's PATH.
- Execute the following command to initialize Leiningen:

```
lein
```

Leiningen will download necessary artifacts and set up directories, initializing itself for the first time:

```
Downloading Leiningen to /home/user/.lein/self-installs/leiningen-2.9.3-standalone.jar now...
```

3. Choosing and Setting Up an Editor or IDE

Several editors and IDEs support Clojure development, with features like syntax highlighting, REPL integration, and project management. Emacs with CIDER and IntelliJ IDEA with Cursive are among the most popular choices.

3.1 Emacs with CIDER

- Install Emacs from its official repository or package manager.
- Start Emacs and install the CIDER package. Add the following configuration to your Emacs init file (.emacs or init.el):

```
(require 'package)
(add-to-list 'package-archives
             '("melpa" . "https://melpa.org/packages/"))
(package-initialize)
```

```
(unless (package-installed-p 'cider)
  (package-refresh-contents)
  (package-install 'cider))
```

- Save the file and restart Emacs. CIDER should now be available, providing an integrated development experience with REPL support.

3.2 IntelliJ IDEA with Cursive

- Download and install IntelliJ IDEA from JetBrains' official website.
- Open IntelliJ IDEA and navigate to File >Settings >Plugins.
- Search for Cursive and install it.
- Restart IntelliJ IDEA after installation.

4. Verifying the Development Environment

Ensure the development environment is configured correctly by creating and running a simple Clojure project using Leiningen:

- Create a new Leiningen project:

```
lein new app my-clojure-app
```

- Navigate into the project directory:

```
cd my-clojure-app
```

- Run the project:

```
lein run
```

The output should confirm the project is running correctly:

```
Hello, World!
```

Having a robust development environment significantly enhances productivity and ensures the tools work harmoniously. Properly setting up initial configurations minimizes potential friction and errors in the development workflow.

9.3 Using Leiningen for Project Management

Leiningen is a build automation tool for Clojure, designed to simplify the setup and management of Clojure projects. It handles tasks such as project creation, dependency management, running tests, and packaging applications. Understanding how to use Leiningen is essential for an efficient Clojure development workflow.

To install Leiningen, download the lein script from the official project website and make it executable. The installation steps for Unix-based systems are as follows:

```
wget https://raw.githubusercontent.com/technomancy/leiningen/stable/bin/lein
chmod +x lein
sudo mv lein /usr/local/bin/
```

For Windows, download the lein.bat script and place it in a directory that is included in your system's PATH.

After installing Leiningen, verify the installation by running:

```
lein version
```

The output should display the installed version of Leiningen.

```
Leiningen 2.9.1 on Java 1.8.0_222 OpenJDK 64-Bit Server VM
```

Leiningen projects are defined by a project.clj file. To create a new Clojure project, use the following command:

```
lein new app my-project
```

This command generates a new project named my-project with the following directory structure:

```
my-project/
  project.clj
  README.md
  doc/
  resources/
  src/
    my_project
      core.clj
  test/
    my_project
      core_test.clj
  target/
```

project.clj is the configuration file for Leiningen. It includes information about the project, dependencies, and build instructions. A typical project.clj file looks like this:

```
(defproject my-project "0.1.0-SNAPSHOT"
  :description "A sample Clojure project"
  :dependencies [[org.clojure/clojure "1.10.1"]]
  :main ^:skip-aot my-project.core
  :target-path "target/%s"
  :profiles {:uberjar {:aot :all}})
```

The dependencies vector specifies the libraries needed for the project. In this example, the project depends on Clojure version 1.10.1. To add more dependencies, list them in the dependencies vector:

```
:dependencies [[org.clojure/clojure "1.10.1"]
               [ring/ring-core "1.8.0"]
               [compojure "1.6.2"]]
```

After modifying project.clj, run lein deps to download and cache the new dependencies.

Leiningen supports running the REPL, a vital tool in Clojure development. Start the REPL with:

```
lein repl
```

Inside the REPL, load project namespaces and experiment with your code interactively. Leiningen also supports running Clojure programs directly:

```
lein run
```

The above command executes the main function defined in my-project.core. Ensure that the namespace and function are correctly specified in project.clj.

Running tests in Clojure projects is straightforward with Leiningen. Place test files in the test directory and use the following command to run them:

```
lein test
```

Leiningen will automatically detect and execute test files matching the pattern *_test.clj. For more advanced testing configurations, consider using profiles within project.clj.

Creating deployment artifacts, such as uberjars, is another essential feature of Leiningen. To generate an uberjar, which contains all dependencies and can be executed as a standalone JAR file, use:

```
lein uberjar
```

The resulting JAR file will be located in the target directory, following the naming convention my-project-0.1.0-SNAPSHOT-standalone.jar. This JAR can be deployed and executed using:

```
java -jar target/my-project-0.1.0-SNAPSHOT-standalone.jar
```

Leiningen also integrates with various plugins to extend its functionality. Plugins can be specified in the :plugins vector within project.clj. For instance, to include the lein-ring plugin for Ring-based web applications:

```
:plugins [[lein-ring "0.12.5"]]
```

After adding the plugin, use its tasks, such as lein ring server, to start the web server.

To automate repetitive tasks, Leiningen supports defining custom tasks. These are specified in the :aliases vector within project.clj. For example:

```
:aliases
{"run-tests" ["do" "clean," "test," "jar"]}
```

Running lein run-tests will perform a clean build, run tests, and create a JAR file, streamlining the development workflow.

By leveraging Leiningen effectively, developers can manage Clojure projects with ease, focusing more on coding and less on build logistics.

9.4 Overview of Popular Clojure Editors and IDEs

The effectiveness of a development environment is paramount in the programming workflow, significantly impacting productivity and code quality. In this section, we will delve into the most popular editors and Integrated Development Environments (IDEs) geared towards Clojure development. We will explore their features, strengths, and how they integrate with Clojure-specific tools and workflows.

Emacs with CIDER

Emacs, a highly customizable text editor, has a significant user base in the Clojure community, mainly when paired with CIDER (Clojure Interactive Development Environment that Rocks). CIDER provides robust support for interactive programming in Clojure and ClojureScript, leveraging the power of the REPL within Emacs.

To get started with Emacs and CIDER, the following steps are typically required:

1. Install Emacs from the official website or using a package manager.
2. Install CIDER via Emacs package manager.
3. Configure Emacs to use CIDER by adding the following to the init.el file:

```
(require 'package)
(add-to-list 'package-archives
             '("melpa" . "https://melpa.org/packages/") t)

(package-initialize)

(unless (package-installed-p 'cider)
  (package-refresh-contents)
  (package-install 'cider))

(require 'cider)
```

CIDER offers features such as on-the-fly code evaluation, interactive debugging, and easy navigation of project dependencies. Emacs users benefit from advanced code editing capabilities, including powerful text manipulation commands, extensive plugins, and support for multiple programming languages.

IntelliJ IDEA with Cursive

IntelliJ IDEA, a widely used IDE from JetBrains, supports Clojure development through the Cursive plugin. Cursive aims to provide a seamless development experience that leverages the rich feature set of IntelliJ IDEA, including smart code completion, code refactoring, and comprehensive project navigation.

To install Cursive in IntelliJ IDEA:

1. Open IntelliJ IDEA and navigate to File > Settings > Plugins.
2. Search for Cursive in the plugin marketplace and install it.
3. Restart IntelliJ IDEA to enable the plugin.

Cursive provides tight integration with Leiningen, facilitating project management and dependency resolution within the IDE. It also supports advanced REPL interactions, allowing developers to evaluate code snippets, debug Clojure code, and utilize interactive development workflows.

Visual Studio Code with Calva

Visual Studio Code (VS Code) is an increasingly popular editor known for its versatility and extensive extension ecosystem. For Clojure developers, the Calva extension delivers an integrated REPL environment, inline code evaluation, and detailed syntax highlighting.

To set up Calva in Visual Studio Code:

1. Install Visual Studio Code from the official website.
2. Navigate to Extensions in VS Code and search for Calva.
3. Install the Calva extension.
4. Open a Clojure project and use the command palette (Ctrl+Shift+P) to start the REPL with Calva: Start REPL and Connect.

Calva's feature set includes Paredit support for structural editing, interactive code evaluations, and integration with test runners, providing a streamlined development experience consistent with Clojure's emphasis on REPL-driven development.

Other Editors and IDEs

While Emacs, IntelliJ IDEA, and Visual Studio Code are among the most popular environments for Clojure development, several other editors and IDEs provide varying levels of support for Clojure.

- **Atom** – With packages such as chlorine and proto-repl, Atom offers basic REPL interaction and code editing capabilities.
- **Sublime Text** – Extensions such as SublimeREPL and syntax highlighting packages provide minimal Clojure support.
- **Light Table** – Originally conceived with Clojure in mind, Light Table offers real-time feedback and interactive development features.

Each editor or IDE has its strengths, and the choice often depends on personal preference and specific project requirements. The rich ecosystem of Clojure-compatible tools ensures that developers can find an environment that fits their workflow, enabling efficient and productive development practices.

9.5 Configuring Emacs for Clojure Development

Emacs is a highly extensible and customizable text editor which is particularly suited for Clojure development due to its powerful and flexible features. Configuring Emacs to streamline your Clojure development workflow involves setting up essential packages such as CIDER, enabling syntax highlighting, and configuring REPL integration.

Begin by installing Emacs. Most Linux distributions provide the Emacs package, which can be installed using the native package manager. For Windows and macOS, Emacs can be downloaded from the official GNU Emacs website.

```
sudo apt-get install emacs        # For Debian-based systems
brew install --cask emacs         # For macOS using Homebrew
choco install emacs               # For Windows using Chocolatey
```

Next, set up the Emacs package manager MELPA (Milkypostman's Emacs Lisp Package Archive) to install the necessary packages. Append the following lines to your .emacs or init.el file to configure MELPA.

```
(require 'package)
(add-to-list 'package-archives
             '("melpa" . "https://melpa.org/packages/") t)
(package-initialize)
```

Install the CIDER (Clojure Interactive Development Environment that Rocks) package by adding it to the init.el file or by using the package manager within Emacs.

```
M-x package-refresh-contents
M-x package-install [RET] cider [RET]
```

CIDER provides powerful capabilities such as interactive development, debugging, and introspection. It requires a running instance of a Clojure REPL to connect to. To launch a REPL in Emacs, run:

```
M-x cider-jack-in
```

This command initiates a REPL session within Emacs, connecting directly to your Clojure project. Ensure you have Leiningen installed, as cider-jack-in uses it to start the REPL. The configuration of Leiningen is covered in another section of this chapter.

Enable syntax highlighting and parenthesis matching by installing the following packages: clojure-mode and paredit.

```
M-x package-install [RET] clojure-mode [RET]
M-x package-install [RET] paredit [RET]
```

Add the following lines to your init.el to enable these modes and integrate them with Clojure files:

```
(require 'clojure-mode)
(add-hook 'clojure-mode-hook #'paredit-mode)
(add-hook 'clojure-mode-hook #'subword-mode)
(add-hook 'clojure-mode-hook #'cider-mode)
(add-to-list 'auto-mode-alist '("\\.clj\\'" . clojure-mode))
```

clojure-mode enables proper syntax highlighting and indentation specific to Clojure code. paredit enhances Lisp editing by ensuring balanced parentheses, a crucial component when working with Clojure's syntax. subword-mode allows navigation through camelCase words, improving the editing experience.

For additional conveniences such as auto-completion, error checking, and linting, install company (Complete Anything) and flycheck.

```
M-x package-install [RET] company [RET]
M-x package-install [RET] flycheck [RET]
```

Configure these features by adding the following lines in your init.el:

```
(add-hook 'after-init-hook 'global-company-mode)
(add-hook 'after-init-hook #'global-flycheck-mode)
```

To further enhance your development experience, integrating projectile, a project interaction library for Emacs, can be highly beneficial.

```
M-x package-install [RET] projectile [RET]
```

Activate and configure projectile by adding these lines to init.el:

```
(projectile-mode +1)
(define-key projectile-mode-map (kbd "C-c p") 'projectile-command-map)
(setq projectile-completion-system 'ivy)
```

Enable ivy for efficient completion and search functionalities:

```
M-x package-install [RET] ivy [RET]
(ivy-mode 1)
```

To improve the user interface and streamline interaction, consider installing the smex package, enhancing M-x command selection with a more intuitive and efficient interface:

```
M-x package-install [RET] smex [RET]
(smex-initialize)
(global-set-key (kbd "M-x") 'smex)
(global-set-key (kbd "M-X") 'smex-major-mode-commands)
(global-set-key (kbd "C-c C-c M-x") 'execute-extended-command)
```

Configuring Emacs for Clojure development effectively consolidates a range of tools and packages that significantly improve the development workflow. Through careful setup, developers can leverage Emacs' extensibility to create a highly productive Clojure coding environment.

9.6 Configuring IntelliJ IDEA and Cursive

IntelliJ IDEA is a widely used integrated development environment (IDE) that offers comprehensive support for various programming languages, including Java, Scala, Kotlin, and Clojure. With the addition of the Cursive plugin, IntelliJ IDEA becomes a powerful environment for Clojure development, providing features such as syntax highlighting, linting, REPL integration, and seamless project management.

To begin configuring IntelliJ IDEA for Clojure development, it is necessary first to install the IntelliJ IDEA itself and then the Cursive plugin. These steps will be detailed to ensure a correct installation and optimal setup for efficient Clojure programming.

Step 1: Installing IntelliJ IDEA

IntelliJ IDEA can be downloaded from the JetBrains official website. The Community Edition is available for free and supports Cursive, but the Ultimate Edition offers additional features that might be beneficial for advanced users.

Proceed with the following steps to install IntelliJ IDEA:

- Visit the JetBrains IntelliJ IDEA download page at: https://www.jetbrains.com/idea/download/
- Download the appropriate installer for your operating system (Windows, macOS, or Linux).
- Run the installer and follow the on-screen instructions to complete the installation.

Step 2: Installing the Cursive Plugin

Once IntelliJ IDEA is installed, the next step is to add the Cursive plugin to your IDE. The Cursive plugin is designed specifically for Clojure and provides a range of features to enhance productivity and simplify development.

To install Cursive:

- Open IntelliJ IDEA.
- Navigate to File > Settings (or IntelliJ IDEA > Preferences on macOS).
- In the Settings/Preferences dialog, select Plugins from the left-hand pane.
- Click on the Marketplace tab.
- In the search bar, type Cursive.
- Locate the Cursive plugin from the search results and click the Install button.
- Once the installation is complete, restart IntelliJ IDEA to apply the changes.

Step 3: Setting Up a New Clojure Project

With IntelliJ IDEA and Cursive installed, you can proceed to set up a new Clojure project. Cursive simplifies the process of creating and managing Clojure projects, especially those that utilize Leiningen for project management.

To create a new Clojure project:

- Launch IntelliJ IDEA.
- From the Welcome screen, click on Create New Project.
- In the New Project wizard, select Clojure from the list of project types.
- Choose Leiningen as the build tool and click Next.
- Specify the project name, location, and necessary SDK (typically, the Java JDK).

- Click Finish to create the project.

Step 4: Configuring REPL Integration

One of the key benefits of using Cursive with IntelliJ IDEA is the seamless integration of the REPL (Read-Eval-Print Loop), which allows for interactive development and immediate feedback. To configure REPL in your newly created Clojure project:

- Open your Clojure project in IntelliJ IDEA.
- Navigate to Run > Edit Configurations.
- Click the + icon to add a new configuration and select Clojure REPL.
- Choose the desired REPL type (nREPL or REPL from source).
- For nREPL, specify the host and port if needed, or use the defaults for local development.
- Save the configuration and click OK.
- Start the REPL by navigating to Run > Run and selecting the created configuration.

Step 5: Leveraging IntelliJ IDEA's Features for Clojure Development

With the Clojure project set up and the REPL configured, you can now leverage the myriad features offered by IntelliJ IDEA and Cursive to enhance your development workflow. Some key features include:

Code Navigation: IntelliJ IDEA offers powerful navigation capabilities, allowing you to quickly jump to definitions, find usages, and navigate between related files. Use shortcuts such as Ctrl+B (Go to Declaration) and Shift+Shift (Search Everywhere) to enhance your productivity.

Syntax Highlighting and Error Checking: Cursive provides comprehensive syntax highlighting for Clojure, making the code more readable and helping identify errors early. Errors and warnings are highlighted in real-time as you code.

Refactoring Tools: IntelliJ IDEA includes robust refactoring tools that support Clojure. These tools help in renaming symbols, extracting functions, and restructuring code, ensuring that your codebase remains clean and maintainable.

Version Control Integration: IntelliJ IDEA seamlessly integrates with version control systems such as Git. You can commit changes, create branches, merge code, and resolve conflicts directly from the IDE.

Leiningen Integration: Cursive supports Leiningen projects, allowing you to run tasks, manage dependencies, and generate project files directly from the IDE.

Unit Testing: IntelliJ IDEA supports running Clojure tests using frameworks like clojure.test. You can run tests directly from the editor and view the results in the run tool window.

Here is an example of running a simple unit test in a Clojure project:

```
(ns myproject.core-test
  (:require [clojure.test :refer :all]
            [myproject.core :refer :all]))

(deftest test-sum
  (testing "Sum function test"
    (is (= 5 (sum 2 3)))))
```

To run the test:

- Right-click on the test namespace file or the test function.
- Select Run 'test-sum' to execute the test.
- View the results in the run tool window.

The configuration of IntelliJ IDEA with Cursive prepares a robust development environment, allowing users to harness the powerful features and tools provided by the IDE. This setup is conducive to efficient, interactive Clojure development, ensuring that professionals and enthusiasts alike can maximize their productivity and code quality.

9.7 Using REPL-driven Development

REPL-driven development is a powerful approach in Clojure that leverages the interactive Read-Eval-Print Loop for rapid development and testing. This section offers a comprehensive exploration of REPL-driven development and its integration into the Clojure workflow.

The process begins with launching a REPL. In the context of Leiningen, the REPL is started with the following command:

```
lein repl
```

Upon execution, an interactive REPL session becomes available, allowing for real-time code evaluation. The prime advantage of REPL-driven development is the instantaneous feedback during the development process.

To illustrate a basic interaction with the REPL, consider the following example where we define and evaluate a simple function:

```
;; Define a function named 'square' that takes a number and returns its square
(defn square [x]
  (* x x))

;; Evaluate the 'square' function with argument 4
(square 4)
```

The REPL evaluates the 'square' function and returns:

```
16
```

This instant feedback loop is invaluable for testing individual components of code without the need for compilation or restarting the application, thus fostering rapid iteration.

Moreover, the REPL can be connected to a running application, which facilitates live coding and modification of a running system. This is typically done in a development environment, where the REPL can directly interact with the application context.

For advanced usage, integrating the REPL into an editor or an IDE enhances the experience. Emacs, for instance, with the CIDER plugin, offers seamless REPL integration. A buffed CIDER REPL session can be initiated within Emacs with the command:

```
M-x cider-jack-in
```

Similarly, IntelliJ IDEA with the Cursive plugin provides robust support for REPL-driven development. You can open a REPL within Cursive and perform live evaluations in the same manner.

One of the strengths of Clojure's REPL is its support for 'ns' (namespace) and 'require' operations, which are fundamental for managing the scope and dependencies of the code being evaluated. Here is an example demonstrating the use of namespaces:

```
;; Create and switch to a new namespace
(ns example.core)

;; Define a function in the new namespace
(defn add [a b]
  (+ a b))

;; Evaluate the function in the REPL
```

```
(add 3 5)
```

The REPL returns:

```
8
```

Properly managing the REPL environment is crucial for effective development. Commands such as 'clojure.tools.namespace.repl' assist in reloading modified namespaces, significantly speeding up the development cycle.

```
(require '[clojure.tools.namespace.repl :refer [refresh]])

;; Refresh all namespaces
(refresh)
```

Furthermore, REPL-driven development aligns well with test-driven development (TDD). Unit tests can be run directly within the REPL by including testing libraries such as 'clojure.test'. Here is an example:

```
;; Require clojure.test for testing support
(require '[clojure.test :refer :all])

;; Define a sample test
(deftest test-add
  (is (= 8 (add 3 5))))

;; Run the test in the REPL
(run-tests)
```

The REPL provides immediate feedback for the test results, which can appear as follows:

```
Testing example.core

Ran 1 tests containing 1 assertions.
0 failures, 0 errors.
```

Finally, REPL-driven development also extends to debugging capabilities. By utilizing the 'break' macro from 'clojure.tools.namespace.repl', developers can halt code execution to inspect the state and modify variables in real time. This is especially useful for identifying and resolving issues during development.

REPL-driven development, characterized by its interactive and iterative nature, significantly enhances the developer experience, facilitating quick experimentation, immediate feedback, and seamless troubleshooting, which together culminate in a highly efficient and productive development workflow.

9.8 Running Tests and Test Suites

Testing is a critical component of software development, ensuring that code behaves as expected and remains maintainable over time. In Clojure, the predominant testing framework is clojure.test, which is integrated into the Clojure standard library. This section will explore how to use clojure.test to write, organize, and run tests, leveraging Leiningen for project management and test execution.

To begin, an understanding of the clojure.test namespace is essential. This namespace provides macros and functions to define tests and assertions. The following example demonstrates a simple test definition:

```
(ns myproject.core-test
  (:require [clojure.test :refer :all]
            [myproject.core :refer :all]))

(deftest addition-test
  (testing "Testing addition function"
    (is (= 4 (add 2 2)))))
```

In this snippet, deftest defines a test function named addition-test. Within this function, the testing macro provides a description for a group of related assertions. The is macro performs the actual test assertion, checking if the expression evaluates to true. In this case, it verifies that the result of the add function with arguments 2 and 2 equals 4.

To run tests using Leiningen, the project configuration must specify the test paths. Typically, test files reside in the test directory. Ensure your project.clj file includes the following configuration:

```
(defproject myproject "0.1.0-SNAPSHOT"
  ;; other configurations
  :test-paths ["test"]
  ;; dependencies, plugins, etc.
)
```

With the infrastructure in place, use the Leiningen test task to execute tests:

```
$ lein test
```

This command runs all tests located in the test directory. The output will indicate the number of tests and assertions, along with details of any failures or errors.

Clojure projects may require organizing tests into multiple namespaces and files. It's often useful to follow the same namespace hierarchy as the source code, placing test files in corresponding directories under the test root. For instance, tests for myproject.core would be placed in myproject/core_test.clj. This organizational strategy facilitates locating and maintaining tests.

To enhance the testing process, various assertion functions and macros are available in clojure.test, such as:

- is: Basic assertion macro.
- are: Allows for multiple related assertions in tabular format.
- thrown?: Asserts that an exception is thrown.
- thrown-with-msg?: Asserts an exception with a specific message.

Examples demonstrate their usage as follows:

```
(deftest exception-test
  (testing "Division by zero should throw an exception"
    (is (thrown? ArithmeticException (/ 1 0))))

  (testing "Exception message should match"
    (is (thrown-with-msg? ArithmeticException #"Divide by zero" (/ 1 0))))
```

For more extensive projects, it is beneficial to group related tests into test suites. While clojure.test does not explicitly support test suites, they can be emulated through namespaces and Leiningen's test selectors. Define tests in separate namespaces according to their functionality, and use metadata or naming conventions to organize them into suites.

Consider categorizing tests as unit tests, integration tests, or regression tests by adding metadata:

```
(deftest ^:unit addition-unit-test
  (is (= 5 (add 2 3))))

(deftest ^:integration addition-integration-test
  (is (= 10 (add 5 5))))
```

Then, configure project.clj to include test selectors:

```
(defproject myproject "0.1.0-SNAPSHOT"
  ;; other configurations
  :test-selectors {:default (complement :integration)
                   :unit :unit
                   :integration :integration})
```

Specify test selectors when running tests:

```
$ lein test :unit
$ lein test :integration
```

This approach refines test execution, allowing focused running of specific test categories.

Integrating continuous testing practices, such as using lein-test-refresh, ensures instant feedback during development:

```
(defproject myproject "0.1.0-SNAPSHOT"
  ;; other configurations
  :plugins [[com.jakemccrary/lein-test-refresh "0.24.1"]])
```

Start the continuous test runner with:

```
$ lein test-refresh
```

The lein-test-refresh plugin watches for file changes, automatically running tests and displaying results.

Thoroughly leveraging Clojure's testing capabilities ensures robust and maintainable code, underpinning a reliable development workflow. This detailed examination initiates proficiency in running tests and test suites, fortifying confidence in the code's correctness and stability.

9.9 Debugging and Profiling Clojure Code

Debugging and profiling are essential tasks in software development, providing insights into the behavior and performance of code. In Clojure, these tasks can be handled using a range of tools and practices tailored to the language's functional programming paradigm and its hosted environment on the Java Virtual Machine (JVM).

Clojure.tools.logging is a popular library that integrates various logging frameworks, making it easier for developers to embed log statements in their code. To use this library, include the dependency in your project.clj file:

```
:dependencies [[org.clojure/clojure "1.10.1"]
               [org.clojure/tools.logging "1.2.0"]
               [ch.qos.logback/logback-classic "1.2.3"]]
```

To incorporate logging into a Clojure namespace, first require the clojure.tools.logging namespace, and then use the provided macros for logging:

```
(ns my.project.core
  (:require [clojure.tools.logging :as log]))

(defn example-fn [x]
  (log/info "Starting example-fn with" x)
```

```
  (if (even? x)
    (log/debug "x is even")
    (log/debug "x is odd"))
  x)
```

log/info and log/debug are used to log information at appropriate levels, providing insight during execution.

Another valuable tool is the clojure.tools.trace library, which can trace the execution of functions. To use it, add it to your project.clj dependencies:

```
:dependencies [[org.clojure/clojure "1.10.1"]
               [org.clojure/tools.trace "0.7.10"]]
```

Trace a function by using the trace macro:

```
(require '[clojure.tools.trace :refer [trace-vars]])

(defn factorial [n]
  (if (<= n 1)
    1
    (* n (factorial (dec n)))))

(trace-vars factorial)
(factorial 5)
```

The output will show each function call and its evaluation results:

```
TRACE t8776: (factorial 5)
TRACE t8777: | (factorial 4)
TRACE t8778: | | (factorial 3)
TRACE t8779: | | | (factorial 2)
TRACE t8780: | | | | (factorial 1)
TRACE t8779: | | | | => 1
TRACE t8780: | | | => 2
TRACE t8781: | | => 6
TRACE t8782: | => 24
TRACE t8783: => 120
```

For more in-depth inspection, use a REPL debugger like cider.nrepl if you are working within Emacs or CIDER for nREPL. It provides capabilities such as setting breakpoints and stepping through code.

Profiling helps identify performance bottlenecks. The clojure.java.jmx library accesses JVM metrics, while VisualVM and YourKit are comprehensive, GUI-based profilers suitable for Clojure and Java ecosystem users. Start by adding the following dependency for JMX profiling:

```
:dependencies [[org.clojure/clojure "1.10.1"]
               [clojure.java.jmx "0.3.1"]]
```

To retrieve JVM metrics:

```
(require '[clojure.java.jmx :as jmx])
```

```
(jmx/mbean "java.lang:type=Memory")
```

This returns a map containing memory usage metrics:

```
{:ObjectName "java.lang:type=Memory",
 :HeapMemoryUsage
  {:init 268435456, :committed 651894784, :max 3817865216, :used 24123840},
 :NonHeapMemoryUsage
  {:init 2555904, :committed 77484032, :max -1, :used 72376824},
 :ObjectPendingFinalizationCount 0,
 :Verbose false}
```

VisualVM can attach to live JVM processes running Clojure applications, providing real-time profiling data. Ensure you run your application with the JVM argument for remote debugging:

```
-Xrunjdwp:transport=dt_socket,server=y,suspend=n,address=5005
```

Attach VisualVM to the process using the remote host and port.

Consider criterium for precise benchmarking of Clojure functions. Add it to your projects:

```
:dependencies [[org.clojure/clojure "1.10.1"]
               [criterium "0.4.4"]]
```

Use with-progress-reporting to obtain detailed benchmarks:

```
(require '[criterium.core :as crit])

(crit/quick-bench (factorial 10))
```

Output provides statistical insights, helping detect performance deviations:

```
Evaluation count : 384 in 6 samples of 64 calls.
             Execution time mean : 1.480411 µs
    Execution time std-deviation : 87.370887 ns
   Execution time lower quantile : 1.382117 µs ( 2.5%)
   Execution time upper quantile : 1.592131 µs (97.5%)
   Overhead used : 1.658233 ns
```

Conclusively, effective debugging and profiling require familiarity with tools that align with Clojure's dynamic and functional characteristics, ensuring the code is both correct and optimized.

9.10 Version Control and Dependency Management

Version control and dependency management are two fundamental aspects of modern software development that ensure codebase stability and reproducibility. This section delves into the intricacies of these approaches within the context of Clojure development.

Version control systems (VCS) facilitate collaborative development, enable tracking changes, and provide mechanisms for merging contributions from multiple developers. Among various VCS options, Git has become the industry standard due to its distributed nature and robust suite of features.

Git usage in Clojure projects typically begins with initializing a new repository or cloning an existing one. To initialize a repository, navigate to your project directory and execute the following command in the terminal:

```
git init
```

This command creates a new hidden directory, .git, which houses all version control data. To clone an existing repository, use:

```
git clone <repository_url>
```

Ensuring your clojure source files and relevant configurations are tracked necessitates the addition and committing of these files. The following series of commands illustrates this process:

```
git add .
git commit -m "Initial commit"
```

Effective dependency management is equally crucial in Clojure development. Leiningen, the de-facto build automation tool for Clojure, simplifies the management and resolution of dependencies. This is accomplished through its project.clj file, which specifies project-specific information, including dependencies.

Consider the following example of a project.clj file:

```
(defproject my-clojure-project "0.1.0-SNAPSHOT"
  :description "Example project for demonstrating dependency management"
  :dependencies [[org.clojure/clojure "1.10.1"]
                 [cheshire "5.10.0"]
                 [ring/ring-core "1.8.2"]
                 [compojure "1.6.1"]])
```

The :dependencies vector contains tuples specifying each dependency's group ID, artifact ID, and version. Leiningen leverages the popular Maven Central Repository to resolve these dependencies, ensuring they are available at compile and runtime.

To fetch and store these dependencies locally, run:

```
lein deps
```

This command downloads all specified dependencies' jars and places them in the .m2/repository directory in the user's home folder, adhering to the Maven repository structure.

Version control integration with dependency management is crucial for maintaining a consistent and reproducible development environment. This is typically achieved by versioning the project.clj file. Any changes to this file, such as adding new dependencies or upgrading existing ones, should be committed to the version control system:

```
git add project.clj
git commit -m "Updated dependencies"
```

When collaboratively working on a Clojure project, team members must ensure they operate on the same dependency versions to avoid conflicts. Adherence to this practice maintains a cohesive development environment where builds and tests are reliable.

Further sophistication in dependency management is afforded by Leiningen profiles. Profiles allow for the segregation of dependencies and configurations based on different environments or use cases. For instance, one can define separate profiles for development, testing, and production. Below, the project.clj is extended with profiles for a testing environment:

```
(defproject my-clojure-project "0.1.0-SNAPSHOT"
  :description "Example project for demonstrating dependency management"
  :dependencies [[org.clojure/clojure "1.10.1"]
                 [cheshire "5.10.0"]
                 [ring/ring-core "1.8.2"]
                 [compojure "1.6.1"]]
  :profiles {:dev {:dependencies [[org.clojure/tools.nrepl "0.2.12"]]}
             :test {:dependencies [[midje "1.9.9"]
                                   [org.clojure/test.check "0.9.0"]]}})
```

This configuration delineates additional dependencies required in the development and testing environments, ensuring core dependencies remain distinct from those used only under specific conditions.

Finally, continuous integration (CI) systems play a pivotal role in the modern software development lifecycle, automating the testing and deployment stages while ensuring that all dependencies are correctly resolved. By integrating with CI tools such as Jenkins or GitHub Actions, Clojure projects benefit from automated workflows that facilitate code quality and reliability. A typical CI configuration, in the form of a GitHub Actions workflow, ensures dependencies are resolved, and tests are executed upon each commit:

```
name: Clojure CI

on: [push, pull_request]

jobs:
  build:
    runs-on: ubuntu-latest

    steps:
    - uses: actions/checkout@v2
    - name: Set up Clojure
      uses: DeLaGuardo/setup-clojure@v1
      with:
        leiningen: 'yes'
    - name: Install Dependencies
      run: lein deps
    - name: Run Tests
      run: lein test
```

This workflow script, specified in a .github/workflows/ci.yml file, ensures that every commit is thoroughly tested, significantly enhancing the stability and reliability of the Clojure project.

Using these tools and best practices, developers maintain a well-organized and efficient development environment, ensuring both version control and dependency management contribute to a smooth and reliable workflow.

9.11 Continuous Integration and Deployment

Implementing a robust Continuous Integration (CI) and Continuous Deployment (CD) strategy is paramount for the effectiveness and reliability of Clojure software development projects. CI/CD pipelines automate the process of integrating code changes, running tests, and deploying applications to various environments, significantly reducing potential errors and increasing development velocity.

Continuous Integration involves the frequent merging of individual developer changes into the main codebase. Automating this process ensures that integrations are verified by automated builds and tests, which helps to detect and address mistakes early. Clojure projects typically use tools such as Jenkins, CircleCI, Travis CI, or GitHub Actions to set up CI pipelines.

Algorithm 1: Basic Continuous Integration Pipeline

```
Input: Source code repository (repository)
Output: Build status (build_status), Test results (test_results)
// Step 1: Clone the Repository
clone(repository);
// Step 2: Install Dependencies
lein deps;
// Step 3: Compile the Code
lein compile;
// Step 4: Run Tests
test_results ← lein test;
if test_results == Pass then
    // Step 5: Create Build Artifacts
    lein uberjar;
    build_status ← Success;
else
    build_status ← Failure;
return build_status, test_results
```

Here is a practical example of a CI setup using GitHub Actions for a Clojure project. GitHub Actions allows you to automate, customize, and execute your software development workflows directly in your repository. Here's an example workflow file:

```
name: CI

on: [push, pull_request]

jobs:
  build:
    runs-on: ubuntu-latest

    steps:
    - name: Checkout code
      uses: actions/checkout@v2

    - name: Set up JDK 11
      uses: actions/setup-java@v1
      with:
        java-version: '11'

    - name: Install Leiningen
```

```
        run: |
          sudo apt-get update
          sudo apt-get install -y leiningen

      - name: Install dependencies
        run: lein deps

      - name: Compile the code
        run: lein compile

      - name: Run tests
        run: lein test
```

Using the above setup ensures that each push or pull request triggers the CI pipeline steps: checking out the repository code, setting up the necessary JDK version, installing Leiningen, dependencies, compiling the code, and running the tests.

Continuous Deployment extends CI by automatically deploying the code changes that pass the CI pipeline to the production environment. This practice is crucial for maintaining deployment consistency and reducing manual intervention risks. A deployment pipeline may integrate with cloud services such as AWS, Azure, or GCP or utilize container orchestration platforms like Kubernetes or Docker Swarm.

For instance, integrating with AWS can be automated using the aws CLI within the CI pipeline. Here is an extension to the previous example, deploying your Clojure application to AWS S3 as a static website upon successful tests:

```
name: CD

on:
  push:
    branches:
      - main

jobs:
  deploy:
    runs-on: ubuntu-latest
    steps:
      - name: Checkout code
        uses: actions/checkout@v2

      - name: Set up JDK 11
        uses: actions/setup-java@v1
        with:
          java-version: '11'

      - name: Install Leiningen
        run: |
          sudo apt-get update
          sudo apt-get install -y leiningen

      - name: Install dependencies
        run: lein deps
```

```
- name: Compile the code
  run: lein compile

- name: Run tests
  run: lein test

- name: Package application
  run: lein uberjar

- name: Deploy to S3
  run: |
    aws s3 cp target/uberjar/your-app.jar s3://your-bucket-name/
```

With this configuration, pushing to the main branch will trigger the CD pipeline to deploy the built JAR file to an S3 bucket, ready to be served as needed.

Best practices for setting up CI/CD pipelines in Clojure development include maintaining a clean and efficient codebase, writing comprehensive automated tests, ensuring environment consistency, and continuously monitoring pipeline performance metrics. Moreover, it's advised to secure the CI/CD pipeline by managing sensitive information such as access tokens and credentials using encrypted secrets.

By adhering to these practices and leveraging automated pipelines effectively, Clojure developers can ensure their projects are reliable, maintainable, and swiftly responsive to changing requirements and environments.

9.12 Best Practices for Clojure Development Workflow

Effective workflows are essential for maximizing productivity and maintaining code quality in Clojure development. Adopting best practices ensures efficient collaboration, reliable software, and smooth project management. This section discusses several best practices, focusing on REPL-driven development, proper use of Leiningen, dependency management, and leveraging version control systems.

1. Prioritize REPL-Driven Development

REPL-driven development (RDD) is a powerful methodology in Clojure programming. By interacting with the Read-Eval-Print Loop (REPL), developers gain immediate feedback on code execution. This interactivity fosters rapid experimentation and iteration.

```
;; An example of defining a function in REPL
(defn add [a b]
  (+ a b))

;; Testing the function immediately
(add 5 3)
```

The output from the REPL would be:

```
8
```

This approach allows you to refine functions iteratively before integrating them into your codebase, enhancing productivity and code quality. Always keep the REPL session running side-by-side with your editor to streamline testing and debugging.

2. Utilize Leiningen for Comprehensive Project Management

Leiningen is the de facto build automation and dependency management tool for Clojure projects. Its capabilities extend beyond mere build automation to managing project dependencies, running tests, packaging applications, and generating documentation.

```
;; Create a new project using Leiningen
lein new app my-clojure-app

;; Change into the project directory
cd my-clojure-app

;; Start the REPL
lein repl
```

Make sure to define dependencies in the `project.clj` file. Properly managed dependencies ensure that the correct library versions are used, preventing conflicts and ensuring reproducible builds.

```
(defproject my-clojure-app "0.1.0-SNAPSHOT"
  :description "A simple Clojure app"
  :dependencies [[org.clojure/clojure "1.10.3"]])
```

Always update dependencies judiciously, testing thoroughly to ensure compatibility.

3. Embrace Version Control with Git

Version control is indispensable for any collaborative software development effort. Git, a distributed version control system, is widely used for managing Clojure projects. Key practices include committing often, using meaningful commit messages, and branching effectively for feature development and bug fixes.

```
# Initialize a new Git repository
```

```
git init

# Add all files to staging
git add .

# Commit with a meaningful message
git commit -m "Initial commit"

# Create a new branch for a feature
git checkout -b feature/my-new-feature
```

GitHub, GitLab, and Bitbucket are popular platforms for hosting Git repositories, offering additional features like pull requests, code reviews, and CI/CD integrations.

4. Ensure Robust Testing

Testing is critical for maintaining robust code. Clojure encourages a test-driven development (TDD) approach, facilitated by libraries like clojure.test. Always aim for comprehensive test coverage, including unit tests, integration tests, and system tests.

```
(ns my-clojure-app.core-test
  (:require [clojure.test :refer :all]
            [my-clojure-app.core :refer :all]))

(deftest test-add-function
  (testing "Addition of two numbers"
    (is (= (add 2 3) 5))
    (is (= (add -1 1) 0))))
```

Run tests frequently to catch regressions early. Use Leiningen's testing commands to streamline this process.

```
lein test
```

5. Leverage Continuous Integration and Deployment (CI/CD)

CI/CD practices are essential for automated testing and deployment. Tools like Jenkins, CircleCI, and Travis CI automate the process of integrating code changes, running tests, and deploying applications. Define your CI/CD pipelines in configuration files, and include steps for building, testing, and deploying your Clojure applications.

Example of a basic .travis.yml configuration:

```
language: clojure
script:
  - lein test
```

Automated deployments reduce the risk of human error and ensure consistent release processes.

6. Practice Effective Dependency Management

Managing dependencies effectively prevents version conflicts and ensures project stability. Use Leiningen's dependency management features to specify and resolve dependencies.

To check for outdated dependencies, use:

```
lein ancient
```

Regularly update dependencies with caution, focusing on compatibility and thorough testing.

7. Code Consistency and Style

Adhering to coding standards is vital for maintaining readability and maintainability. Follow the Clojure community's conventions, such as naming standards, indentation rules, and idiomatic constructs.

Use tools like cljfmt for code formatting and eastwood for linting, ensuring that code adheres to these standards.

```
lein cljfmt fix
lein eastwood
```

By integrating these practices into your daily workflow, you ensure a sustainable and efficient Clojure development process.

Chapter 10

Building and Deploying Clojure Applications

This chapter focuses on the processes involved in building and deploying Clojure applications. It covers structuring application code, managing dependencies with Leiningen, and creating standalone JAR files. Topics include packaging and distributing Clojure libraries, automating builds with CI/CD tools, and various deployment strategies. The chapter also addresses deploying applications to the cloud, using Docker with Clojure, monitoring and maintaining applications, and scaling Clojure applications effectively.

10.1 Introduction to Building Clojure Applications

Building Clojure applications involves combining multiple components and processes to create a functional and deployable software product. In this section, we explore the foundational concepts necessary for successfully constructing Clojure-based projects, focusing on essential tools, frameworks, and methodologies used within the Clojure ecosystem.

The first step in building any Clojure application is establishing a structured development environment. Clojure typically relies on the Java

Virtual Machine (JVM) given its interoperability with Java libraries and tools. Ensuring that your system has Java Development Kit (JDK) installed is crucial. Most Clojure projects use Leiningen, a powerful build automation tool that simplifies project configuration and dependency management.

To create a new Clojure project using Leiningen, execute the following command in your terminal:

```
lein new app my-clojure-app
```

This command creates a new directory named my-clojure-app with a standard Clojure project structure. Here is an outline of the generated directory structure:

```
my-clojure-app/
  project.clj
  README.md
  doc/
  src/
    my_clojure_app/
      core.clj
  test/
    my_clojure_app/
      core_test.clj
  resources/
```

The project.clj file is the heart of any Leiningen project, containing essential information about the project, such as its dependencies, build settings, and metadata. Here is a simplified example of a typical project.clj configuration:

```
(defproject my-clojure-app "0.1.0-SNAPSHOT"
  :description "A sample Clojure application."
  :url "http://example.com/my-clojure-app"
  :license {:name "Eclipse Public License"
            :url "http://www.eclipse.org/legal/epl-v10.html"}
  :dependencies [[org.clojure/clojure "1.10.3"]]
  :main ^:skip-aot my-clojure-app.core
  :target-path "target/%s"
  :profiles {:uberjar {:aot :all}})
```

In this configuration, we declare the leiningen project name, version, description, URL, license, dependencies, and other critical settings. The :dependencies vector lists libraries that the application depends on, such as the Clojure language itself. The :main setting specifies the namespace containing the -main function to run when the application starts.

Let us explore the contents of the src/my_clojure_app/core.clj file, which typically contains the entry point for your application:

```
(ns my-clojure-app.core
  (:gen-class))
```

```
(defn -main
  [& args]
  (println "Hello, Clojure World!"))
```

This file defines a namespace my-clojure-app.core and a -main function, which prints a greeting message to the console. The defn macro is used to define functions in Clojure. When executed, the -main function takes an arbitrary number of arguments, denoted by & args, and prints "Hello, Clojure World!".

We execute our application using the following Leiningen command:

```
lein run
```

The output in the terminal should display the following message:

Hello, Clojure World!

With the basic project structure in place, developers often include additional libraries and tools to enhance functionality. Managing these dependencies is made simple through the :dependencies vector within project.clj. Below is an example of adding Ring, a popular Clojure web application library, to the project:

```
:dependencies [[org.clojure/clojure "1.10.3"]
               [ring/ring-core "1.8.2"]
               [ring/ring-jetty-adapter "1.8.2"]]
```

Updating the :dependencies vector facilitates the use of these libraries within your application. For web applications, defining routes and handlers in an additional handler.clj file may look like the following:

```
(ns my-clojure-app.handler
  (:require [ring.adapter.jetty :refer [run-jetty]]
            [ring.util.response :refer [response]]))

(defn hello-handler
  [request]
  (response "Hello from Ring!"))

(defn -main
  [& args]
  (run-jetty hello-handler {:port 3000}))
```

Here, the run-jetty function starts an HTTP server on port 3000, responding with the message "Hello from Ring!" whenever a request is made to the server.

In the context of building Clojure applications, emphasis should also be placed on and testing. Clojure provides robust testing libraries such as clojure.test, which can be included and configured in the project.clj. The test/my_clojure_app/core_test.clj file provides a template for writing unit tests:

```
(ns my-clojure-app.core-test
  (:require [clojure.test :refer :all]
            [my-clojure-app.core :refer :all]))

(deftest test-main
  (is (= 1 1)))
```

Executing the test suite is done via the command:

```
lein test
```

Ensuring all tests pass provides confidence in the correctness of the application before moving on to packaging, deploying, and scaling steps covered in the subsequent sections.

By establishing a strong foundation in building Clojure applications, developers are well-prepared to tackle more advanced topics and challenges, ensuring the continued success and scalability of their projects.

10.2 Structuring Your Application Code

When developing a Clojure application, it is crucial to structure your code in a way that promotes maintainability, modularity, and scalability. This section delves into best practices for organizing your application's source files, namespace conventions, and leveraging Clojure's inherent capabilities to write clean and efficient code.

Clojure applications generally follow a conventional directory structure that can be easily navigated by developers and tools alike. A typical layout resembles the following:

```
src
    your_namespace
        core.clj
        components.clj
        utils.clj
test
    your_namespace
        core_test.clj
        components_test.clj
        utils_test.clj
resources
project.clj
README.md
```

```
target
```

src is the directory where all source files are housed. Inside src, the code is typically organized into namespaces which correspond to the directory structure. For instance, a file named your_namespace/core.clj corresponds to the namespace your-namespace.core. This convention allows Clojure to resolve namespaces and their dependencies effectively.

Using Namespaces Effectively

Namespaces in Clojure are essential for organizing and managing your code. A namespace is a mapping from simple names (like core, utils) to fully qualified names (like your-namespace.core). Use the ns macro to define a namespace at the top of each Clojure source file. Here is an example:

```
(ns your-namespace.core
  (:require [clojure.string :as str]
            [your-namespace.utils :as utils]))
```

This snippet demonstrates a few key points: - The namespace is defined using the ns macro. - Dependencies are included using :require, enabling the current namespace to use functions from clojure.string and your-namespace.utils.

Defining Namespace Conventions

Adopt consistent naming conventions to simplify collaboration and maintenance. Standard practices include: - Use hyphens instead of underscores in namespace names (your-namespace.core instead of your_namespace.core). - Organize related functionalities into sub-namespaces. For example, your-namespace.db might handle database interactions, while your-namespace.api could manage HTTP endpoints.

Structuring Core and Component Files

The core.clj file typically contains the entry point of your application and essential initialization logic. For example:

```
(ns your-namespace.core
  (:require [your-namespace.components :as comps]))

(defn -main []
  (comps/start-app))
```

In this example, -main is the entry function, calling a start-app function from the your-namespace.components namespace. Component files, such as components.clj, are responsible for modular parts of the application, such as initializing and managing services, database connections, or background tasks.

Utility Functions

It is advisable to keep helper or utility functions in a separate file, such as utils.clj. This isolates commonly used, generic functions that are not tied to specific business logic:

```
(ns your-namespace.utils)

(defn greet [name]
  (str "Hello, " name "!"))
```

Practicing Modularization

To build a modular application, break down your code into small, reusable functions and place them into logically coherent namespaces. This practice not only makes your codebase easier to test and maintain but also promotes code reuse and separation of concerns.

Testing and Validation

Follow a parallel structure in your test directory to keep your tests organized in the same way as your source files. For instance, to test utils.clj, you would create a corresponding utils_test.clj file:

```
(ns your-namespace.utils-test
  (:require [clojure.test :refer :all]
            [your-namespace.utils :refer :all]))

(deftest test-greet
  (is (= "Hello, John!" (greet "John"))))
```

Utilize the clojure.test framework to create your tests, ensuring that each functionality gets validated independently.

Dependency Management

Ensure that all your dependencies are properly declared and managed through your project.clj file. Dependencies should be scoped appropriately to avoid conflicts and promote clear accountability for which components or namespaces rely on specific libraries.

Summary

The detailed structuring of your Clojure application code is foundational to the creation of robust, maintainable, and scalable software. By adhering to standard directory structures, utilizing namespaces effectively, and modularizing your codebase, you ensure that your application remains organized and comprehensible both to you and other developers.

10.3 Managing Dependencies with Leiningen

Leiningen is a build automation tool for Clojure, which simplifies the task of managing project dependencies, building projects, running tests, packaging code, and deploying applications. This section will delve into managing dependencies with Leiningen, providing an in-depth understanding of how to specify, retrieve, and manage dependencies in a Clojure project.

Dependencies in Leiningen are specified in a project.clj file, which contains a map called :dependencies. This map includes library names and versions required by the project. The project.clj file is crucial for ensuring that your Clojure project has all the necessary libraries and versions to compile and run successfully.

```
(defproject your-project "0.1.0-SNAPSHOT"
  :description "A sample Clojure project"
  :dependencies [[org.clojure/clojure "1.10.3"]
                 [cheshire "5.10.0"]
                 [clj-http "3.12.1"]])
```

In the example above, the project has three dependencies: org.clojure/clojure, cheshire, and clj-http, each followed by their respective versions. Leiningen uses these declarations to fetch the specified libraries from central repositories such as Clojars or Maven Central.

To update and retrieve dependencies, you can use the following Leiningen command:

```
lein deps
```

This command reads the project.clj file and downloads the specified libraries and their transitive dependencies to the local $HOME/.m2/repository directory. This ensures that all the needed code is available locally.

In addition to declaring dependencies, you can also specify dependency exclusions to prevent conflicts or unnecessary bloat in your project. This is done by using the :exclusions keyword in the dependency vector.

```
:dependencies [[cheshire "5.10.0" :exclusions [org.clojure/clojure]]
               [clj-http "3.12.1"]]
```

In this example, the cheshire dependency is configured to exclude the default org.clojure/clojure library, which might otherwise cause a version conflict.

Leiningen also supports specifying dependencies for different environments, such as development (:dev), testing (:test), and production (:prod). This can be done using profiles.

```
:profiles {:dev {:dependencies [[ring/ring-mock "0.4.0"]]}
           :test {:dependencies [[midje "1.9.9"]]}
           :prod {:dependencies [[compojure "1.6.2"]]}}
```

Here, ring/ring-mock is added only to the development environment, midje is used for the testing environment, and compojure is included in the production environment. This separation ensures that development and test libraries do not unnecessarily inflate the production build.

To activate a specific profile when running Leiningen tasks, use the with-profile command:

```
lein with-profile dev run
```

This command executes the project using dependencies specified under the :dev profile.

Leiningen also supports repository management. While Maven Central and Clojars are the primary repositories, you can add other repositories in the project.clj file under the :repositories key.

```
:repositories {"private-repo" {:url "https://mycompany.repo/releases"
                               :username :env/repo_user
                               :password :env/repo_pass}}
```

This configuration adds a private repository alongside specifying environment variables for authentication. Leiningen retrieves these values at runtime from the environment, ensuring secure management of repository credentials.

Snapshot dependencies are another critical aspect managed by Leiningen. Snapshots are intermediate versions of a library that are under active development. They are represented with a -SNAPSHOT suffix in the version.

```
:dependencies [[my-library "1.0.0-SNAPSHOT"]]
```

Leiningen treats snapshot dependencies with special care, frequently checking for updates to ensure the project always uses the latest development version.

To summarize, managing dependencies with Leiningen consists of declaring the needed libraries in the project.clj file, handling exclusions to avoid conflicts, organizing environment-specific dependencies using profiles, and securely managing repository access. By mastering these strategies, you can ensure that your Clojure projects are well-organized, maintainable, and easily reproducible across different environments.

10.4 Building Standalone JAR Files

In this section, we will explore the process of building standalone JAR files for Clojure applications. A standalone JAR file contains all the necessary classes, resources, and dependencies required to run a Clojure application, making it an executable archive. Creating such JAR files is crucial for deploying Clojure applications, as it ensures that the application can run in various environments without additional configuration.

To begin with, let us revisit the basic project structure of a Clojure application managed by Leiningen. Typically, the project directory consists of the following:

- src/ directory: Contains the source code.
- resources/ directory: Contains resources such as configuration files.
- test/ directory: Contains test code.
- project.clj file: Defines the project configuration including dependencies and build instructions.

Leiningen, the build tool for Clojure, facilitates the creation of standalone JAR files via its uberjar command. The process consolidates all project dependencies and the compiled classes into a single JAR file. Below is an example of a project.clj configuration set up for building an uberjar:

```
(defproject my-clojure-app "0.1.0-SNAPSHOT"
  :description "A sample Clojure application"
  :url "http://example.com/my-clojure-app"
  :license {:name "EPL-2.0"
```

```
           :url "https://www.eclipse.org/legal/epl-2.0/"}
  :dependencies [[org.clojure/clojure "1.10.3"]
                 [ring/ring-core "1.9.1"]
                 [ring/ring-jetty-adapter "1.9.1"]]
  :main ^:skip-aot my-clojure-app.core
  :target-path "target/%s/"
  :profiles {:uberjar {:aot :all}})
```

In this configuration, the :main directive specifies the main namespace containing the -main function that serves as the entry point of the application. The :profiles section defines a profile for the uberjar with :aot (Ahead-Of-Time compilation) set to :all, which compiles all namespaces. By setting the :target-path, we ensure the artifacts are placed in designated directories, distinguished by profiles like dev and uberjar.

To create the standalone JAR file, navigate to the project directory and run the following Leiningen command:

```
lein uberjar
```

Execution of this command results in the generation of two files in the target/uberjar directory:

- my-clojure-app-0.1.0-SNAPSHOT.jar: A traditional JAR e.g., contains the project's compiled bytecode and resources.

- my-clojure-app-0.1.0-SNAPSHOT-standalone.jar: The standalone (or uberjar) containing both the project's bytecode and all of its dependencies.

The my-clojure-app-0.1.0-SNAPSHOT-standalone.jar is the standalone JAR file that can be distributed and executed independently. To run this JAR file, use the following command:

```
java -jar target/uberjar/my-clojure-app-0.1.0-SNAPSHOT-standalone.jar
```

This command launches the application by initiating the -main function in the my-clojure-app.core namespace.

To summarize the entire process programmatically, let us consider a concise algorithm that encapsulates the steps necessary to build a standalone JAR file using Leiningen:

Algorithm 2: Building a Standalone JAR File

```
Data: Clojure project directory
Result: Standalone JAR file
begin
    /* Step 1: Define Project Configuration                          */
    Modify project.clj to include dependencies and build
     instructions;
    Set :main to the entry point namespace;
    Define :profiles with :uberjar and :aot;
    /* Step 2: Build Uberjar                                         */
    Execute command lein uberjar from the project root;
    /* Step 3: Verify and Run the JAR                                */
    Verify the standalone JAR in the target/uberjar directory;
    Run the JAR using java -jar command;
```

Care must be taken to ensure all dependencies are correctly specified in the project.clj file, as missing dependencies will result in a non-functional JAR file. Additionally, manage the project version properly, to avoid conflicts and ensure compatibility with other projects and libraries. Remember, the aim is to produce a standalone executable that encapsulates the entire runtime environment of the application.

Using this structured approach to create standalone JAR files streamlines the deployment process, providing consistency and reliability in deploying Clojure applications across various environments.

10.5 Packaging and Distributing Clojure Libraries

When packaging and distributing Clojure libraries, it is essential to ensure that your code is portable, reusable, and easily accessible to other developers. The process generally involves preparing the library for release, managing dependencies, and uploading the library to a central repository. This section covers each of these steps in detail to ensure a smooth and efficient distribution of your Clojure libraries.

To begin with, structuring your Clojure project correctly is critical. For libraries that you intend to distribute, follow the conventions that the Clojure community typically adheres to. Make use of the Leiningen build tool, which simplifies the packaging and deployment process.

```
(defproject my-library "0.1.0-SNAPSHOT"
  :description "A sample Clojure library"
  :url "http://example.com/my-library"
  :license {:name "Eclipse Public License"
            :url "http://www.eclipse.org/legal/epl-v10.html"}
  :dependencies [[org.clojure/clojure "1.10.3"]])
```

In the Leiningen project configuration file, project.clj, it is crucial to include descriptive metadata such as :description, :url, and :license. This metadata provides essential information about the library and ensures that it is easily understood and accessible by potential users and contributors.

Next, include unit tests to make sure your library functions as expected. Place your test files in the test directory, parallel to the src directory. For example, if you have a source file src/my_library/core.clj, the corresponding test file should be test/my_library/core_test.clj.

```
(ns my-library.core-test
  (:require [clojure.test :refer :all]
            [my-library.core :refer :all]))

(deftest a-test
  (testing "Example test"
    (is (= 1 1))))
```

Ensure that all tests pass before proceeding to the packaging step. Execute the tests using Leiningen via the command:

```
lein test
```

After confirming that all tests are successful, you can define a deployment profile in your project.clj file to facilitate the release process. This profile can include additional dependencies or plugins necessary for deployment.

```
:profiles {:deploy {:plugins [[lein-deploy "0.4.1"]]
                    :repositories [["clojars" {:url "https://repo.clojars.org"}]]}}
```

The :deploy profile above includes the lein-deploy plugin and specifies Clojars as the target repository. Clojars is a popular repository for Clojure artifacts. You need to add your credentials to your ~/.lein/credentials.clj.gpg file for authentication.

```
{"https://repo.clojars.org"
 {:username "your-username"
  :password "your-password"}}
```

To deploy your library to Clojars, run the following Leiningen commands:

```
lein deploy clojars
```

Leiningen will package your project, sign it with GPG if configured, and upload it to the specified repository. Once uploaded, your library will be publicly available, and other developers can include it as a dependency in their projects.

You can also automate the release process using Continuous Integration (CI) tools like Travis CI or GitHub Actions. Configure these tools to run tests and deploy your library whenever changes are pushed to the main branch.

Here is an example configuration for GitHub Actions in a .github/workflows/deploy.yml file:

```
name: Clojure CI/CD

on:
  push:
    branches:
      - main

jobs:
  build:
    runs-on: ubuntu-latest
    steps:
      - uses: actions/checkout@v2
      - name: Set up JDK 11
        uses: actions/setup-java@v1
        with:
          java-version: 11
      - name: Install Leiningen
        run: sudo apt-get install leiningen
      - name: Test
        run: lein test
      - name: Deploy to Clojars
        if: github.ref == 'refs/heads/main'
        run: lein deploy clojars
        env:
          CLOJARS_USERNAME: ${{ secrets.CLOJARS_USERNAME }}
          CLOJARS_PASSWORD: ${{ secrets.CLOJARS_PASSWORD }}
```

In this configuration, GitHub Actions will check out your repository, set up Java and Leiningen, run your tests, and deploy the library to Clojars if all tests pass and the changes are pushed to the main branch. You need to store your Clojars username and password in GitHub Secrets for secure access.

By adhering to these best practices, you will ensure that your Clojure libraries are well-structured, tested, and readily available for the community. This streamlined approach to packaging and distributing libraries not only enhances code reusability but also fosters collaborative development and innovation.

10.6 Creating and Managing Build Configurations

Creating and managing build configurations is a critical aspect of developing robust and maintainable Clojure applications. This section delves into the specifics of setting up and handling build configurations using Leiningen, the most widely adopted build automation tool for Clojure.

Leiningen uses a project.clj file to hold the configuration settings needed to build, run, and manage Clojure projects. The project.clj file is written in Clojure syntax and includes various parameters that specify project metadata, dependencies, plugins, and build profiles.

Basic Structure of project.clj

A typical project.clj file includes the following basic elements:

```
(defproject my-clojure-app "0.1.0-SNAPSHOT"
  :description "A sample Clojure application"
  :url "http://example.com/my-clojure-app"
  :license {:name "Eclipse Public License"
            :url "http://www.eclipse.org/legal/epl-v10.html"}
  :dependencies [[org.clojure/clojure "1.10.1"]]
  :main ^:skip-aot my-clojure-app.core
  :target-path "target/%s"
  :profiles {:uberjar {:aot :all}})
```

Metadata

The initial part of the project.clj file includes project metadata such as defproject, followed by the project name and version. The metadata also includes optional fields such as :description, :url, and :license that provide information about the project.

Dependencies

Dependencies are specified in the :dependencies vector. Each dependency is represented by a vector containing the group ID, artifact ID, and version. For example:

```
:dependencies [[org.clojure/clojure "1.10.1"]
               [compojure "1.6.1"]
               [ring/ring-defaults "0.3.2"]]
```

Main Namespace

The :main key specifies the main namespace of the application. The use of ^:skip-aot denotes skipping Ahead-Of-Time (AOT) compilation for the specified namespace except when creating an uberjar.

Target Path

The :target-path key defines the directory where build artifacts will be placed. Using "target/%s" makes Leiningen place build-specific artifacts into appropriate subdirectories in the target folder.

Profiles

Build profiles are a powerful feature in Leiningen that enable you to define different configuration settings for various environments and build scenarios. The :profiles map can contain multiple profile configurations. For example:

```
:profiles {:dev {:dependencies [[ring/ring-mock "0.4.0"]]
                 :source-paths ["env/dev"]}
           :test {:dependencies [[midje "1.9.9"]]
                  :plugins [[lein-midje "3.2"]]
                  :source-paths ["env/test"]}
           :uberjar {:aot :all}}
```

- :dev Profile: Contains dependencies and source paths specific to the development environment.
- :test Profile: Adds dependencies and plugins needed for testing, as well as source paths specific to the test environment.
- :uberjar Profile: Used to create an uberjar (a standalone JAR file that includes all dependencies). The :aot :all key enables Ahead-Of-Time compilation for all namespaces in the project.

Plugins

Leiningen supports a range of plugins that extend its functionality. Plugins are typically specified in the :plugins vector. For example:

```
:plugins [[lein-ring "0.12.5"]
          [lein-environ "1.2.0"]]
```

Build Configurations

Leiningen allows custom tasks and commands through build configurations. The project.clj file can include custom tasks, aliases, and hooks to automate repetitive tasks. For instance, adding the following alias to run tests and generate a coverage report:

```
:aliases {"test-all" ["do" "test" ["run" :unit-tests] ["run" :integration-tests]]}
```

This alias runs unit tests followed by integration tests, combining these into a single command for efficiency.

Environment Variables

Environment variables can be managed using the lein-environ plugin, allowing configuration to change based on the environment. You must first include the plugin in your :plugins vector, and then define environment variables in profiles.clj.

```
:profiles {:dev {:env {:database-url "jdbc:postgres://localhost/devdb"}}
           :prod {:env {:database-url "jdbc:postgres://prod-server/proddb"}}}
```

Here, the database URL changes depending on whether the :dev or :prod profile is active.

Leiningen's build configuration system provides an extensive and flexible toolset for managing Clojure project builds, catering to varying environments and scenarios with ease and precision.

10.7 Automating Builds with CI/CD Tools

The advancement in software development methodologies has profoundly influenced the ways in which applications are built, tested, and deployed. Continuous Integration (CI) and Continuous Deployment (CD) are pivotal practices within modern development environments that greatly enhance software quality and development pace. This section delves into automating the build process of Clojure applications using CI/CD tools.

Continuous Integration involves regularly merging code changes into a central repository, with automated builds and tests executed to ensure that new changes do not break the existing application. Conversely, Continuous Deployment extends this by ensuring that every successful build is automatically deployed to a production environment, albeit with proper gating mechanisms in place for human oversight if required.

Setting Up Continuous Integration (CI)

To set up CI for a Clojure application, one typically configures a CI server to monitor the source code repository for changes. Popular CI tools include Jenkins, Travis CI, CircleCI, and GitHub Actions. We will provide an example configuration using Travis CI.

Firstly, ensure that your Clojure project is correctly structured and includes a project.clj file for Leiningen. Below is an example of a minimal project.clj file:

```
(defproject sample-ci-cd "0.1.0-SNAPSHOT"
```

```
:description "A Sample Clojure Project"
:url "http://example.com/sample-ci-cd"
:license {:name "Eclipse Public License"
          :url "http://www.eclipse.org/legal/epl-v10.html"}
:dependencies [[org.clojure/clojure "1.10.3"]]
:main ^:skip-aot sample-ci-cd.core
:target-path "target/%s"
:profiles {:uberjar {:aot :all}})
```

Next, create a .travis.yml file at the root of your project directory. This YAML file is where you will define the CI configuration for Travis CI:

```
language: clojure
lein: 2.9.8

jdk:
  - openjdk11

script:
  - lein clean
  - lein deps
  - lein test
```

In this configuration:

- language: clojure specifies the programming language.
- lein: 2.9.8 specifies the version of Leiningen to use.
- jdk: openjdk11 sets the OpenJDK version to be used in the build environment.
- script defines the sequence of Leiningen commands to execute during the CI process.

Commit and push these files to your repository. Upon each commit, Travis CI will execute the defined steps, performing a clean build, resolving dependencies, and executing tests. An excerpt of Travis CI build output might look like this:

```
$ lein clean
$ lein deps
Retrieving org/clojure/clojure/1.10.3/clojure-1.10.3.pom ...
Retrieving org/clojure/spec.alpha ...
$ lein test
Running tests...
All tests passed.
```

Continuous Deployment (CD)

For Continuous Deployment, additional configuration is required to deploy the application artifacts upon successful builds. We will continue with the Travis CI example and configure deployment to an Amazon S3 bucket.

Update your .travis.yml file to include deployment settings:

```
deploy:
  provider: s3
  access_key_id: $AWS_ACCESS_KEY
  secret_access_key: $AWS_SECRET_KEY
  bucket: my-clojure-app-bucket
  skip_cleanup: true
  acl: public_read
  on:
    repo: username/sample-ci-cd
    branch: main
```

In this configuration:

- provider: s3 specifies that the deployment provider is Amazon S3.
- access_key_id and secret_access_key references are environment variables (configured securely in the Travis CI settings) that store AWS credentials.
- bucket identifies the S3 bucket name for deployment.
- skip_cleanup: true ensures that the target folder's contents are retained for deployment.
- acl: public_read sets permissions for the deployed artifacts.
- on: ensures deployment only occurs from the specified repository and branch.

Upon successful completion of a build on the main branch, the generated artifacts will be deployed to the defined Amazon S3 bucket, effectively automating the end-to-end CI/CD pipeline.

Monitoring and Maintaining CI/CD Pipelines

Maintaining robust CI/CD pipelines demands continuous monitoring and updating. Review build logs to identify and resolve failures promptly. Ensure that dependencies and tools are up-to-date to avoid pitfalls due to deprecations or security vulnerabilities. As Clojure and its ecosystem evolve, periodically revisiting and refreshing your project.clj and CI/CD configurations is imperative for sustained efficiency and security.

Automating builds with CI/CD tools in a Clojure development environment significantly reduces manual intervention, increases build reliability, and accelerates delivery of high-quality software. Such practices align with industry standards, facilitating seamless integration, daily testing, and consistent deployment of applications.

10.8 Deployment Strategies for Clojure Applications

Successfully deploying Clojure applications involves several strategies that can be adapted based on the specific requirements and constraints of your environment. Understanding and utilizing these deployment strategies ensures that your applications run smoothly, are easy to update, and can scale efficiently.

Deployment, in the context of Clojure applications, refers to the process of making your application available for use, typically within a production environment. This entails several steps, including preparing your application, packaging it, transferring it to the target environment, and starting it up. Common strategies for Clojure application deployment include using standalone JAR files, containerization with Docker, cloud deployment, and orchestration tools like Kubernetes.

Standalone JAR Files enable simple and straightforward deployment. The Clojure code is compiled and packaged into a Java ARchive (JAR) file. This JAR file can then be transferred to the target environment and executed using the Java Virtual Machine (JVM). The primary advantages of this approach are simplicity and portability, as the JAR file encapsulates the entire application along with its dependencies.

```
$ java -jar your-app-standalone.jar
```

This method aligns well with environments where Java is already utilized extensively, as it leverages the existing JVM infrastructure.

Containerization with Docker provides a more robust and isolated environment for your Clojure applications. Docker allows applications to run in containers, which encapsulate the application along with its dependencies in a standardized unit of software. This approach ensures that your application behaves the same way, regardless of where it is deployed.

Here's an example of a simple Dockerfile for a Clojure application:

```
# Use an official OpenJDK runtime as a parent image
FROM openjdk:11-jre-slim

# Set the working directory in the container
WORKDIR /usr/src/app

# Copy the application JAR file to the container
COPY target/your-app-standalone.jar /usr/src/app/

# Run the application
CMD ["java", "-jar", "your-app-standalone.jar"]
```

To build and run the Docker container, use the following commands:

```
$ docker build -t your-app .
$ docker run -p 8080:8080 your-app
```

Docker simplifies deployments by providing an immutable infrastructure, which makes managing dependencies and reproducing environments straightforward.

Cloud Deployment involves deploying your Clojure applications on cloud platforms like AWS, GCP, or Azure. These platforms offer various services and tools that facilitate the deployment and scaling of applications. Using cloud services often includes combining multiple strategies, such as using container orchestration (Kubernetes) and serverless deployments.

For instance, deploying to AWS involves using services like:

- Elastic Beanstalk for automatic scaling and deployment management.
- Lambda for serverless, event-driven functions.
- ECS (Elastic Container Service) for container orchestration.

A CI/CD pipeline can integrate these steps for seamless deployment. Here's an example of a basic configuration for deploying a Dockerized Clojure application using Amazon ECS:

```
version: '3'
services:
  web:
    image: your-docker-repo/your-app:latest
    ports:
      - "8080:8080"
```

Kubernetes Orchestration allows you to manage containerized applications at scale. Kubernetes provides features like load balancing, scaling, and automated rollouts and rollbacks, making it an ideal choice for complex deployment scenarios. To deploy a Clojure application using Kubernetes, define your deployment and service configuration, such as:

```
apiVersion: apps/v1
kind: Deployment
metadata:
  name: your-app-deployment
spec:
  replicas: 3
  selector:
    matchLabels:
      app: your-app
  template:
    metadata:
      labels:
        app: your-app
    spec:
      containers:
      - name: your-app
        image: your-docker-repo/your-app:latest
        ports:
        - containerPort: 8080
---
apiVersion: v1
kind: Service
metadata:
  name: your-app-service
spec:
  type: LoadBalancer
  ports:
  - port: 8080
    targetPort: 8080
  selector:
    app: your-app
```

CI/CD pipelines, such as those provided by Jenkins, GitLab CI, and GitHub Actions, can automate the building, testing, and deployment processes. Here is a basic Jenkinsfile for a Clojure application:

```
pipeline {
    agent any
    stages {
        stage('Build') {
            steps {
                sh 'lein uberjar'
            }
        }
        stage('Docker Build') {
            steps {
                sh 'docker build -t your-app .'
            }
        }
        stage('Deploy') {
            steps {
                withCredentials([string(credentialsId: 'dockerhub-password', variable: '
                        DOCKER_HUB_PASSWORD')]) {
                    sh 'echo $DOCKER_HUB_PASSWORD | docker login -u your-
                        dockerhub-username --password-stdin'
                    sh 'docker push your-dockerhub-username/your-app:latest'
```

```
            }
            sh 'kubectl apply -f k8s/deployment.yaml'
        }
      }
    }
}
```

These deployment strategies enable you to choose the best method for your specific needs, taking into consideration factors such as simplicity, scalability, and the familiarity of your team with the tools involved.

Each deployment strategy offers distinct benefits and challenges. Adopting a particular strategy depends on the application's requirements, the deployment environment, and the scalability needs. Careful planning and implementation of the chosen strategy contribute to the robustness and reliability of the deployed Clojure application.

10.9 Deploying Clojure Applications to the Cloud

Cloud deployment of Clojure applications involves a series of steps that ensure your application is accessible, scalable, and maintainable when hosted on cloud platforms such as AWS, Google Cloud Platform (GCP), and Microsoft Azure. This section provides an in-depth look into these steps, from configuring your environment to monitoring your deployed application.

To begin, ensure you have a basic understanding of cloud services and their offerings. This knowledge will guide your selection of resources and configurations.

Configuring Your Environment

Start by configuring your development environment to suit cloud deployment requirements. Configuration typically includes setting environment variables, modifying application settings for production environments, and ensuring security parameters like credentials and API keys are properly managed.

```
(defn load-config []
  {:db-uri (System/getenv "DB_URI")
   :api-key (System/getenv "API_KEY")
   :port (or (System/getenv "PORT") 3000)
   :log-level (System/getenv "LOG_LEVEL")})
```

In this example, load-config retrieves environment variables, providing necessary configurations for database connections and API integrations.

Creating a Production Build

Prepare your Clojure application for a production build by generating a standalone JAR file. Ensure all dependencies are included. Use Leiningen for packaging:

```
lein uberjar
```

The lein uberjar command creates a self-contained JAR file in the target directory.

Choosing a Cloud Provider

Selecting a cloud provider depends on your project requirements. Here, an example of deploying on AWS using Elastic Beanstalk is demonstrated.

Deploying to AWS

Begin by installing the AWS CLI and Elastic Beanstalk CLI. Configure your AWS settings:

```
aws configure
```

This command prompts you to enter your AWS access key, secret key, region, and output format.

Next, initialize your project for Elastic Beanstalk:

```
eb init
```

This command guides you through the setup, including selecting the appropriate region and application name.

Create an environment and deploy your application:

```
eb create my-env
eb deploy
```

Review the deployment logs to ensure the application is running correctly.

Deploying to Google Cloud Platform (GCP)

For GCP, you will primarily use Google Kubernetes Engine (GKE). First, configure the gcloud CLI:

```
gcloud init
```

Set up your Kubernetes cluster:

```
gcloud container clusters create my-cluster --num-nodes=3
```

Create a Docker image of your application and push it to Google Container Registry:

```
docker build -t gcr.io/[PROJECT_ID]/my-app:latest .
docker push gcr.io/[PROJECT_ID]/my-app:latest
```

Deploy the Docker image to your GKE cluster using a Kubernetes YAML configuration:

```
apiVersion: apps/v1
kind: Deployment
metadata:
  name: my-app-deployment
spec:
  replicas: 3
  selector:
    matchLabels:
      app: my-app
  template:
    metadata:
      labels:
        app: my-app
    spec:
      containers:
      - name: my-app
        image: gcr.io/[PROJECT_ID]/my-app:latest
        ports:
        - containerPort: 8080
```

Apply the configuration to your Kubernetes cluster:

```
kubectl apply -f deployment.yaml
```

Verify your deployment:

```
kubectl get pods
```

Security Considerations

Ensure proper security measures are in place. Avoid hardcoding secrets; use secure storage solutions provided by your cloud provider, such as AWS Secrets Manager or GCP Secret Manager.

Monitoring and Logging

Monitoring and logging are crucial for maintaining the health of your deployed application. Use cloud-native monitoring tools like AWS CloudWatch, Google Cloud Monitoring, or Azure Monitor to track metrics and set up alerts for anomalies.

```
(require '[clojure.tools.logging :as log])

(defn handler [request]
  (log/info "Request received" request)
  {:status 200 :body "Hello, Cloud!"})
```

Integrate logging into your application to record significant events and errors, facilitating easier debugging and maintenance.

Scaling Your Application

Configure auto-scaling to handle increased traffic. In AWS, configure an auto-scaling group and define scaling policies. For Kubernetes, use Horizontal Pod Autoscaler:

```
kubectl autoscale deployment my-app-deployment --cpu-percent=50 --min=1 --max=10
```

This command sets up automatic scaling for your deployment based on CPU utilization.

Effective deployment of Clojure applications in the cloud requires careful planning, attention to security, and active monitoring to ensure optimal performance and reliability.

10.10 Using Docker with Clojure

Docker is a powerful tool that allows developers to containerize applications, making them more portable and easier to deploy across different environments. In this section, we will cover the essential steps involved in using Docker with a Clojure application. This includes creating a Dockerfile, building Docker images, running containers, and integrating Docker into your development workflow for efficient and consistent deployment.

Creating a Dockerfile

Begin by creating a Dockerfile in the root directory of your Clojure project. A Dockerfile is a script containing instructions on how to build a Docker image for your application. Below is an example Dockerfile for a basic Clojure application:

```
# Use the official Clojure image as a base
FROM clojure:openjdk-11-lein

# Set the working directory
WORKDIR /app

# Copy the project files
```

```
COPY project.clj /app/
COPY src /app/src

# Install dependencies and compile the application
RUN lein deps
RUN lein uberjar

# Expose the application port (e.g., 3000)
EXPOSE 3000

# Command to run the application
CMD ["java", "-jar", "target/uberjar/your-app-name-standalone.jar"]
```

This Dockerfile performs the following steps:

- Uses an official Clojure Docker image with OpenJDK 11 and Leiningen pre-installed.
- Sets the working directory to /app.
- Copies the project.clj file and src directory into the container.
- Installs the project dependencies using lein deps.
- Compiles the project to create a standalone JAR file using lein uberjar.
- Exposes port 3000 for the application.
- Specifies the command to run the application using the generated standalone JAR file.

Building the Docker Image

To build a Docker image from your Dockerfile, navigate to your project directory in the terminal and run the following command:

```
docker build -t your-app-name .
```

Here, the -t option tags the image with a name of your choice (e.g., your-app-name). The . specifies the current directory as the context for the build. The output will display each step of the build process, culminating in a successfully built Docker image.

Running the Docker Container

Once the image is built, you can run a container based on the image using the following command:

```
docker run -p 3000:3000 your-app-name
```

This command tells Docker to run a container from the your-app-name image, mapping port 3000 on your local machine to port 3000 in the container, thus making your Clojure application accessible at http://localhost:3000.

Dockerizing Development Workflow

Integrating Docker into your development workflow can streamline the process of running and testing your application in a consistent environment. Create a docker-compose.yml file for managing multi-container applications and services. Here is an example configuration file:

```
version: '3'

services:
  app:
    build: .
    ports:
      - "3000:3000"
    volumes:
      - .:/app
    command: ["lein", "trampoline", "run"]
```

This docker-compose.yml file:

- Defines a service named app that builds the Docker image from the current directory (.).
- Maps port 3000 on the local machine to port 3000 in the container.
- Mounts the current directory to /app inside the container, allowing live updates to the code.
- Runs the application using the lein trampoline run command, which ensures Leiningen tasks run in the same JVM process as the application.

To start the services defined in your docker-compose.yml, use the command:

```
docker-compose up
```

This will build and run the containers as specified, allowing you to develop and test your Clojure application efficiently within a Dockerized environment.

By leveraging Docker and Docker Compose, you can ensure that your Clojure application runs consistently across different environments, simplifying both development and deployment processes.

10.11 Monitoring and Maintaining Clojure Applications

Monitoring and maintaining Clojure applications is an integral part of ensuring their robustness, reliability, and performance in production environments. This section delves into effective strategies, tools, and practices for monitoring and maintaining applications built with Clojure, focusing on key aspects such as logging, metrics collection, health checks, and issue detection.

Effective monitoring begins with the systematic collection of application logs. Logging is essential for tracking the behavior and performance of an application over time. In Clojure, logging can be implemented using libraries like 'clojure.tools.logging' and 'logback'. Below is an illustrative example of configuring logging within a Clojure application using 'clojure.tools.logging':

```
(ns my-app.core
  (:require [clojure.tools.logging :as log]))

(defn some-function []
  (log/info "Executing some-function...")
  ;; Additional function logic
)
```

In this example, log/info is used to log informational messages. The logging library provides various levels of logging, such as debug, info, warn, and error, which help in categorizing logs based on severity.

To manage and analyze these logs, integrating with tools like ELK (Elasticsearch, Logstash, Kibana) stack or Grafana Loki is common practice. These tools assist in the aggregation, storage, and visualization of log data. Configuring Logback for log management might look like this:

```
<configuration>
    <appender name="STDOUT" class="ch.qos.logback.core.ConsoleAppender">
        <encoder>
            <pattern>%d{yyyy-MM-dd HH:mm:ss} %-5level %logger{36} - %msg%n</
                pattern>
        </encoder>
    </appender>

    <root level="info">
        <appender-ref ref="STDOUT" />
    </root>
</configuration>
```

Apart from logging, collecting and monitoring metrics is crucial. Metrics provide quantitative data about the application's performance and resource usage. Libraries like ‘metrics-clojure‘ enable seamless integration with the Dropwizard Metrics library, providing facilities to track JVM metrics, request times, and custom application metrics. Below is a sample setup using ‘metrics-clojure‘:

```
(ns my-app.monitoring
  (:require [metrics.core :refer [default-registry]]
            [metrics.meters :refer [defmeter mark!]]))

(defmeter request-meter "request-meter")

(defn handle-request [request]
  (mark! request-meter)
  ;; Handle the request
)
```

In this snippet, defmeter defines a new meter, request-meter, and mark! increments the meter each time handle-request is called. By tracking these metrics, potential issues such as increased latencies or request failures can be detected early.

Health checks are another vital component of application maintenance, ensuring that the application is running correctly. Health checks can be implemented using libraries like ‘com.stuartsierra/component‘ and ‘clojurewerkz/quartzite‘. An example of a simple health check function:

```
(ns my-app.health
  (:require [com.stuartsierra.component :as component]))

(defrecord HealthCheckComponent []
  component/Lifecycle
  (start [this]
    (println "Health check started")
    ;; Perform startup health checks
    this)
  (stop [this]
    (println "Health check stopped")
    ;; Perform cleanup if needed
    this))

(defn new-health-check []
  (map->HealthCheckComponent {}))
```

The HealthCheckComponent record implements the Lifecycle protocol to define startup and shutdown behavior, including important health checks required at each stage.

Automated alerting mechanisms complement monitoring by proactively notifying when issues are detected. Integrating with alerting tools such as Prometheus Alertmanager or PagerDuty ensures timely notifications are sent to the operations team.

For application maintenance, implementing continuous integration and deployment (CI/CD) practices ensures that code changes are tested and deployed efficiently. Tools like Jenkins, CircleCI, and GitHub Actions facilitate creating pipelines for build, test, and deployment processes. Here is an example of a simple CI configuration using GitHub Actions for a Clojure project:

```
name: Clojure CI

on: [push, pull_request]

jobs:
  build:
    runs-on: ubuntu-latest

    steps:
    - uses: actions/checkout@v2
    - name: Set up JDK 11
      uses: actions/setup-java@v1
      with:
        java-version: 11
    - name: Install Leiningen
      run: sudo apt-get install leiningen
    - name: Build
      run: lein do clean, test
```

This configuration sets up a workflow that runs on every push and pull request, checks out the code, sets up JDK 11, installs Leiningen, and runs the tests.

Adding to these practices, regular maintenance tasks such as dependencies updates, security patches, and application performance profiling are essential to keep the application in optimal condition. Profiling tools like YourKit or VisualVM can be used during performance tuning, and dependency management tools like 'lein-ancient' help in keeping project dependencies up to date.

Continuous monitoring and maintenance ensure that the Clojure applications remain resilient, performant, and capable of scaling according to demand. Integrating these practices into the development lifecycle is crucial for achieving sustainable and reliable software operations.

10.12 Scaling Clojure Applications

Scaling Clojure applications involves addressing increased load and demand while ensuring that performance remains robust and reliable. This section will delve into strategies and techniques for effectively scaling applications written in Clojure. The topics covered include horizontal and vertical scaling, leveraging concurrency and parallelism, employing caching, and using appropriate profiling and monitoring tools.

Horizontal vs. Vertical Scaling

Horizontal scaling, or scaling out, involves adding more nodes or instances to distribute the load across multiple servers. Vertical scaling, or scaling up, entails enhancing the capacity of a single server by adding more resources such as CPU, memory, or storage.

- Horizontal Scaling (Scaling Out): Adding more servers or instances to distribute the load. This approach is essential for web-based applications that need to manage numerous concurrent users. It involves deploying the application across several machines to balance the traffic.
- Vertical Scaling (Scaling Up): Increasing the power of an existing server by adding more CPU, RAM, or disk space. This is effective for applications that require substantial computational resources or for services that need to maintain strong performance benchmarks.

Concurrency and Parallelism in Clojure

Clojure provides robust facilities for concurrency and parallelism, which are critical for scaling applications. By leveraging these features, Clojure applications can handle multiple tasks simultaneously, thus improving throughput and performance.

```
;; Example of Clojure's asynchronous programming with core.async
(require '[clojure.core.async :refer [go <! >! chan]])

(defn async-task [input]
  (go
    (let [result (* 2 input)]
      (println "Processed" input "into" result)
      result)))

(defn parallel-processing []
  (let [c (chan 100)]
    (doseq [i (range 10)]
      (>! c (async-task i)))
    (loop [results []]
      (if (= 10 (count results))
        (println "All tasks completed" results)
        (recur (conj results (<! c)))))))
```

In the example above, core.async library is utilized to perform asynchronous tasks. The go blocks execute tasks in parallel, allowing efficient processing of multiple inputs without blocking the main thread.

Caching

Caching is another essential technique for scaling Clojure applications. By storing frequently accessed data in memory, applications can reduce the number of expensive database queries or computations, thereby improving response times and reducing the load on backend services.

```
;; Using Atom for an in-memory cache
(def cache (atom {}))

(defn get-cached [key]
  (get @cache key))

(defn set-cache [key value]
  (swap! cache assoc key value))

;; Example usage
(let [key "user-data"
      value {:name "Alice" :age 30}]
  (set-cache key value)
  (println "Cached value:" (get-cached key)))
```

The example shows how an atom can be used as an in-memory cache. This approach is useful in scenarios where the cached data is mutable and needs to be updated frequently.

Profiling and Monitoring

Effective scaling is incomplete without appropriate profiling and monitoring. By continuously monitoring the performance and resource utilization of your application, you can identify bottlenecks and optimize accordingly.

- Profiling Tools: Tools like YourKit, VisualVM, or Clojure's own core.async tap can be used to profile the application, identifying hotspots and areas where performance may be improved.
- Monitoring Tools: Monitoring solutions such as Prometheus, Grafana, or Datadog can be integrated to track metrics like CPU usage, memory consumption, request latency, and error rates.

The combination of profiling and monitoring ensures that the application performs efficiently under different loads, helping to make well-informed decisions about scaling strategies.

Load Balancing

Load balancing distributes incoming traffic across multiple instances of the application, ensuring that no single instance is overwhelmed. Solutions like NGINX, HAProxy, or cloud-based services such as AWS Elastic Load Balancing can manage load distribution effectively.

- NGINX example configuration:

```
http {
    upstream clojure_app {
        server 127.0.0.1:3000;
        server 127.0.0.1:3001;
        server 127.0.0.1:3002;
    }

    server {
        listen 80;

        location / {
            proxy_pass http://clojure_app;
            proxy_set_header Host $host;
            proxy_set_header X-Real-IP $remote_addr;
            proxy_set_header X-Forwarded-For $proxy_add_x_forwarded_for;
            proxy_set_header X-Forwarded-Proto $scheme;
        }
    }
}
```

This configuration file for NGINX sets up a load balancer that distributes incoming requests to three different instances of the Clojure application running on ports 3000, 3001, and 3002.

State Management

In a distributed environment, managing state becomes challenging. Clojure applications can leverage external storage systems like databases or distributed cache systems (e.g., Redis) to manage state consistently.

```
;; Example of using Redis with Clojure
(require '[carmine :as redis])

(def conn-pool (redis/make-conn-pool))
(def conn-spec (redis/make-conn-spec :host "127.0.0.1" :port 6379))

(defn set-redis-key [key value]
  (redis/wcar
    conn-pool
    conn-spec
    (redis/set key value)))

(defn get-redis-key [key]
  (redis/wcar
    conn-pool
    conn-spec
    (redis/get key)))

;; Usage example
(set-redis-key "session" "active")
(println "Session state:" (get-redis-key "session"))
```

By using Redis, this example demonstrates how to set and get state in a distributed environment, ensuring data consistency across multiple instances of the application.

Scaling Clojure applications requires a combination of strategies, each addressing different aspects of performance and demand. Concurrency and parallelism leverage Clojure's strengths for managing tasks efficiently. Caching reduces the load on backend services, while profiling and monitoring provide insights into performance bottlenecks. Load balancing ensures even distribution of requests, and proper state management maintains consistency in a distributed setup. By employing these techniques, Clojure applications can be scaled to handle increased load and complexity effectively.

Made in the USA
Monee, IL
05 November 2026

67911524R00174